THE ART OF
BONSAI

Color Plate 1 (see overleaf). A semiformal Japanese arrangement for exhibiting bonsai. The principal tree is a beautifully proportioned common Ezo spruce in the semi-cascade style, on a stand made of a carved and polished tree trunk. This is balanced on the left by the subordinate bonsai, an excellent rock planting in the clinging-to-a-rock style, created four years ago by Lt. Col. and Mrs. John M. Anderson, U.S. Air Force, while attending Mr. Yoshimura's classes. The scroll painting of wild camellias and bird harmonizes with the seasonal motif of this winter arrangement.

Technical data. **Principal tree:** 3 ft. wide. Age about 50 yrs. Produced by layering about 20 yrs. ago, from a naturally stunted tree found in northern Japan. Unglazed Chinese pot. **Rock planting:** consists of dwarf bush clover (3 pieces, 5 yrs. old, from cuttings), dwarf flowering quince (2 pcs., 5 yrs., cuttings), golden fern (1 yr., dividing), ibota ligustrum (3 pcs., 7 yrs., cuttings), Japanese tamarack (3 pcs., 8 yrs., natural), Sargent juniper (5 pcs., 7 yrs., cuttings), and dwarf star jasmine (3 pcs., 5 yrs., cutings).

Color Plate 1. See overleaf for caption.

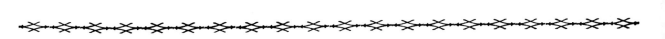

THE ART OF BONSAI

CREATION, CARE, AND ENJOYMENT

by YUJI YOSHIMURA *and* GIOVANNA M. HALFORD

CHARLES E. TUTTLE COMPANY
Rutland, Vermont   Tokyo, Japan

Published by the Charles E. Tuttle Company, Inc.
of Rutland, Vermont & Tokyo, Japan
with editorial offices at
2-6 Suido 1-chome, Bunkyo-ku, Tokyo 112

LCC Card No. 57-8794
ISBN 0-8048-2091-0

First published as
The Japanese Art of Miniature Trees and Landscapes, 1957
Thirty-fifth printing, 1996

Printed in Singapore

PUBLISHER'S NOTE

This book could only have resulted from the combination of two authors which it happily found, - a Japanese authority on bonsai with long teaching experience and a Western student of the art with the ability to anticipate the Western reader's questions and problems and to describe an intricate subject in lucid English Collaboration on a technical book, however, is never easy; and in this case the difficulties have been compounded by the fact that the authors suddenly found themselves separated by the oceans and seas—to say nothing of canals—between Japan and North Africa. Fortunately, the book had already been written, but there still remained the tasks of final editing, choosing photographs, drafting line drawings, preparing captions, proofreading, indexing, and coordinating all the various parts. In these circumstances the publishers have had to assume more responsibility and make more decisions than were rightfully theirs. They must, then, thank both authors for patience and understanding, and must also take upon themselves the blame for any acts of commission or omission which do injustice to the authors' intentions.

TABLE OF CONTENTS

LIST OF ILLUSTRATIONS

TEXT FIGURES

1 ● *INTRODUCTION*

THE ART OF GROWING AND caring for miniature trees is one which may be enjoyed practically anywhere in the world, although it has reached its apex in Japan. Owning a particularly fine *bonsai*, as the Japanese call these trees—the word is written with characters meaning "tray" or "pot" and "to plant"—is a responsibility, not to be undertaken lightly. A Japanese who owns bonsai has nearly always taken the trouble to turn himself into an expert; he has studied the art and is probably acquiring a collection of these little masterpieces. He gives up a good deal of his time to their care, belongs perhaps to a bonsai society, allows his best trees to appear in exhibitions, and attends the annual auctions, sometimes to buy, sometimes to sell, sometimes just to "study form." He may well have inherited his most valuable trees from his father and grandfather, for bonsai lovers, like bonsai growers, are both born and made, artists and craftsmen with a long tradition behind them. The all-too-common practice among Western visitors to Japan of buying a bonsai and then allowing it to die through neglect or ignorance is shocking to the Japanese. They know that the dead tree, flung on the rubbish heap with a rueful "Oh, well, it wasn't so very expensive anyway," represents many years of loving care by some unknown gardener, whose grandfather may have sown the seed.

But the amateur should not be discouraged by this talk of many years and heavy responsibilities involved in making and caring for a perfect specimen. Perfection is rare, and enjoyment does not depend on it; and, as will be pointed out, there are short cuts and "tricks of the trade" by which a handsome bonsai can be created in months rather than years. It is certainly not difficult to learn at least the basic rules which will keep a bonsai alive. With a little trouble anyone who loves plants can give it proper attention, water it sufficiently, keep it free from disease, do simple pruning, and even change the soil when necessary. The smallness of the bonsai is so wonderful that many people believe that there must be some mystery about them, some special treatment known only to the initiates so that, as one often hears, "bonsai always die in two or three months in a Western house." But this is not the case. The authors hope that this book will help Western people who own bonsai to care for them and increase their own enjoyment. They also hope it will encourage those who like gardening to experiment in making and training their own miniature trees.

It might be difficult for a person with absolutely no experience in gardening who lives in an apartment in a city to grow a bonsai from seed and train it, but there is no reason why he should not care for a ready-made one successfully, provided he has a convenient fire escape or window box for the tree to live on and can take it from time to time to a reliable nursery for advice and inspection. But the man or woman who is accustomed to a garden, who knows about seedlings and shrubs and young fruit trees, will find from this book that the technique of growing bonsai is largely an adaptation of what he knows already. If

he is prepared to embark upon an undertaking—no longer, after all, than the development of a mature apple orchard and in many cases much shorter—which will require a good deal of patience, the performance of little, fiddling jobs which may not take more than a few minutes of his time every day but which must not be neglected, then he may enjoy the satisfaction of possessing a treasure of his own making. The technique is here in this book.

What we cannot teach by rule of thumb, although we have tried to indicate the fundamental principles, is the art which makes the bonsai perfect. The final beauty of the bonsai lies in its training, and each person must see for himself just how the tree can be displayed to greatest advantage, whether its form should be austerely classical or gracefully cascading, whether this branch spoils the symmetry or the addition of a rock or tiny shrub may not give balance to the whole. The choice of pot, the posi-

Color Plate 2. Japanese persimmon. Informal upright style. 2'2". About 30 yrs. Produced from a seedling and potted about 20 yrs. ago. Glazed Chinese pot.

Color Plate 3. Japanese millettia. Informal upright style. 1'3". About 15 yrs. Produced from a cutting or by dividing. Glazed Japanese pot.

Color Plate 4. English holly. Informal upright style. 11". About 35 yrs. Produced from a seedling or cutting or by layering. Glazed Chinese pot of Kuang-tung ware, the color contrasting harmoniously with the red berries, which remain for most of the winter.

Color Plate 2

Color Plate 3

Color Plate 4

tion of the tree in the pot, the angle at which the trunk is set, the way in which the exposed roots are arranged, all these go to make the masterpiece.

In this book there are numerous photographs of finely trained bonsai, which will help the novice to "get his eye in" and realize what to aim at. They will also help the owners of full-grown bonsai to keep their trees in proper shape when they show a tendency to grow out sideways or otherwise spoil the line which art has so carefully given them. It is, in fact, a good idea to photograph a newly acquired bonsai for reference in years to come, although this does not mean that the shape of a trained bonsai cannot be improved. The owner may find, as he studies these illustrations, that by planting his tree at a different angle or training a branch to fill an ugly hiatus he can give the whole a more satisfying beauty.

Owners of bonsai should always try to have more than one tree. The temptation to keep the tree in the house so as to enjoy it and see the enjoyment of others is almost too strong for most Western people. But if there are several which can be brought into the house in rotation they will not suffer. It is also worth while to arrange a suitable setting for the bonsai, a special place in the room where it will look its best. With this in mind we have made some suggestions at the end of the book as to how a substitute for the Japanese alcove can be arranged in a Western room. Bonsai have such a very Japanese look about them, even when grown by someone who is not Japanese, that there is good reason for adapting the room to the tree rather than the tree to the room.

Until the turn of the century bonsai had never been seen outside Japan, and their first appearance, at an exhibition in London in 1909, created a sensation. The idea of age with smallness is fascinating and has led many Western people to give undue importance to the age of a tree. They tend to expect a bonsai to be hundreds of years old and are disappointed to learn that it is not. They forget that the most important thing about a bonsai is its beauty. Many people do not realize that the creation of bonsai is, for Japan, a comparatively new art. A good deal of confusion comes from the fact that certain trees are said to be six or eight hundred years old, and Western people assume that the practice of dwarfing is older than that. This is not the case. These very old trees have probably been entitled to the name of bonsai for less than half that time, although their age is fully documented. The Japanese have always loved miniature things,

and since very early times naturally stunted trees have been collected and treasured. But these are not bonsai; they are classified by the Japanese as "potted trees" to indicate that there has been no attempt to improve on nature. The oldest existing bonsai started in this way.

The early history of bonsai is a subject of some dispute and is not important for the purposes of this book. Certainly by the early years of the Meiji era (1868–1912) the art had become quite well established in its present form. And it was probably during the late sixteenth century, at the close of the Muromachi period (which might be described as Japanese Rococo), that the idea of artificially improving the shape of potted trees came into existence. At first it was merely a question of training these trees so as to compensate for natural defects, and it may be noted that to this day the most treasured bonsai are still those which are naturally stunted. Potted trees were to be found only in the houses of wealthy nobles, who could afford to pay the price for a thing so rare. But as the idea of improving on nature took hold, gardeners began to realize that it would be possible to create artificial dwarfs from seed or cuttings. These could be produced in quantity and were often as beautiful as the older trees, with a natural-

ness outrivaling nature, a factor which the taste of the period found particularly appealing. Moreover, there was a new and inexhaustible market for bonsai among the wealthy and cultivated merchant class, then beginning to rival the aristocracy as a patron of the arts.

Thus bonsai came into being. Their creation remains one of the cherished arts of Japan, and the care and patience which go into the making of one miniature tree is infinite. Of course, not all bonsai are exhibition pieces. We have laid some stress on the time and trouble required to create a fully matured tree, but again we emphasize that this should not discourage the novice from trying his hand. It is true that there are no short cuts to perfection, and bonsai growers generally think in terms of months and years instead of days and weeks. But, although to the connoisseur only a fully trained tree is worthy of note, that does not mean that to the grower, and particularly to the amateur grower, the tree is not both beautiful and exciting from its early stages. The very fact that it exists at all, that it puts out leaves and behaves like an ordinary tree, is a wonder in itself. And there are many bonsai of real beauty which have been in training for only three years, or even less.

Not all trees are equally slow in growing,

and trees which begin as cuttings or layerings—or, faster yet, as a small and untrained but promising potted tree such as can be discovered at any nursery—have a good start over trees grown from seed. The willow is a particularly good subject for a beginner as a willow cutting takes very easily and is extremely hardy. It grows fast and training can begin as soon as shoots develop—within a month or two of planting the cutting. In two or three years the willow will be a fair-sized tree with graceful drooping branches and can be used very effectively in rock plantings, where it can be made to hang over a miniature pool.

Even if the young tree must stay in its training pot for some years, it has all sorts of charms—some perhaps visible only to the eye of its creator. A tree that is five years old and has still not outgrown its three-inch pot is a triumph. Its shape may not be remarkable, but that will come. The tiny lilac tree grown from a cutting taken ten years ago and now covered with minute clusters of flowers is as much a treasure as the splendid two-hundred-year-old pine whose branches spread so gracefully.

After all, the pine was once a seedling, one among many. It grew into a gawky little sapling, and its tender branches were first persuaded to follow the line which would lend it most beauty when a full-grown tree. For years it received unceasing care. Perhaps the first owner never lived to see the completion of his work. His son may have watched the tree develop into a handsome bonsai, worthy of a fine pot. But it is his grandsons and great-grandsons who inherit the full benefit of all this thought and labor and continue the work, pruning the old tree, wiring wayward twigs, watching for signs of disease, and above all enjoying its beauty.

The miniature "Japanese garden" with tiny houses, bridges, people, animals, and the like, which is often seen in the West, is regarded by the Japanese bonsai lover as a rather vulgar object. But the tiny landscapes formed of group plantings and rock plantings belong to quite another category. They have the advantage of making use of young trees and dwarf shrubs which can be easily obtained from a nursery, if they are not available in the reader's own garden, and may be shown with pride within a week or two of their completion. The pleasure of arranging one of these group plantings is enormous. Japanese tend to prefer groups all of one species, but Western people often like to make a "mixed wood" like their groves at home. The little landscape can have a rocky cliff hanging over it or a grotto made from a hollow stone. It can be provided with a "river" of sand or made in the form of a gentle mossy slope which looks like a heath in Lilliput. On the practical side, these arrangements make excellent table centers and, if they consist of evergreens, go far to solve the winter flower problem. The same may be said of rock plantings, in which the pleasure of creating a miniature landscape is enhanced by the search for an interesting stone to build it on.

The bonsai owner finds that his trees become part of the family; he has a tendency to gravitate toward them at any spare moment of the day, just to make sure that all is well. Each one has its moment of glory, when it is the favorite child. The plum, quince, and apple follow each other in the spring; the deciduous trees are brilliantly green in early summer; in autumn the maples turn red, gold, and orange; and in winter there is the rich, dark color of the pines. And even though the maples and the fruit trees stand bare and leafless through the winter months, their owner can still take pleasure not only in the delicate tracery of their branches, but in the strong buds on every twig. Spring never seems far away with these reminders.

2 ◉ PROPAGATION

BONSAI ARE ORDINARY TREES which, whether naturally or artificially dwarfed, have been trained in pots to grow into naturally beautiful shapes. It is important to bear this in mind, for the chief beauty of the bonsai is its form, and even when that form is fantastic it still must not be grotesque. Anyone studying the photographs in this book will understand this. Even the strange "cascade" trees, which grow down over the edge of the pot instead of upwards, should look like trees clinging to a ledge of rock above a precipice; and the type known as the "literati's tree"— so called from its resemblance to the trees seen in paintings by the scholar-artists of the Southern school of Chinese art—should not be distorted more than nature will at times distort. Above all, the bonsai should never be trained into a shape that does not naturally become its species; it should remain a forest tree, seen through the wrong end of a telescope. This training is the antithesis of topiary work, which at one time was almost as great a passion in England as bonsai are in Japan. Bonsai art aims at creating artificially perfect trees, while topiary art aims at amazing by the ingenuity with which trees can be made to look like anything but themselves. Yet there is a similarity between the two, for without constant care the products of neither would reach and retain perfection.

Because a bonsai is a forest tree it takes as long to come to maturity as it would if it were growing in a wood. It has the same span of life, except that, since it is cared for and protected, it may well outlive an ordinary tree, sometimes achieving a very great age indeed. Evergreens such as pines, cryptomeria, or cypresses reach maturity more slowly than most deciduous trees, but also live longer. On the whole, fruit trees and flowering trees mature fastest, but do not as a rule achieve a very great age, although there are cherry trees and wisteria

which are known to be two or three hundred years old. As a general rule, a tree should be at least thirty years old to have reached maturity and at least fifty to have put on its full beauty, although not necessarily all these years as a bonsai. The tree should be judged as a whole. As pointed out in more detail in Chapter 8, the healthy color of the leaves, the pattern of trunk and branches, the spread of the roots, and the moss growing round them are all important.

The authors have written from the point of view of bonsai cultivation in Japan because it is there they have gained their experience. The trees here described are the Japanese varieties and the climatic conditions are those of Japan. This does not mean, of course, that other trees are not equally suitable. Any tree that flourishes is a potential bonsai, and many different types have been grown successfully in America and Europe. The great thing to remember is that to achieve satisfactory results it is preferable to choose varieties with small leaves and, particularly, small fruits and flowers. The trunk and branches can be dwarfed by pruning and even the leaves will become much smaller with the years of restriction as a bonsai, but fruit and flowers will always remain proportionate to their species. Thus a dwarf chestnut would have awkwardly large burs and

its leaves would tend to be as long as its branches, and the tiny-leafed Japanese maple is more suitable than the larger Canadian variety. When making a bonsai by layering it is often possible to find a natural sport, a branch with dwarfed leaves which will make an especially fine tree.

Japan has a fairly average temperate climate. It is similar to that of large parts of America and most of Europe. It is damper than Oklahoma or Italy; hotter in summer than Colorado or England; colder in winter than Florida or Spain; but these are minor differences for which adjustments can be made. Bonsai should survive in any country with normal seasons. In the tropics, where the temperature and humidity hardly vary throughout the year, they have never so far been kept alive for more than six months, and the same would probably be true of subarctic countries. It is, however, possible that a bonsai of an indigenous tree, such as the mangosteen, might be reared successfully in Malaya and a local variety of pine or fir in Northern Canada or Sweden.

We have tried in this book to explain how the Japanese cultivate, care for, and enjoy their bonsai. The Japanese are an etiquette-loving people; they like to tabulate their experience and deduce rules from it. This can be seen in the elaborate rules which govern the art of flower arrangement, the tea ceremony, and indeed good manners in everyday life. There are also rules and etiquette where bonsai are concerned. We do not mean the basic principles for the cultivation of a healthy tree, but the etiquette which decides the form most suited to the species of tree, the choice of pot, the presentation, and even the manner in which the bonsai should be appreciated. We have tried to give the basic rules of Japanese taste underlying this etiquette, not because we think Western people must slavishly imitate the Japanese, but because these rules are interesting in themselves and will perhaps help others to realize the value set in Japan upon the bonsai. The reader will, we hope, understand why things are done and arranged in a certain way and by studying the pictures see the end result of the application of these principles. With this knowledge behind him he can create his own practical experience and adapt the rules evolved in Japan to his personal taste.

Japanese bonsai naturally resemble trees in Japan — those fantastic, wind-twisted trees that make a glorious pattern in paintings and prints but, until seen actually growing, seem like the figment of an artist's imagination. The trees of every country have their own peculiar beauty. A dwarf olive tree could be equally symbolic of Mediterranean lands, a little group of firs at the top of a slope of rocks and dwarf heather could recall moorland all over the world, and the satin trunk of the silver birch would lend beauty to a Scots or Canadian bonsai.

Bonsai may be grown in five different ways: they may be found already matured in places where natural conditions have stunted them; they may be grown from seed; or they may be made from cuttings, from graftings, or from layerings or dividings. The following descriptions of these five methods, together with Appendix 3, which indicates the most practical methods for various types of trees, should put anyone who is truly interested well on the way to the creation of a bonsai. It might be noted here that miniature bonsai (these are small enough to be held easily in the palm of one hand, pot and all; see classification on page 62) can be made only from seedlings or cuttings; trees with variegated leaves, only from cuttings; and crossbreeds, only from seedlings.

BONSAI FROM NATURALLY STUNTED PLANTS

In Japan these bonsai are the most highly prized of all and the finest trees are natural

dwarfs. They are collected from high up in the mountains or on the seashore, where the soil is poor and where strong winds tend to distort the trunk (see Plates 1–10). The shape of the trunk is of paramount importance as, being old wood, it cannot be altered. The branches of natural dwarfs are usually poor but this need not discourage the finder as they can be improved by careful pruning. Wild seedlings can also be collected and trained, being especially suitable for group plantings. The greatest advantage of this type of bonsai, adding no little zest to the hunt, is that, given luck and persistence, the collector may find a natural dwarf which can be made into a really good bonsai in record time. We ourselves have seen such bonsai which, after about a year's training, looked older and more finished than others which had been in training for many years.

The hunt for natural bonsai can be a most pleasant sport in itself, one which has been practiced so assiduously for so many generations in Japan, and even in nearby countries, that good specimens are today almost never found outside the protected areas of national parks. Other countries, where such stunted trees have not been prized, offer much better hunting grounds, but even so, the hunter should scrupulously abide by local regulations in the interest of conservation and, as a nature lover, should always collect his specimens with moderation and in such a way as to do no harm to the natural scenery.

The best season for collecting is in early spring before the new buds open. Pines may also be transplanted in early autumn, after the end of the summer growth but before the winter hardening of the twigs begins. In the case of deciduous trees, it is possible, although not advisable, to transplant them when they are in leaf, but this should on no account be done until the summer, and half the leaves should be stripped off as soon as the tree has been dug up. The most dangerous season for transplanting deciduous trees is when the leaves are newly opened and still tender.

Before setting out on a collecting expedition, it is well to prepare the following articles, which are described in more detail in Appendix 1: a small trowel or shovel, sharp scissors, a quantity of sphagnum moss, oiled paper or plastic sheeting, and some string. A small crowbar may sometimes be needed to break rocks, and a hook on the end of a stick is also convenient.

When a suitable tree has been found, it is important to retain as large a quantity as possible of the surrounding earth. The tree must be dug out very carefully, if possible without cutting the taproot. If this is unavoidable. the root should be cut as low down as possible, particularly in the case of pines. The earth and roots are then covered with wet sphagnum moss and tied up in the paper or plastic sheet.

During transportation back to the nursery, the tree should be propped up carefully so that it does not roll about or get unduly jolted. It must be kept in the open air and not put for any great length of time into any place so tightly enclosed as, say, the luggage compartment of a car. During the journey it needs protection from the sun and wind and the leaves must be sprayed with water often enough to keep them damp. A large perfume-spray is useful for this purpose.

The tree should be planted as soon as its destination is reached. If it has small, fine roots near the trunk (this can be judged by whether the soil falls away from the trunk, for, if there are small roots, they will hold the soil), it is planted in a deep training pot without removing the original soil. Any root ends showing through the soil are trimmed off with a sharp knife. If the tree has only one or two large, thick roots, it is best planted out, together with its own soil, in a garden bed or a field.

After being planted, all trees should be protected from direct sun and wind, the earth kept moist, and the leaves sprayed at least three or four times a day. After three or four months of this initial care the tree will begin to form new roots, at which point it is sufficiently established to benefit by manuring and may be allowed direct sunlight. Now it is no longer necessary to spray the leaves, though the earth of course should still be kept moist. If the tree is in good condition strong new buds will appear on the branches.

At the end of the first year the tree is transplanted from its training pot or from the ground into a pot suitable to its dimensions. Some of the original soil is still retained and the roots are trimmed. If there is an abundant growth of new roots at the base of the trunk, the roots are cut as described in the case of repotting (Chapter 3). If, however, only a few fine roots have formed round the thick taproot, this is only slightly pruned; if it is cut back drastically, the tree will die. The taproot is pruned again at the end of the second year, and finally cut off short at the end of the third year. This final cutting, however, should only be done when new roots have appeared at the base. This type of root formation is very common in pines and needs very careful treatment.

Once the tree is strong and well established, the branches may be wired and shaped, usually about three months after

the second repotting, that is, when it has been in the nursery for rather more than two years. As described in the chapter on training, the branches should be arranged so as to display to best advantage the beauty of the trunk.

Not all trees lend themselves to natural dwarfing. Pines and junipers are perhaps the most common since mountains and sea-shore are their natural habitats. Among deciduous trees, maples, elms, hornbeams, etc., are occasionally to be found.

Bonsai from Seed

Bonsai of any species may be bred from seed, although of course this method takes the most time (see Plates 11–13). For good results, it is essential to use fresh seed, which should be collected in the autumn and is best planted directly. If it is necessary to keep the seed till the following spring, it is enclosed in an airtight container and kept dry and cool, in the refrigerator if desired, and then sown in the early spring, before the budding season.

The seed may be sown in a pot, a box, or prepared ground. Before sowing, it is soaked overnight and, in the case of fruit stones or other hard-shelled seeds, the shell is broken to help germination. The pot is

filled with soil in the same way as for repotting (Chapter 3). The seed is placed on the surface of this soil, (if there is more than one seed, care should be taken that they do not touch each other) and the whole covered with topsoil to about twice the depth of the seed. The pot is then watered, never with a can, but by standing it in a container of water long enough for the moisture to permeate upwards to the surface of the soil; this procedure will take only a few minutes if the level of the water in the container is as high as the surface of the soil in the pot. The topsoil is next covered with a layer of damp sphagnum moss, chaff, or wood shavings. This should be lifted from time to time to make sure that the soil is not getting too dry. The pot may be kept either outside or indoors. At the end of a week the entire moss covering should be lifted and, if there are signs of germination, removed altogether. The pot

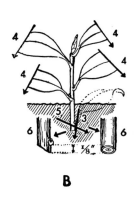

B

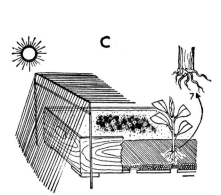

C

Fig. 1.—Ordinary cutting (camellia). *A)* Parent branch. 1) Remove flower buds. 2) Scissor-cuts (to produce four cuttings). *B)* Prepared cutting (from topmost cut of A). 3) Remove lower leaves. 4) Scissor-trim upper leaves. 5) Knife-cut stem. 6) Cut stem, 2 views. *C)* Cutting planted about 6 mos. 7) Root development. *D)* Transplanted to training pot.

must be set out of doors where it can get direct sunshine and the seedlings watered regularly (from a can) and kept well weeded.

Pine seedlings should be left undisturbed for a full year, but deciduous seedlings can be lifted after six months except in the case of very slow-growing trees. The seedlings are separated and transferred either to individual small pots or to the open ground. The latter produces quicker results, but is less convenient. The seedlings require normal all-year-round care until they are fit for training.

BONSAI FROM CUTTINGS

With the exception of pines, almost all trees can be bred from cuttings (see Plates 14–17). The cuttings are taken in the same way as for ordinary full-sized trees. There are two seasons for taking cuttings: early spring, when the new buds are beginning to swell; and early autumn (September in a normal temperate climate), when plants make a last growing effort before becoming dormant. In Japan the rainy season in June is also considered suitable.

A cutting should be from three to five inches long with three or five nodes on it (see Fig. 1). It is taken from the parent branch by cutting straight across with sharp scissors, just below a node. If the tree is of the large-leafed variety and the cutting is made after the budding season, one-third of each leaf must be cut off. All buds or leaves should be removed for half an inch at the bottom of the shoot. This end is then cut on the slant with a knife just below a node as this node will form the lowest root. If the shoot is thicker than an ordinary pencil, a double cut will be needed on either side of the stem, one cut being

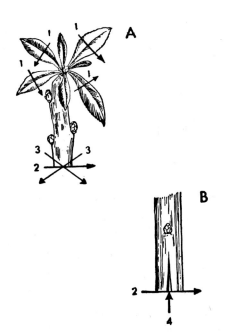

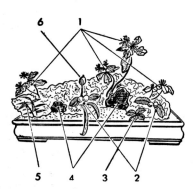

Key to Color Plate 5. 1) Winter chrysanthemum. 2) Ardisia. 3) Bird's-eye.
4) Stones. 5) Dwarf bamboo. 6)Japa-
nese ground orchid.

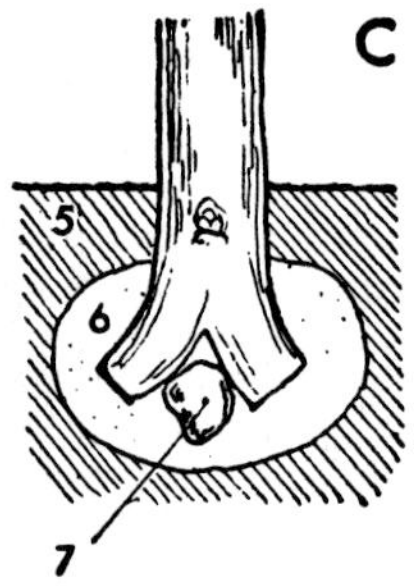

Fig. 2.—Very thick cutting (flowering
quince). A) Tapering method. 1) Scissor-
cuts. 2) Knife-cut from parent branch. 3)
Tapering knife-cuts. B & C) Notch method.
4) Knife-cut notch. 5) Soil. 6) Clay. 7)
Pebble or piece of wood.

longer than the other. When the shoot is
a very thick one (Fig. 2) it is necessary
either to make two tapering cuts in the end,
or else to make a deep notch, into which a
small stone or piece of wood is inserted to
prevent its closing, after which the aperture
is filled with clay or loam.

In the case of evergreens, the prepared
cutting must be laid in water for several
hours, the leaves, if any, above the surface.
Leaves should not be pruned away entirely,
as they assist growth.

Thus prepared, the shoot is planted to
the depth of about an inch in a pot or box
of coarse, well aerated, sandy soil and

watered thoroughly both from below and
from above. The soil must be kept moist
and the leaves sprayed, particularly in the
evening. Roots develop readily from the
nodes, and at the end of six to twelve
months, depending upon the species, the

Color Plate 5. Seasonal group planting: New Year's.
See planting chart above.

Color Plate 6. Weeping forsythia. Clump style. 10".
About 25 yrs. Produced by dividing. Glazed Chinese
pot of Kuang-tung ware.

Color Plate 7. Wild-thyme azalea. Clinging-to-a-rock
style. 1'. 7 yrs. Produced from a cutting and planted
on rock 3 yrs. ago. Bronze container by Houn Harada
of Tokyo, in the shallow depth particularly suited to
this style. This type of azalea blooms twice yearly.

Color Plate 5

Color Plate 6

Color Plate 7

cutting may be transplanted into a training pot or, as in the case of seedlings, into the ground. The pot should be kept out of doors but protected, during the first three months, from wind and direct sunlight. If the cutting has taken successfully, fresh buds and leaves will appear, after which normal everyday care is sufficient.

BONSAI BY GRAFTING

With the exception of the rough-barked black pine (*nishiki*), which cannot be bred successfully by other means, first-quality bonsai can never be created by grafting. The method is often used, however, in the interest of speed, particularly in the case of the cheaper commercial bonsai; it may be readily detected by the unsightly scar which the graft leaves on the trunk. It is fairly common to find a five-needle pine grafted onto an ordinary black pine as the latter quickly produces a handsome trunk.

Grafting should be done in early spring. It is important to choose the right moment. The accompanying Table of Graftings indicates the appropriate times for the Tokyo area only, but the general rule is that the scion must still be dormant, with no sap yet rising in it, while in the stock the sap has already begun to rise. The shoot from which the scions are taken will have been cut from its tree, to a length of less than a yard and with winter buds on it, in the

TABLE OF GRAFTINGS

Stock	Scion	Tokyo Grafting Season
Apple Wild crab-apple	Apple	Mid-March
Wild crab-apple	Crab apple	Mid-March
Oshima cherry	Cherry	Late February to mid-March
Trifoliata citron	Citrus family	Late April to early May
Black pine	Five-needle pine	Late February to early March
Peach Plum	Peach	Mid-March
Pear	Pear	Early March
Persimmon Dwarf persimmon	Persimmon	Late March to early April
Japanese flowering apricot *(ume)*	Japanese flowering apricot	Early to mid-March
Wisteria	Wisteria	Early to mid-March

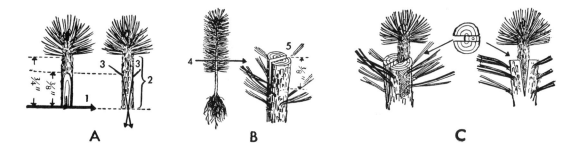

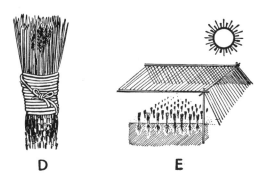

Fig. 3.—Top grafting (five-needle pine on-to black pine). **A)** Prepared scion, 2 views. 1) Knife-cut stem. 2) Knife-cut needles. 3) Knife-trim stem. **B)** Preparing stock. 4) First scissor-cut and then knife-cut smooth. 5) Knife-cut cleft. **C)** Inserting scion in stock, 3 views. **D)** Bound graft. **E)** After 2-3 mos.

late autumn of the previous year and kept buried up to two-thirds of its length in the ground (see Fig. 5). Now, depending upon the thickness of the scion required for a particular grafting, all but the upper and lower few inches of this shoot may be cut into sections to make a number of scions; each should be between an inch and a half and two inches long with one or two strong buds on it (see Fig. 5). The stock should be a seedling about two or three years old and in vigorous condition.

There are a number of grafting methods. Two principal methods—top and side grafting—are described below in detail. See also Figs. 3–7 and Plates 18–25.

Top grafting (Fig. 3). This method is particularly suitable for pines and is the easier of the two. The stock should not be thicker than a pencil and the top is cut off straight across, leaving four or five bunches of needles adhering to the stem. The stock is then split down the middle with a sharp knife to the depth of about half an

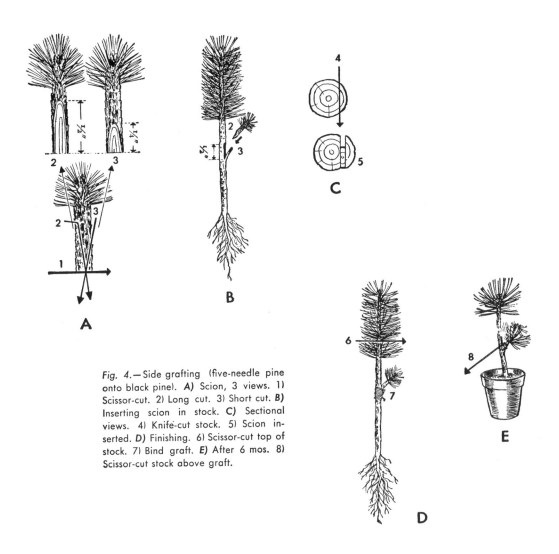

Fig. 4. — Side grafting (five-needle pine onto black pine). *A)* Scion, 3 views. 1) Scissor-cut. 2) Long cut. 3) Short cut. *B)* Inserting scion in stock. *C)* Sectional views. 4) Knife-cut stock. 5) Scion inserted. *D)* Finishing. 6) Scissor-cut top of stock. 7) Bind graft. *E)* After 6 mos. 8) Scissor-cut stock above graft.

inch. The scion should be about an inch long and, if possible, of the same thickness as the stock. The lower end is cut into a wedge which will fit into the split in the stock, approximately a third of an inch each of bare stem and needles remaining above this point. If, when the scion is inserted into the stock, it is found to be slightly smaller, it must be placed to one side so that one edge of the bark of the scion is flush with the bark of the stock. The needles are all gathered up together and the graft bound with raffia (this must be removed at the end of the year) or rice straw (this need not be removed, as it will decay naturally). The plant is then put in a shady place, protected from the wind, for two weeks, after which its care is the same as for ordinary bonsai.

Side grafting (Fig. 4). This method may be used for all types of trees, including pines. It requires a rather heavier stock. A slanting cut is made in the trunk, about two-thirds of an inch deep. The scion is

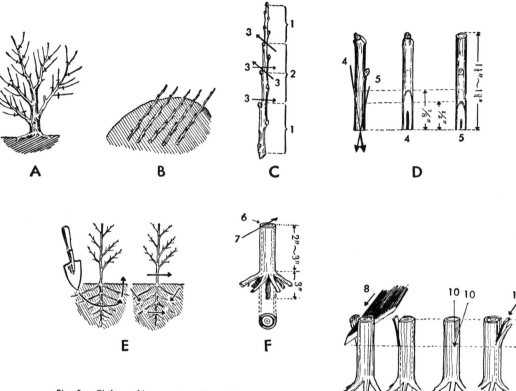

Fig. 5.—Cleft grafting, preparation. **A)** Parent tree showing scissor-cutting points. **B)** Dormant shoots buried in mound of earth. **C)** Cutting shoot into scions. 1) Portions discarded. 2) Portion used. 3) Scissor cuts, leaving 1-2 nodes on each scion. **D)** Trimming scion, 3 views. 4) Long cut. 5) Short cut. **E)** Stock trimming. **F)** Trimmed stock. 6) Slightly bevel entire circumference. 7) Slice off a segment. **G)** Single-cut cleft for thin scion. 8) Knife-cut downward. 9) Cut through cambium. **H)** Double-cut cleft for heavy scion. 10) Knife cuts. 11) Remove section from cut.

trimmed so that the inner side has a long cut and the outer side a short one. In the case of a needle tree, if the needles of the scion are too long, they should be trimmed back to about one inch. The scion is inserted and bound into place and cared for in the same way as in the case of top grafting. After about six months the stock extending above the joint is cut off.

Cleft grafting. See Figs. 5 & 6.

Inarching grafting. See Fig. 7.

Bonsai by Layering and Dividing

The advantages of this way of creating bonsai are that it is possible to make a full-grown tree in a comparatively short time and that full use can be made of the branch of a tree which is a natural sport, one with unusually small leaves or a particularly suitable shape.

There are three simple methods of layering, and also five of dividing, which, tech-

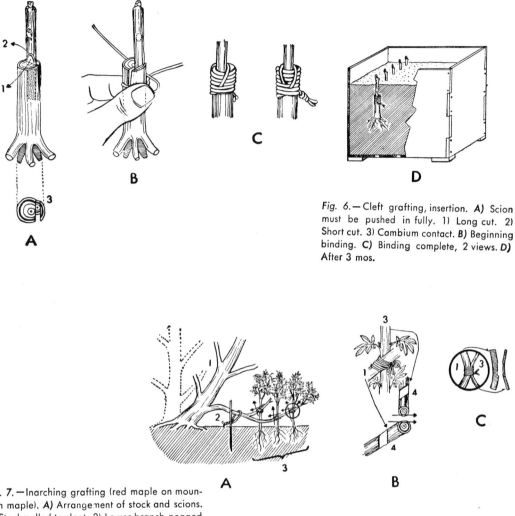

Fig. 6.—Cleft grafting, insertion. A) Scion must be pushed in fully. 1) Long cut. 2) Short cut. 3) Cambium contact. B) Beginning binding. C) Binding complete, 2 views. D) After 3 mos.

Fig. 7.—Inarching grafting (red maple on mountain maple). A) Arrangement of stock and scions. 1) Stock pulled to slant. 2) Lower branch pegged down. 3) Seedling scions. B) Cross-branch connection. 4) Bark peeled off at points of contact. C) Parallel-branch connection (not shown in A).

nically, are considered either natural or induced layering:

Method A (Figs. 8 & 9). A tourniquet of copper wire is put round the trunk or branch about an inch below the place where the new roots are desired. This should be done in spring at the beginning of the growing season and will keep the sap in the upper part of the branch. The area immediately above the tourniquet is then wrapped in tightly packed, moist sphagnum moss and covered with agricultural plastic. Ordinary plastic should not be used as it is not porous. This plastic cover is particularly important as it makes it possible to watch the development of the new roots as they push their way through the moss.

In the case of trees which form roots quickly, such as the Sargent juniper, cryptomeria, maple, willow, crape myrtle, and camellia, the cover may be tied at both ends and no extra watering will be needed.

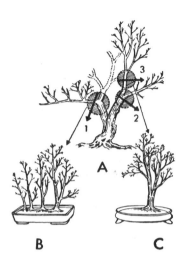

B   C

Fig. 8.—Layering by Methods A & B. *A)* Parent tree showing 3 possible layering points. *B)* Bonsai from layering at point 1. *C)* From layering at point 3.

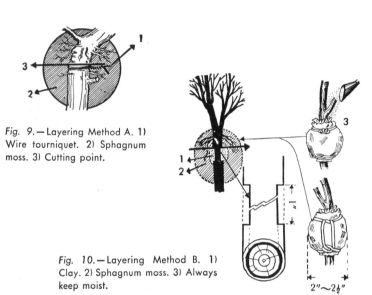

Fig. 9.—Layering Method A. 1) Wire tourniquet. 2) Sphagnum moss. 3) Cutting point.

Fig. 10.—Layering Method B. 1) Clay. 2) Sphagnum moss. 3) Always keep moist.

2"~2½"

Roots will develop in from three to six months, and if the layering is done early enough in the season, the tree can be separated from the parent stem in September and be established within a year.

Slow root-forming trees, such as the pine, or any branch over five years old, require the upper end of the plastic cover to be left open so that the moss can be moistened. The wrapping must be left in place from one to three years, fresh moss being applied once a year in the early spring. It is better to leave the wrapping for a longer rather than a shorter period.

Once the new roots are well developed, the tree is then cut off from the parent trunk and the moss carefully removed with pincers. It is planted in the ordinary way, but special care must be taken not to damage the tender new roots. Maples and other deciduous trees potted before September should have all their leaves cut off with scissors.

Method B. (Figs. 8, 10 & Plate 26).

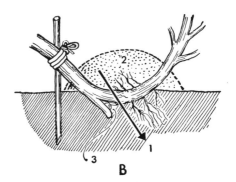

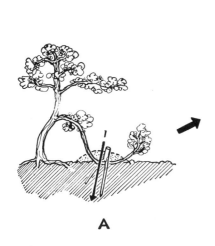

Fig. 11.—Layering Method C. **A)** Branch pegged to ground. 1) Point of eventual cutting. **B)** Detail of a similar arrangement. 2) Soil. 3) Clay and small stone or piece of wood.

Instead of using a wire tourniquet, the bark may be peeled off for an inch and a half below the place where the roots are to form. The peeled area is then coated with moist clay or red loam, wrapped in moist sphagnum moss which has been packed fairly tightly, and again covered with plastic. This method produces quicker results than Method A but is more dangerous as it may kill the tree, particularly if it is a pine.

Method C. (Fig. 11 & Plate 26). This method is safe and simple if a branch can be found that is long enough to reach the ground. A slit is made in the branch at a point which will touch the ground, and a small stone or piece of wood is inserted in the slit. The aperture is filled with clay or red loam. The branch is then pegged to the ground and the area with the slit is covered with soil, which must be kept damp. The roots will take about as long to form as in Method A. The earth should be carefully removed from time to time to see whether the roots have appeared; when they do so, the branch can be cut off just below them and the tree potted in the ordinary way.

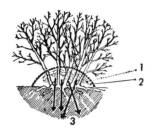 

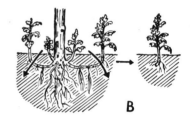

Fig. 12. — Dividing Method **1,** entire plant and roots. 1) New roots developing. 2) Mound of earth. 3) Cutting points.

Fig. 13. — Dividing Method 2, shoots and roots. **A)** Pomegranate. **B)** Chrysanthemum.

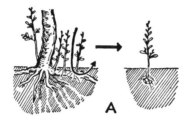

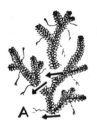 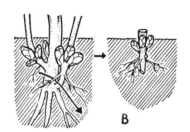

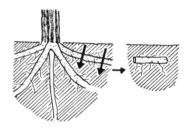

Fig. 15. — Dividing Method **4,** roots without buds. Wisteria.

Fig. 14. — Dividing Method 3, buds and roots. **A)** Kurama moss. **B)** Polygonum.

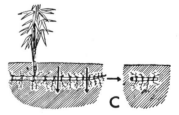

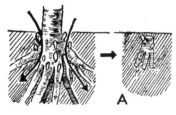 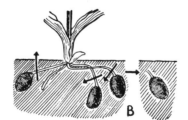

Fig. 16.—Dividing method 5, roots, bulbs, or rootstock, with buds. **A)** Chinese bellflower. **B)** Pecteilis. **C)** Bamboo.

Dividing. (Figs. 12–16). Certain plants, as indicated in Appendix 3, may be propagated by dividing (1) the entire plant and roots, (2) the shoots, over three inches long, with their roots, (3) the buds, under three inches long, with roots, (4) the roots without buds, or (5) roots, bulbs, or rootstock, with buds on them.

Plate 1. A naturally stunted rhododendron as found in the mountains. The scale measures 1'8" in each direction.

Plate 2. Collecting the rhododenron, together with some pumila pines found nearby.

Plate 3. A similar rhododendron after being trained for 20 yrs.

Plate 4. Pumila pines in Ibaragi Prefecture, north of Tokyo, suitable for making into large-size bonsai.

Plate 5. Pumila pine found high in the mountains. The scale measures 10″ by 16″.

Plate 6. Five-needle pines planted in earth after being collected from the mountains.

Plate 7. A naturally stunted five-needle pine after being planted on a rock and trained for 4 yrs.

Plate 9. A single tree from the group shown in Plate 8; note its few needles and long primary root All the soil was removed from the roots for this photograph; actually, as much of the original soil as possible should be retained.

Plate 8. Black pines collected from a rocky moor, after a 4-day trip by mail packed in a wooden box with sphagnum moss.

Plate 10. Two black pines aged 15-20 yrs. and collected 2 yrs. ago.

Plate 11. Sowing seed. Shown are the seed (which have been soaked in water 24 hrs.), being sown over a bed of No. 5 main soil; containers of various sizes of soil; and working tools such as the revolving table, pincettes, brush, whisk, and trowel.

Plate 12. Seedlings. **Back row,** left to right: 1) Mountain maple, 8 mos. 2) Common Ezo spruce, 1 yr. 3) Black pine, 8 mos. 4) Five-needle pine, 1 yr. 5) Seeds covered with top soil and then sphagnum moss. **Front row:** 1) Mountain maple, 3 yrs. 2) Same, 8 mos. 3) Common Ezo spruce, 1 yr. 4) Black pine, 2 yrs. 5) Same, planted in group at 3 mos. 6) Five-needle pine, 1.5 yrs. 7) Same, 2 yrs.

Plate 13. Final products. 1) Japanese mountain maple, 9", 10 yrs. 2) Five-needle pines, 4", 13 yrs., made into a group 4 yrs. ago.

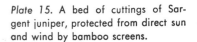

Plate 14. Potted cuttings. **Back row:** 1) Common camellia, 8 mos. 2) Common Ezo spruce, 1 yr. 8 mos. 3) Dwarf dog-rose, 1 mo. 4) Hemlock, 1 yr. **Front row:** 1) Common camellia, also 8 mos. 2) Common Ezo spruce, 2.5 yrs. 3) Dwarf dog-rose, 1 yr.

Plate 15. A bed of cuttings of Sargent juniper, protected from direct sun and wind by bamboo screens.

Plate 16. The bonsai emerges. **Left to right:** 1) Wild-thyme azalea, 1 yr. 2) English holly, 4 yrs. 3) Common Ezo spruce, 6 yrs. 4) Hemlock, 6 yrs. 5) Dwarf azalea, 2 yrs. 6) Dwarf flowering quince, 8 yrs.

Plate 17. These 10-yr.-old cuttings of Ezo spruce were planted on a rock only 1 yr. ago. 9". Blue Japanese pot of Tosui ware.

Plate 18. Top grafting made 2 yrs. 4 mos. ago. A five-needle-pine scion on a 2-yr.-old black-pine seedling stock.

Plate 19. Close-up of Plate 18.

Plate 20. Five-needle pine branches on corticata pine trunk. 1'7". Red unglazed Chinese pot. All the branches were top- and side-grafted onto the trunk about 10 yrs. ago.

Plate 21. Side grafting made 2 yrs. 4 mos. ago. Five-needle-pine scion (the shorter branch) on 2-yr.-old black-pine seedling stock.

Plate 23. Cleft grafting made 1 yr. 7 mos. ago; stock is a 2-yr.-old sand-pear cutting; scion is also a sand pear. *a)* Stock. *b)* Scion. *c)* lst year's growth. *d)* 2nd year's growth.

Plate 24. Close-up of Plate 23.

Plate 22. Close-up of Plate 21.

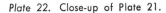

Plate 25. Cleft grafting made 4 yrs. ago; orange-tree scion on a tri-foliata-citron stock (2-yr.-old cutting). The grafting point is the knot just at the rim of the pot.

Plate 26. Layering a mountain maple. The larger tree is being layered in three places: the two plastic wrappings cover Method B layerings and the pulled-down branch is a Method C. The smaller trees were produced 6 mos. ago by Method B.

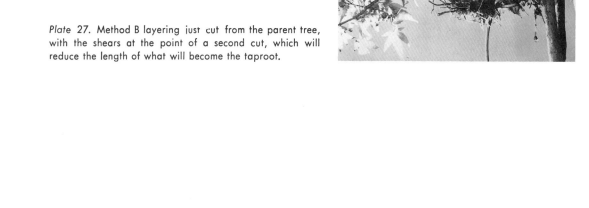

Plate 27. Method B layering just cut from the parent tree, with the shears at the point of a second cut, which will reduce the length of what will become the taproot.

3 ⦿ *POTTING AND REPOTTING*

BONSAI EXIST ONLY IN POTS; IT is a combination of training and the confining action of the pot that makes the bonsai. The training of a sapling cannot begin until it is put into a pot, and the healthy condition of all dwarf trees depends to a great extent on the way in which the earth in the pots is changed and the roots pruned. A healthy bonsai puts out new roots every year and these roots make it increasingly difficult for water and air to penetrate the soil. The surface roots will get all the nourishment and the main root near the trunk will harden and atrophy. It is therefore periodically necessary to cut back the main root and thin out the surface roots.

How often this is done depends on the tree's rate of growth. Evergreens, such as pines and spruces, require repotting only once in from three to five years; broadleaved evergreens, such as the camellia and the laurel, and deciduous trees, once every two or three years; flowering trees and fruit trees, every second year, but when the blossom or crop is very heavy it may be necessary to repot after a year; willows and crape myrtle, which are very quick growing, twice a year. It should be remembered that these intervals apply to healthy trees which have received proper care.

The best season for repotting is in the early spring when the first new buds appear. A secondary season occurs in late summer or early autumn when for a short time the roots check their growth before the final autumn shooting. Fruit trees such as plum and apricot, which flower before the leaves appear, should be repotted after flowering, but before the leaves open. Fruit trees such as the cherry and apple, which flower in late spring, should be repotted before flowering. A bonsai must never be repotted in winter. In cold weather the tree is in a dormant state and therefore

unable to establish itself in the new soil and put out new roots. It is equally dangerous to repot in late spring and early summer when the leaves are fully open but still tender.

If it is absolutely essential to repot in an off-season, say because the pot has been broken or the soil is in dangerously poor condition, the leaves of deciduous trees must all be cut off first, unless it is late in August, by which time they may be left on without ill effects. When a pine tree requires such an emergency repotting, the new, soft needles should be pulled off, leaving the old ones.

Soils

The soils used in potting bonsai may be classified according to texture and type, different mixtures being used for the bottom, the main, and the top layers in any one pot. The appropriate textures are determined by the size of the pot, while the appropriate types are determined by two factors: the species of tree and whether the tree is still being trained or its training has been completed. These different requirements will be set forth in tables which follow, but first a few general observations are needed.

The soils used in Japan are much the same types as those found in any temperate climate. They should be collected at a depth of about three feet below the surface of the ground, to avoid contamination and insects, and should be spread out and dried in the sun for about a week before sieving. All soils should be sieved and separated, being placed in separate boxes according to type and texture. Powdery soil prevents good drainage and, except in cases where powdered black loam is specifically mentioned, should never be used. The mixtures indicated are those used in Japan, that is to say in a moderate climate with a tendency toward dampness. In a dry, hot climate the mixture should be varied by replacing the specified amount of sand with a similar amount of a mixture of heavy clay, leaf mould, and sphagnum moss in equal parts, as this will hold moisture; if sphagnum moss is unavailable, then use equal parts of clay and leaf mould only. In a climate cooler than Japan's there is no need to alter the basic mixtures given below.

The following tables should answer most practical needs so far as bonsai soils are concerned (see also Fig. 19). More precise, technical information may be found in the soil analyses given in Appendix 2.

TABLE OF SOIL TEXTURES

No. used to designate texture	Size of sieve (in approx. no. of holes per linear inch)
1	3
2	4
3	7
4	10
5	14
6	24
7	35

TABLE OF TEXTURES USED IN DIFFERENT POTS

Note: Where more than one texture is indicated, the coarser should predominate.

Size of pot (in inches)		Number of texture		
Depth	Length of longest side or diameter	Bottom Soil	Main Soil	Top Soil
Under 2	Under 2	5	5 and 6	6
2 — 5	Over 2	4	5	6
5 — 7	Over 2	3 and 4	5	6
7 — 9	Over 2	2, 3, and 4	5	6
Over 9	Over 2	1, 2, 3, and 4	5	5

TABLE OF SOIL TYPES

Symbol used to designate type	Description
S	Sand or fine gravel such as river sand
BS	Black loam, sieved
BP	Black loam, powdered
C	Clay soil or reddish loam (35 to 50% clay)
K	Light clay soil mixed with sand (*Kanuma-tsuchi*)
P	Peat (used for group and rock plantings)
L	Leaf mould or humus (to encourage growth)
SM	Sphagnum moss (fresh for propagating and potting; partially decayed for mulching and packing)

TABLE OF TYPES USED IN DIFFERENT MIXTURES

Note: Letters designate the type of soil; numerals indicate the percentage to be used.

Kind of plant	While being trained			After completing training		
	Bottom Soil	Main Soil	Top Soil	Bottom Soil	Main Soil	Top Soil
Evergreen needle trees	S60, C40	S20, C50, BS30, plus BP10	S20, C40, B40	S60, C40	S30, C60, BS10	S20, C40, BS40
Evergreen broad-leaved trees & deciduous trees	S40, C40, BS20	C30, BS70, plus BP10	S10, C30, BS60	S40, C40, BS20	S20, C40, BS40	S10, C30, BS60
Flowering & fruit trees	S40, C40, BS20, plus L10	C20, BS80, plus L10	S10, C30, BS60	S40, C40, BS20, plus L10	S20, C40, BS40, plus L10	S10, C30, BS60
Rhododendron & azaleas	K50, SM50	K50, SM50	S10, C30, BS60	K50, SM50	K50, SM50	S10, C30, BS60
Maples & zelkovas	S40, C40, BS20	C70, BS30, plus BP10	S10, C30, BS60	S40, C40, BS20	C70, BS30, plus S10	S10, C30, BS60
Cuttings*	S60, C40	C100	C100	Same as while being trained		
Bamboo & willows	S40, C40, BS20	C20, BS60, L20, plus BP10	S10, C30, BS60	"	"	"
Grasses & herbs	S40, C40, BS20	C10, BS40, BP50	C10, BS40, BP50	"	"	"
Group & rock plantings	See Chapter 5					

* For cuttings use texture No. 6 in main soil irrespective of size of pot.

METHODS

1 Cleansing (Fig. 17 & Plates 28–32). Before this operation is begun, the old soil should be allowed to dry slightly—but not too much otherwise the tree will suffer— so that it comes away easily from the sides of the pot and from the roots. It should be noted that when loosening the soil with a chopstick (any strong, slender stick with a point will do) the stroke must always follow the direction in which the roots grow, that is to say from the trunk outwards and downwards. *First Step.* Any moss on the surface of the old soil is removed with tweezers and set aside on a board for future use. The tree is then eased out of the pot together with its soil, which can be loosened from the sides if necessary, and placed on a revolving table. *Second Step.* A mark is drawn on the surface of the soil so that one-third of the surface is inside the mark, round the trunk of the tree, and two-thirds are outside the mark. If a new and different-sized pot is to be used, this mark should be drawn in such a way that the area inside the mark represents one-third of the surface area of the new pot. All soil outside the mark is removed by jabbing a chopstick into the hard-packed soil, beginning at the surface and working downwards to the bottom. If the soil is very hard indeed, it may be necessary to use an iron bar to remove the outer crust, but this should be done with great care and in such a way as not to injure the roots. *Third Step.* From the one-third of the original soil which remains, one-half is now removed, this time by calculating the depth of the soil, dividing it in two and removing the lower half. *Fourth Step.* The remaining ball of soil round the roots is now further thinned out as follows: looking down on the surface of the soil, as if it were the crust of a pie divided into slices by the roots radiating out from the trunk and showing above the surface, the gardener removes every second slice of earth. Such soil as remains after this final treatment is left round the roots until the next repotting. This step is essential when the soil is old and hard but will, in fact, prove beneficial in all cases.

2. Root Trimming (Figs. 17, 18 & Plates 33, 34). Surface roots are never cut straight across but always on a slant. If the tree is healthy, long roots will hang down from it when the cleansing is completed. The main lateral roots are cut back by about a third, that is to say, the length of root finally showing beyond the nucleus of old soil should be roughly the same as the length between the trunk and

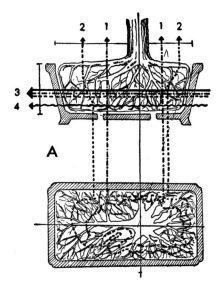

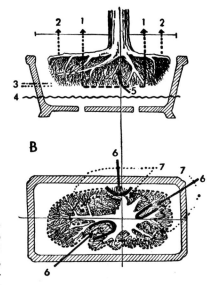

Fig. 17.—Removing old soil and trimming roots. A) Before beginning. 1) Lines mark two-thirds of old soil to be removed in 2nd Step
of cleansing. 2) Lines mark one-third of lateral roots to be trimmed
away. 3) Lines mark one-half of old soil to be removed in 3rd Step,
and, in the case of deciduous trees only, of bottom roots to be trimmed away. 4) Line marks bottom roots to be trimmed from evergreen
needle trees. B) After finishing. 5) Remaining nucleus of old soil.
6) Alternating slices of old soil removed this potting in 4th Step.
7) Slices to be removed next potting.

the outer edge of the nucleus. The bottom
roots below the trunk and main roots are
usually cut very short, close to the old soil,
but in the case of an evergreen needle tree
they are left somewhat larger. If a heavy
taproot is found, it should be cut off as
close to the trunk as possible, provided the
tree is in a condition to stand such treatment.
If in an unhealthy state, the taproot must
be pruned back gradually over a number
of years as in the making of a bonsai from
a naturally stunted tree (see Chapter 2).

3. *Potting* (Fig. 19 & Plates 30, 35–41).
Meanwhile the pot and its new soil will
have been prepared. The pot is thoroughly cleaned and its drainage hole or holes
covered with a porous material. If coconut
fiber is used for this purpose, it should be
stretched a little to make it sufficiently
porous. The bottom of the pot is covered
with a layer of bottom soil as shown in
Fig. 19. Onto this, main soil is sprinkled
until the pot is about three-quarters full,
care being taken not to mix the soils. If

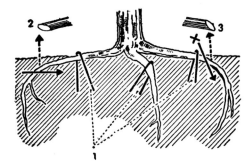

Fig. 18.—Trimming surface roots. 1) Copper hoops. 2) Correct trimming angle. 3) Wrong trimming angle.

the tree has a poor root development so that there will be a wide area of empty pot around it, it is as well to bank up the bottom soil around the inside of the pot, leaving a pocket in the center for the main soil. If the roots have been diseased or are in poor condition so that below the trunk and main roots there is a hollow, a little heap of main soil should be made at the place where the tree will stand. If the root development or the top-heavy shape of the tree prevents it from standing upright in the pot by itself, wires are prepared at this point with which to wire it to the pot.

After the roots have been pruned and the pot prepared, the tree is set in the pot. If the pot is oval or oblong, the tree should be placed slightly off-center, about one-third of the way from one end of the pot. If the pot is round or square, the tree is usually placed in the middle. The tree now rests upon a bed of main soil and should be gently worked a little way into the soil. The pot is then filled to the brim with main soil, which is sifted round the

trunk with a small scoop. The tree must be held firmly in place. If it has a handsome, rough bark, great care must be taken not to damage this. Holding the tree with one hand, the gardener gently prods with a chopstick between the roots so that the new soil can penetrate. This is done to eliminate air pockets under the soil, which are potential breeding places for rot. The prodding must be continued with gentle, firm strokes until no further holes appear between the roots. As long as holes continue to appear, they are filled up with new main soil, which is firmly jabbed down. When the tree is solidly established in the new earth, the excess main soil is brushed away; leaving about a quarter of an inch of the rim of the pot exposed to allow room for watering. Any roots showing above the surface should be pressed back with a chopstick and the earth smoothed over them. If these roots are large and stubborn they must be pinned down with a small hoop of copper wire shaped like a hairpin (see Fig. 18). When small, fine roots persist in ap-

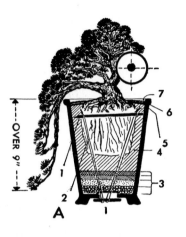
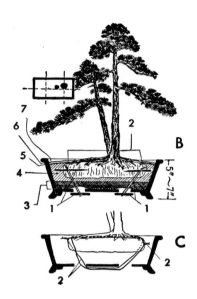

Fig. 19. — Potting, finishing, and fixing in pot. *A)* Centered tree in tall pot. 1) Bamboo sticks. 2) Copper wires. 3) Bottom soils. 4) Main soil. Although not shown, the main soil is worked well into the ball of roots to press firmly against the smaller ball of old soil. 5) Topsoil. 6) Dry moss. 7) Space of one-fourth to one-half inch for watering. *B)* Off-center tree in shallow pot. *C)* Alternate method of wiring B in the pot.

pearing above the surface, they can be trimmed off. Roots which belong below the earth must not be confused with the roots springing from the base of the trunk. The latter can be left exposed and greatly increase the beauty of the tree.

4. Finishing (Fig. 19 & Plates 42–44). The smooth surface of main soil is now covered with a thin layer of topsoil, the merest dusting, which is spread evenly with a soft brush. This fine topsoil prevents the more porous main soil from being washed away by heavy rain or blown away by wind; it also encourages the growth of moss. The topsoil is sprinkled with dried, powdered moss, which is pressed into the surface with a flat trowel; this will encourage the growth of the moss which is so important in preventing the washing away of soil.

5. Fixing in Pot (Fig. 19 & Plates 36, 46). When a bonsai has been newly re-potted it is often found to be unsteady in the pot, moving if touched. This is unavoidable in the case of trees which lean heavily to one side. It can, however, be circumvented by tying the tree into the pot and this is, in fact, to be recommended for all large trees. These wires are left in place for about six months.

When the bonsai to be repotted is one already well established in a pot, that is to say, a tree which has been in a pot for some four or five years, it will have formed a close mat of fine roots. These roots and the earth with them make a firm base for the trunk, and when the excess earth and roots have been removed, the tree can be secured firmly in place by wires passed through the drainage holes of the pot (which in this case are best covered with

STEPS IN REPOTTING

Plate 28. Using an iron hook to loosen the old soil from the edges of the pot.

Plate 29. Using a chopstick to complete the loosening.

Plate 30. Putting in the main soil. Previously the drainage holes have been covered with coconut fiber, two copper wires have been threaded through the holes to be used to fix the tree in the pot, and the bottom soil has been put in.

Plate 31. Loosening the outside roots with the iron hook.

Plate 32. Removing two-thirds of the old soil with a chopstick.

Plate 33. Trimming the roots with sharp scissors.

Plate 34. Root-trimming finished.

Plate 35. Inserting the tree in the pot.

Plate 36. Fixing the tree in the pot with the wires.

Plate 37. Putting in more main soil.

Plate 38. Working the soil down around the roots by prodding with a chopstick.

Plate 39. Brushing away excess main soil.

Plate 40. Pressing surface roots back into the soil.

Plate 41. Trimming back into the soil the fine roots which still show on surface.

Plate 42. Spreading a paper-thin layer of top soil.

Plate 43. Sprinkling dried, powdered moss over surface.

Plate 44. Pressing the powdered moss into the soil with a trowel.

Plate 45. Watering the tree from above and below.

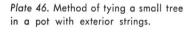

Plate 46. Method of tying a small tree in a pot with exterior strings.

Plate 47. Transplanting seedlings at 6 mos. **Left-hand group:** black pine. **Right-hand group:** mountain maple. Each group shows: 1) a seedling just as it comes from the earth, 2) a seedling with its primary root trimmed back (in an actual case neither so much soil nor so many of the hair roots would be removed as shown here), and 3) a potted seedling.

coconut fiber) and across the ball of roots. If the pot has only one drainage hole, the wire can be looped round a stick across the hole underneath the pot. This method of holding the bonsai in place is excellent as the wires are almost entirely concealed, but when the tree is in poor condition or is being potted for the first time this support is not sufficient. In such cases wires must be passed under the pot, after potting is completed, and attached someway up the trunk, preferably at a fork. A wire is best passed round the rim of the pot to hold the others in place.

6. *Watering* (Plate 45). A large container is prepared beforehand in which the water is sufficiently deep to cover the pot almost to the rim when it is placed in it. A garden trough or old sink is suitable; a baby's bath or large washtub with a flat bottom will also do. It is very important that the water should be either well or rain water; if tap water is used, it must be drawn and left standing in the open air for at least three or four days. The newly potted bonsai is placed in the water to soak. At the same time the tree is watered with a fine-spray can, care being taken to wet all the leaves, but not to wash out the soil. The best way to do this is to wave the can

up and down so that the water falls like rain without being concentrated in one place. The pot should be left standing in the trough for several minutes.

7. *Aftercare.* When a bonsai has been repotted it requires special attention. An evergreen or a tree in leaf should be kept for about a week in a shady place protected from wind and rain. Wind and sun will not harm a leafless tree, but shelter should be given during rain lest the soil be washed away. The tree is watered about three times in the first week. If, however, the earth round the trunk looks dry, this spot is watered with a syringe spray. If the tree is in poor condition, the area round the trunk is covered preferably with wet sphagnum moss, or with a pad of hessian or wood shavings. The moss must not be left in place for more than three weeks as roots may start to form in it. A bonsai should never be manured until one month after repotting. If the season permits, it should not be manured for three months.

8. *Transplanting Seedlings* (Plate 47). A seedling may be transplanted when it has put out three or four new leaves. At the same time the taproot is cut short, leaving five or six small side-roots at the

base of the stem. If the seedling is required for a "small" bonsai, that is to say, one less than six inches high, it is put into a three-inch training pot. The tree remains in this pot until it has been given its final shape (see Chapter 4). If the seedling is to become a normal-sized bonsai with a heavy trunk, it is planted out in the ground. It is dug up every year, the roots are pruned in the ordinary way, and it is replanted in a new place. The tree is left in the ground for three or four years, but during that time it is trained in the same way as a tree in a pot. The roots of seedlings are very tender and should never have the soil removed from them or made firm round them with a stick. If the old soil does not fall away easily it should be washed off. When the tree is repotted, the earth must be settled by either hitting the sides of the pot smartly with the fist or tapping the bottom of the pot lightly against a tabletop or other flat surface without tilting the tree; the pot should never be shaken back and forth as this might displace the hole cover.

9. *Treatment of Cuttings.*

After about six months a cutting may be repotted, provided the season is suitable, that is to say, neither in winter nor early summer. The roots of a cutting break so easily that great care must be taken when removing the tree from the pot. The best way is to remove the earth intact from the pot and soak it in water until the soil becomes soft and falls away easily from the roots. If the roots are longer than the depth of the pot, they are cut back to that length. When a cutting has a naturally attractive shape it can be transplanted straight into a decorative pot; otherwise it should be returned to its training pot. It is repotted in the normal way.

10. *Special Conditions Requiring Immediate Repotting.*

There are various conditions which require immediate repotting, regardless of the season. These are: (a)

Color Plate 8. Japanese wisteria. Semicascade style. 3′ wide. About 25 yrs. Produced by grafting and potted about 15 yrs. ago. Glazed Japanese pot. Tended for the past 5 yrs. by Mr. Frank Judson.

Color Plate 9. Nagasaki crab-apple. Informal upright style. 1′10″. 25 yrs. Produced by cleft grafting. Glazed Chinese pot. Produces small yellow fruit in the autumn.

Color Plate 10. Common Ezo spruce, dwarf garden variety "Yatsubusa." Clinging-to-a-rock style. 1′. About 15 yrs. Produced from a cutting and planted on rock about 5 yrs. ago. Glazed Chinese container.

Color Plate 11. Japanese black pine. Formal upright style. 2′9″. About 80 yrs. Produced from a naturally stunted tree and potted about 50 yrs. ago. Unglazed Chinese pot. Black pine is one of the best species for the formal style; this is a particularly fine example.

Color Plate 8

Color Plate 9

Color Plate 10

Color Plate 11

Pests; when worms or ants are found in the soil and spraying fails to eradicate them. (b) Poor soil; when the soil is either too coarse, so that it forms hard lumps, or too fine and dusty. (c) Damaged roots; when the upper, surface roots are killed by the application of overstrong manure, by manuring too soon after repotting, by water-logged soil due to overwatering, or by parched soil due to neglected watering; in these cases the dead roots must be cut away until living wood is found. Special measures to be taken in such emergency repot-tings have already been described (see page 48).

11. Repotting after Drastic Pruning. If it is decided to alter the shape of a decidu-ous tree by pruning away part of the branches or by removing one large dis-figuring branch, the bonsai must be re-potted immediately after the operation. It is essential to clear the roots completely of old soil and this is best done by washing them with a hose, a quicker and safer method than cleansing them with a stick.

4 🔘 TRAINING

THERE IS NOTHING MORE IN-teresting and rewarding in the care of a bonsai than its training, for upon this training depends its ultimate beauty. Training in the broader sense must, moreover, continue all through the tree's life; perfect shape can only be preserved by constant pruning and periodic wiring.

The training of a bonsai begins when it is strong enough and large enough to stand treatment. In the case of a naturally dwarfed bonsai it is, as has been said, better to wait two years so that the tree is firmly established. In the case of a seedling, cutting, or grafting, a great deal depends upon the speed of growth, but, roughly speaking, provided the tree is strong and healthy, training may begin when the tree has formed shoots about two inches long. A layering has branches already formed, but training should not be undertaken until the tree is well established and showing all the signs of good health, that is to say, strong, new shoots and leaves.

When deciding on the shape of a bonsai, it is essential to study the tree carefully from the point of view of its species and natural form. At the same time it must be settled whether the bonsai is to be a miniature bonsai (less than two inches in height), a small bonsai (from two to six inches), a medium bonsai (from six to twelve inches), or a large bonsai (from twelve to twenty-four or more inches). It is very important to determine at the outset which side of the tree is the front, as a bonsai is always displayed with its best side to the front.

In Japan, no matter what shape is chosen for a bonsai, it is customary to observe the rule of the "three points," the points symbolizing Heaven, Earth, and Humanity, which will be familiar to those who have studied the art of Japanese flower arrangement. These three points form a

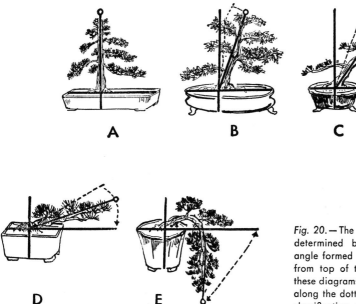

Fig. 20.—The basic styles. In general the style is determined by the number of degrees in the angle formed by a vertical line and a line drawn from top of tree to base of trunk. In each of these diagrams the top point could fall anywhere along the dotted arc without changing the style classification. *A)* Formal upright. *B)* Informal upright. *C)* Slanting. *D)* Semicascade. *E)* Cascade.

triangle, with Heaven (the top of the tree) as the apex and Earth (the point nearest the ground) forming the most acute of the three angles. When the branches which form the Earth angle are inadequate, a rock or a small shrub can be placed near the roots to accentuate it.

CLASSIFICATION OF STYLES

The Japanese have several systems for the classification of bonsai according to the styles in which they are trained, but these systems often seem confusing and overlapping. It has therefore seemed best to us to work out a sort of logical synthesis of the various systems rather than to adopt any one of them.

Basically, most bonsai may be classified into five main styles according to their over-all shapes: the formal upright, the informal upright, the slanting, the semicascade, and the full-cascade (Fig. 20). In the two upright styles (Figs. 21 & 22) and the slanting style the lower branches are always arranged in groups of three, starting about one-third the way up the trunk. Two branches are trained to come forward a little on the best side (that is, the front side) of the tree, one slightly higher than the other, while the third branch of this group lies somewhere between these two and extends out in the back of the tree. These back branches are extremely important from the point of view of both shape and density of foliage. (The lowermost third branch, as it should be at the back, also provides one of the most convenient ways of distinguishing between the front and back sides of a finished bonsai.) When arranging the various groups of

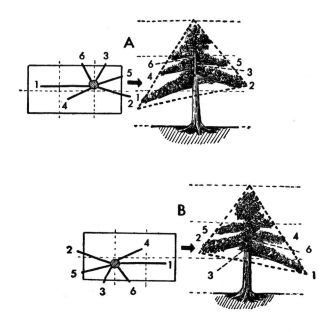

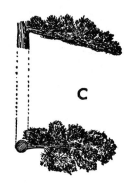

Fig. 21.—Formal upright style: arrangement of branches. **A)** Front view. **B)** Back view. **C)** Shape of each branch, seen from the front and from above.

three, care must be taken that no one branch is immediately above the other as it would then deprive the lower branch of water and sunshine. The branches should be placed closer together toward the top. In the formal upright style, the top is erect, whereas it always bends slightly to the front in the informal upright style. In the slanting style, the trunk should have an agreeable slant or curve, as should also the lower branches; the lowest branch spreads in the opposite direction to that in which the tree slants; and again the top of the tree is bent slightly forward.

Both the cascade styles start by growing upward from the soil, but in the full-cascade, the trunk turns downward so quickly that it reaches a point below the level of the pot, which consequently must be placed on the edge of a table or on a small stand. In the semicascade, the trunk is allowed to grow straight for a certain distance and then "cascaded" down at a less abrupt angle

and without necessarily reaching the level of the bottom of the pot. These cascade styles are also subject to the groups-of-three rule, but in applying it the underside of the "cascade" is thought of as the front of the tree and the third or back branch in each group is trained closer to the trunk than in the other styles.

Presumably all the other many bonsai styles grew out of these five basic shapes, but the variations are so extreme that it would be difficult to try to trace the relationships. Hence in the following classifications, the original form of each of these basic styles is treated simply as one style among many. In any case, a study of the illustrations will show the reader better than any number of words or system of classification exactly what is meant. For this reason each style is followed by a reference to one or more photographs illustrating it. As of possible interest, the Japanese names of the styles are also given. The different

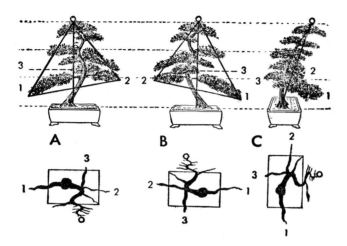

Fig. 22.—Informal upright style: arrangement of branches. *A)* Front view. *B)* Back view. *C)* Side view. Note how the top point slants to the front.

styles are not always mutually exclusive and a tree's most prominent characteristic will generally determine which of two or more possible classifications is most appropriate.

Group I. The following sixteen styles are classified according to the shape of the trunk and generally consist of but a single trunk:

1. Formal upright *(chokkan)* style. See Color Plate 11 & Plates 48–52.
2. Informal upright *(tachiki)*. See Color Plates 2–4, 9, 12, 23 & Plates 53–69.
3. Slanting *(shakan)*. See Color Plate 19 & Plates 70–78.
4. Semicascade *(han-kengai)*. See Color Plates 1, 8 & Plates 79–83.
5. Cascade *(kengai)*. Plates 84–86.
6. "Literati" *(bunjingi)*. See Plate 87.
7. Coiled *(bankan)*. See Plates 90–93.
8. Broom *(hôkidachi)*. Plates 88–89.
9. Split-trunk *(sabamiki)*. See Plates 94–97.
10. "Driftwood" *(sharimiki)*, i.e., portion of trunk or branches is dead and bleached like driftwood. See Color Plates 14, 18 & Plates 98–103.
11. Wind-swept *(fukinagashi)*. See Plates 104–5.
12. Exposed-root *(neagari)*. See Plates 106–7.
13. Root-over-rock *(sekijôju)*, i.e., planted on a rock with the roots extending down into the soil below. See Color Plates 7, 21, 22 & Plates 108–10.
14. Clinging-to-a-rock *(ishitsuki)*, i.e., roots attached to the rock itself. Color Plates 1, 10, 17, 24 & Plates 111–13.
15. Twisted-trunk *(nejikan)*. See Plates 114–16.
16. Octopus *(takozukuri)*. Plate 117.

Group II. The following five styles feature multiple trunks from a single root. The number of trunks may be 2 *(sôkan)*, 3 *(sankan)*, 5 *(gokan)*, 7 *(nanakan)*, 9 *(kyûkan)*, or more. Of these, only the twin-trunk is used as a separate style category, the other numbers being simply appended to one of the other categories (e.g., straight-line 5-trunk style):

17. Twin-trunk *(sôkan)* style. See Color Plate 16 & Plates 118–20.
18. Clump *(kabubuki* or *kabudachi)*. See Color Plate 6 & Plates 121–30.
19. Stump *(kôrabuki)*. *Kôra* means "shell, carapace," as of a turtle; *buki* means "a growth," as of new shoots. Hence, several branches growing from a flat, "turtle back" trunk. See Plates 131–34.
20. Straight-line or raft *(ikadabuki)*. The single root (formerly the trunk of a tree) extends in a straight line; hence the Japanese name, which suggests the horizontal timbers of a raft. See Plates 135–42.
21. Sinuous *(netsunagari)*. The single root twists and turns. See Color Plates 13, 24 & Plates 143–46.

Group III. The following eight styles constitute the category of group plantings *(yose-ue)* which are true bonsai, each consisting of two or more separate trees with their own roots. These styles are discussed in more detail in Chapter 5, but it should be noted here that any group planting is distinguished in the first place by the number of trees it has and, secondly, by whether it is an ordinary group planting (in which

case no further designation is added to that showing the number of trees) or one of two special-category group plantings (in which case the further designation of "natural group" or "clustered group" is added):

22. Two-tree *(sôju)* style. See Plate 147.
23. Three-tree *(sambon-yose)*. See Plate 148.
24. Five-tree *(gohon-yose)*.
25. Seven-tree *(nanahon-yose)*. See Plate 149.
26. Nine-tree *(kyûhon-yose)*. See Color Plate 20 & Plate 150.
27. Multiple-tree *(yose-ue)*, i.e., with more than nine trees. See Plates 151–53.
28. Natural-group *(yamayori)*. See Plates 154–55.
29. Clustered-group *(tsukami-yose)*. See Plate 156.

Group IV. The following three styles are also group plantings but are not true bonsai in the strict meaning of the word:

30. Tray-landscape *(bonkei)* style. See Color Plate 15 & Plates 157–59.
31. Seasonal group plantings. See Color Plate 5.
32. Plantings of herbs, grasses, and shrubs *(kusamono* or *shitakusa)*. See Plates 160–63.

Plate 48. Common cryptomeria. 1'11". About 20 yrs. By cutting or layering. Cobalt-blue glazed Chinese pot.

Plate 49. Common cryptomeria. 2'3". About 80 yrs. From a natural tree or a cutting, trained about 30 yrs. Brown unglazed Chinese pot.

Plate 51. Chabo cypress. 1'7". 30 yrs. From a cutting. This was originally planted on a rock, but after 5 yrs. the tree grew out of proportion and, 10 yrs. ago, was planted in this style. Dark reddish unglazed Chinese pot.

Plate 50. Japanese yew. 2'8". About 50 yrs. From a natural tree, **trained** about 30 yrs. Bluish glazed Japanese pot of Tofukuji ware.

Plate 52. Chinese hackberry. 1'11". About 50 yrs. From a seedling, trained about 30 yrs. Dark reddish unglazed Japanese pot of Tokoname ware.

Plate 53. Common Ezo spruce. 1'9". Between 200 and 300 yrs. This naturally stunted tree was found far in the northern part of Japan in 1926. Poetically named "Crane's Dance," surely this delightful bonsai has been visited by many of these birds of good fortune in its long life. Antique unglazed Chinese pot of pale reddish color.

Plate 54. Corticata pine. 3'2". About 80 yrs. From a natural tree or by grafting. This has been a famed bonsai now for almost 30 yrs. Antique unglazed Chinese pot of dark greyish color.

Plate 55. Orange tree. 1'8". 10 yrs. By cleft grafting on stock of trifoliata citron. White glazed Japanese pot of Kutani ware with reddish design.

Plate 56. Japanese maple, garden variety "Kagiri-nishiki." 3'. About 35 yrs. By cleft grafting on stock of Japanese mountain maple. Blue unglazed Chinese pot.

Plate 57. Japanese flowering apricot, garden variety "Asahi-zuru." 2'. About 100 yrs. By grafting or from a seedling, trained about 80 yrs. This was originally a two-trunk bonsai, but the second trunk died about 30 yrs. ago.

Plate 58. Wild sand-pear. 1' 8". About 50 yrs. From a natural tree, trained about 30 yrs. Green glazed Chinese pot of Kuang-tung ware.

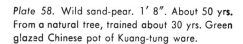

Plate 59. Satsuki azalea, garden variety "O-saka-zuki." 1'8". About 80 yrs. From a cutting, trained about 50 yrs. Reddish-brown unglazed Chinese pot.

Plate 60. Hall crab-apple. 1'9". About 30 yrs. By grafting, at point where trunk becomes abruptly smaller. Green glazed Chinese pot.

Plate 61. Trident maple. 1'10". About 50 yrs. From a natural tree, trained about 30 yrs. The scar left at base of trunk by cutting off a heavy root when training was begun detracts somewhat from the tree's beauty, but new bark will conceal this in another 5 or 6 yrs.

Plate 62. Chinese quince. 2'. About 35 yrs. By layering. Dark reddish unglazed Chinese pot.

Plate 63. Star jasmine. 1'9". About 70 yrs. From a natural tree or by layering, trained about 50 yrs. Dark reddish unglazed Chinese pot.

Plate 64. Five-leaf akebia. 2'. About 25 yrs. By layering or from a natural tree, trained about 15 yrs. Bluish glazed Chinese pot.

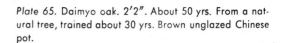

Plate 65. Daimyo oak. 2'2". About 50 yrs. From a natural tree, trained about 30 yrs. Brown unglazed Chinese pot.

Plate 66. Rock cotoneaster. 1'1". About 30 yrs. By dividing or from a cutting. The tree was left unpotted for about 10 yrs. until it had reached its present growth; then it was potted and trained to present shape. In autumn the thick growth of red berries makes a beautiful contrast with the green moss and yellow glazed Chinese pot of Nanking ware. It is also beautiful in spring with tiny, pale-pink flowers.

Plate 67. Japanese red pine. 4'. 380 yrs. From a natural tree or seedling. This was famous as a potted tree almost 350 yrs. ago when travelers used to stop to admire it at Shizuoka. It was probably planted on a rock when it was less than 1' high, as the rock, now almost completely overgrown, still peeps from the base of the trunk. Such large bonsai are repotted only about every 15 yrs. Whitish-yellow unglazed Chinese pot with surface design.

Plate 68. Osteomeles. 1'5" About 80 yrs. From a natural tree, trained 50 yrs. Has tiny, white, rose-like flowers in spring. Whitish-yellow glazed Chinese pot.

Plate 69. Nippon hawthorn. 1'7". About 50 yrs. From a natural tree, trained 30 yrs. The red fruits harmonize well with the dark-blue glazed Chinese pot of Kuangtung ware.

Plate 70. Corticata pine. 2'8". About 75 yrs. From a natural tree collected 45 yrs. ago by Mr. Yoshimura's father, then aged 19, who split and bent down a portion of the top of the trunk both to create a more interesting shape and to make the size smaller. Dark-grey unglazed Chinese pot.

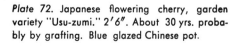

Plate 71. Euonymus oxyphylla. 2'2". About 15 yrs. From a natural tree, trained about 10 yrs. The hanging berries are pale red outside, with dark-red seeds inside; the leaves turn a beautiful red in autumn. White glazed Chinese pot.

Plate 72. Japanese flowering cherry, garden variety "Usu-zumi." 2'6". About 30 yrs. probably by grafting. Blue glazed Chinese pot.

Plate 73. Winged spindle tree. 1'6". 25 yrs. From a natural tree, trained 15 yrs. Red unglazed Chinese pot.

Plate 74. Japanese ivy. 1'7". About 80 yrs. By layering or from a natural tree, trained about 50 yrs. The dark, shiny foliage turns red in autumn. Whitish-yellow glazed Chinese pot.

Plate 75. Same tree in winter

Plate 76. Osmanthus aurantiacus. 2'7". About 30 yrs. By grafting onto stock of Japanese holly, the grafting point being almost at the top of the main trunk. Brown unglazed Chinese pot.

Plate 77. Nagasaki crab-apple. 1'1". 15 yrs. By grafting. Blue glazed Japanese pot.

Plate 78. Spindle tree. 2'. About 50 yrs. From a natural tree, trained about 30 yrs. Blue glazed Chinese pot.

Plate 79. Dogwood. 9". 20 yrs. From a natural tree, trained 13 yrs. Blue glazed Chinese pot.

Plate 80. Thunberg barberry. 11". About 30 yrs. From a natural tree trained 25 yrs. Blue glazed Chinese pot.

Plate 81. Japanese black pine. 1'5". About 50 yrs. From a natural tree, trained about 25 yrs. Brown unglazed Chinese pot.

Plate 82. Needle juniper. 1'3". About 100 yrs. From a natural tree, trained about 30 yrs. Whitish-yellow unglazed Chinese pot.

Plate 83. Lily magnolia, with pink flowers. 3'2" laterally. About 30 yrs. Green glazed Chinese pot of Kuang-tung ware.

CASCADE STYLE

Plate 84. Juneberry. 3'10" laterally. About 60 yrs. From a natural tree, trained about 50 yrs. In late spring the entire tree is covered with white flowers as though with snow. Dark-red unglazed Chinese pot.

Plate 85. Five-needle pine. 3'10". About 80 yrs. From a natural tree, trained about 30 yrs. Whitish-yellow unglazed Chinese pot with surface design.

Plate 86. Star jasmine. 3'. About 50 yrs. From a natural tree, trained 30 yrs. Blue glazed Chinese pot of Nanking ware, on a pedestral made of a polished stump and roots.

LITERATI STYLE

Plate 87. Japanese red pine. 2'3". About 50 yrs. From a natural tree, trained 30 yrs. Red unglazed Chinese pot.

BROOM STYLE

Plate 88. Japanese grey-bark elm in full leaf. 2'3". About 50 yrs. From a seedling or a natural tree, trained about 40 yrs. Whitish-yellow glazed Chinese pot.

Plate 89. Japanese grey-bark elm in winter. 2'. 27 yrs. From a natural tree found in a bamboo grove in Tochigi Prefecture when it was a 5-yr.-old seedling about 1' high; trained 22 yrs. Brown unglazed Chinese pot.

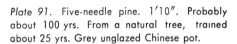

Plate 91. Five-needle pine. 1'10". Probably about 100 yrs. From a natural tree, trained about 25 yrs. Grey unglazed Chinese pot.

Plate 90. Sargent juniper. 3'. Probably about 300 yrs. From a natural tree, trained about 50 yrs. Brown unglazed Chinese pot.

Plate 92. Mongolian redshrub. 1'. 35 yrs. From a natural tree, trained 25 yrs. White glazed Chinese pot.

Plate 93. Five-needle pine. 1'10". Probably about 100 yrs. From a natural tree, trained about 80 yrs. Reddish-brown unglazed Chinese pot.

SPLIT-TRUNK STYLE

Plate 94. Five-needle pine. 2'5". Probably about 100 yrs. From a natural tree, trained about 50 yrs. The design of the trunk was produced artificially. Dark-grey unglazed Chinese pot.

Plate 95. Japanese yew. 1'10". Probably about 180 yrs. From a natural tree, trained about 30 yrs. Red unglazed Chinese pot.

Plate 96. Japanese flowering apricot. 3'. About 80 yrs. From a natural tree dug from ground about 10 yrs. ago. Brown unglazed Chinese pot.

Plate 97. Japanese box. 2'4". Probably about 150 yrs. From a natural tree, trained about 50 yrs. Dark-grey unglazed Chinese pot.

Plate 98. Sargent juniper. 2'8". Probably between 300 and 500 yrs. From a natural tree, trained 80 yrs. The design of the trunk is natural. A very famous example of the driftwood style. Repotted every 10 yrs.

Plate 99. The ancient Chinese pot for the preceding bonsai. 1'10.5" by 1'0.75" by 6". The dark-grey unglazed color is in the "quiet and sober taste" much admired by Japanese and particularly suitable for needle trees. This pot is said to have been used as an incense burner in China over 300 yrs. ago. Note the ample drainage hole in the bottom.

Plate 100. Five-needle pine. 1'8". Probably about 100 yrs. From a natural tree collected 40 yrs. ago in the Japan Alps. The owner has named this bonsai "Gem," probably referring to the gem-like gleam of its trunk. Antique reddish unglazed Chinese pot.

Plate 101. Sargent juniper. 2'2", About 150 yrs. From a natural tree, trained about 30 yrs. The only living part of the trunk is the narrow, dark strip at the right. Dark-red unglazed Chinese pot.

Plate 102. Five-needle pine. 2'1". About 60 yrs. From a natural tree, trained 20 yrs. Brown unglazed Chinese pot.

Plate 103. Sargent juniper. 3'. Probably 300-400 yrs. From a natural tree, trained about 80 yrs. This became very famous 34 yrs. ago when given its present shape by reducing its height almost 1' and cutting away part of its very heavy root, thereby greatly improving its proportions. About 10 yrs. ago a number of its dead branches on the front side decayed so badly they were cut off. Its name is "White-Thread Waterfall."

WIND-SWEPT STYLE

Plate 104. Five-needle pine. 2'2". About 50 yrs. From a natural tree, trained 20 yrs. Brown unglazed Chinese pot in the rough-surface, primitive style.

Plate 105. Five-needle pine. 3' laterally. About 50 yrs. From a natural tree, trained 25 yrs. In same pot as that of the preceding bonsai.

Plate 106. Sargent juniper. 2'3". About 50 yrs. From a natural tree, trained 15 yrs. Dark-brown unglazed Japanese pot of Tokoname ware.

Plate 107. Five-needle pine. 1'10". About 35 yrs. From a natural tree, trained 25 yrs. Dark-red unglazed Chinese pot.

Plate 108. Trident maple. 2'. About 35 yrs. From a seedling, trained about 25 yrs. Named "Yabakei" for the region of that name in southern Japan, famed for its views of rocky riverbanks; the rock also came from this region. Dark-blue glazed Japanese pot of Tosui ware.

Plate 109. Common Ezo spruce. 1'1". About 80 yrs. From a natural tree, planted on rock about 35 yrs. Note that, as in the case of other bonsai that can be classified under more than one style, this is also in the sinuous style. White unglazed Chinese pot.

Plate 110. Trident maple. 2'. About 50 yrs. From a seedling or cutting, trained about 35 yrs. Originally this consisted of 7 individual trees planted in a group on the rock, but now the roots have grown into a single system. Pale cobalt-blue glazed Chinese pot.

Plate 112. Common Ezo spruce. 1'8". About 25 yrs. From a natural tree, planted on rock 13 yrs. May also be classified as sinuous style. Blue glazed Japanese pot of Tosui ware.

Plate 111. Common Ezo spruce. 1'7". 20 yrs. By layering. Planted on rock 13 yrs., with golden fern and dwarf azaleas. Primitive Chinese pot, unglazed, with rough brown surface.

Plate 113. Common Ezo spruce, dwarf variety. 1'3". 20 yrs. From cuttings, planted on rock 13 yrs., with golden fern, Kurama moss, and wild-thyme azalea. Arranged on a naturally flat stone.

TWISTED-TRUNK STYLE

Plate 114. Sargent juniper. 4'2". Probably 200-300 yrs. From a natural tree, trained 80 yrs. The name of this excellent bonsai is "Dragon Flying into the Clouds." Antique pale reddish-grey unglazed Chinese pot.

Plate 115. Sargent juniper. 2'4". Probably 200-300 yrs. From a natural tree, trained about 50 yrs. Such a magnificent trunk could only have been produced by many years of exposure to strong winds, deep snows, and perhaps landslides. Antique red unglazed Chinese pot.

Plate 116. Sargent juniper. 2'5". Probably about 100 yrs. From a natural tree, trained about 50 yrs. Note how this tree is tied to the pot since it does not yet have enough secondary roots to hold it upright. In an ordinary training pot, whose shape insures good drainage.

OCTOPUS STYLE

Plate 117. Five-needle pine. 4'. About 350 yrs. Tradition has it that this was potted early in the 17th cenfury. It is now at the Tokyo Horticulfural School. Blue glazed Japanese pot of Shigaraki ware.

TWIN-TRUNK STYLE

Plate 118. Hornbeam. 2'3". About 35 yrs. From a natural tree, trained about 20 yrs. Whitish-yellow glazed Chinese pot.

Plate 119. Pomegranate, garden variety "Kimpo." 2'. About 50 yrs. By layering or from a cutting. Dark-red unglazed Chinese pot.

Plate 120. Wax tree (female). 2'8". 35-50 yrs. From a natural tree, trained about 30 yrs. White glazed Chinese pot.

CLUMP STYLE

Plate 122. Ibota ligustrum, 5 trunks. 2'4".
35-40 yrs. From a number of seedlings
planted in a group and now grown together.
Brown unglazed Chinese pot in the rough-
surface primitive style.

Plate 121. Common Ezo spruce, 3 trunks. 3'.
Probably between 100 and 200 yrs. From a
natural tree found in northernmost Japan,
trained 37 yrs. Reddish-brown unglazed
Chinese pot.

Plate 123. Hydrangea, 5 trunks. 1'11". 10-
15 yrs. By dividing, potted 7 yrs. White
glazed Chinese pot.

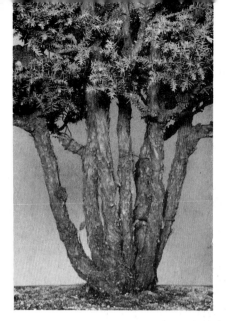

Plate 124. Common cryptomeria, 7 trunks. 2′5″. About 50 yrs. From a layering or cutting, trained about 30 yrs. Dark-brown unglazed Chinese pot with rough surface.

Plate 126. Pourthiaea. 1′4″. About 40 yrs. From a natural tree or seedling, trained about 25 yrs. Cobalt-blue glazed Chinese pot.

Plate 127. Dogwood. 2′. About 50 yrs. From a natural tree, trained about 30 yrs Pale reddish unglazed Chinese pot.

Plate 128. Flowering quince. 1'3". About 100 yrs. From a natural tree, trained about 50 yrs. Has dark-red blossoms in winter. Whitish-yellow glazed Chinese pot.

Plate 129. Thin-leaf nandina. 2'4". About 100 yrs. By dividing. Dark-blue glazed Chinese pot.

Plate 130. Gingko. 1'8". About 50 yrs. By layering. Green glazed Chinese pot of Kuang-tung ware.

Plate 131. Trident maple. 2'. About 40 yrs. Main trunk and stump are from a natural tree, but the smaller trunks were grafted on 7 yrs. ago. This was done by letting top shoots of main trunk grow long enough to bend to base of trunk and then grafting them there by the inarching method. White glazed Chinese pot.

Plate 132. Base of the trunk.

Plate 133. Five-needle pine. 2' About 150 yrs. From a natural tree with a stump, trained about 50 yrs. Dark reddish-brown unglazed Chinese pot.

Plate 134. Base of the trunk.

Plate. 135. Five-needle pine, 3 trunks. 2'9".
About 150 yrs. From a natural tree, trained
about 80 yrs. Brown unglazed Chinese pot.

Plate 136. Five-needle pine, 3 trunks. 1'2".
About 50 yrs. From a natural tree, trained
about 30 yrs. Brown unglazed Japanese pot
of Tokoname ware.

Plate 137. Detail of Plate 136.
Trunks and straight root.

Plate 138. Five-needle pine, 5 trunks. 2' 6".
Probably about 200 yrs. From a natural tree,
trained 80-100 yrs. This is a particularly
good and famous example of the style. Dark-
grey unglazed Chinese pot.

Plate 139. Five-needle pine,
5 trunks. 1' 7". About 100
yrs. From a natural tree,
trained 70-80 yrs. Red unglazed Chinese pot.

Plate 140. Detail of Plate 139.
Trunks and straight root.

Plate 141. Japanese mountain maple, 5 trunks. 1'9". About 35 yrs. From a natural tree, trained about 25 yrs. Whitish-yellow glazed Chinese pot.

Plate 142. Detail of Plate 141. Trunks and straight root.

SINUOUS STYLE

Plate 143. Sargent juniper. 1'6". Probably about 100 yrs. From a natural tree or a layering, trained about 50 yrs. Reddish-brown unglazed Japanese pot of Tokoname ware.

Plate 144. Five-needle pine. 1'2". About 60 yrs. From a natural tree, trained 30 yrs. Blue glazed Japanese pot of Tosui ware.

Plate 145. Five-needle pine. 2'4". About 80 yrs. From a natural tree, trained 40-50 yrs. Reddish-brown unglazed Japanese pot of Tokoname ware.

Plate 146. Common Ezo spruce. 1'10". About 35 yrs. By layering 20 yrs. ago. Brown unglazed Chinese pot in the rough-surface primitive style. Arranged with dwarf azalea, moss, and rocks at base.

Plate 148. Three-tree style: common Ezo spruce. 1'5". About 50 yrs. From natural trees, trained about 30 yrs. White glazed Chinese pot.

Plate 147. Two-tree style: oriental arborvita. 2'. 38 yrs. From seeds planted by the late Dr. Saburo Watanabe on the day of the birth of his first son. Balanced by a water-worn rock. Glazed whitish Chinese pot.

Plate 149. Seven-tree style: common Ezo spruce. 2'8". About 50-80 yrs. From natural trees, grouped about 15 yrs. Red unglazed Chinese pot.

Plate 150. Nine-tree style: white beech 1'8". 15-25 yrs. From natural trees, grouped 5 yrs. Blue glazed Japanese pot of Tosui ware.

Plate 151. Multiple-tree style: common Ezó spruce. 2'2". 30-60 yrs. From natural trees, grouped 15 yrs. Pale-brown unglazed Japanese pot of Hishoku ware.

Plate 152. Multiple-tree style: Japanese black pine. 1'. 20-25 yrs. From natural trees collected on a rocky hillside near Kujukurihama, Chiba Prefecture, 15 yrs. ago, grouped as at present 5 yrs. ago. Whitish-yellow glazed Chinese pot.

Plate 153. Multiple-tree style: trident maple. 9″. 11 yrs. From cuttings, first trained in separate pots and then arranged as shown 6 yrs. ago. Whitish-yellow glazed Japanese pot of Ichiyo ware.

Plate 154. Natural-group style: wild-thyme azalea. 1′10″. Probably 100 yrs. From natural trees collected 60 yrs. ago. Pale-brown unglazed Chinese pot.

Plate 155. Natural-group style: wild-thyme azalea. 1′2″. About 50 yrs. From natural trees collected 20 yrs. ago. On a naturally flat stone from the Kyoto area.

Plate 156. Clustered-group style: Japanese mountain maple. 8″. 7 yrs. From seedlings. Bluish-green glazed Japanese pot of Shigaraki ware.

OTHER GROUP PLANTINGS

Plate 157. Tray landscape. 1′2″. Made 4 yrs. ago. Dark-brown unglazed Japanese pot of Tokoname ware.

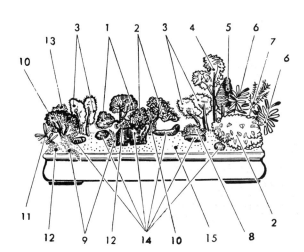

Key to *Plate 157.* **1)** 2 Sargent junipers. 5 yrs., cuttings. **2)** 5 satsuki azaleas, 8 yrs., cuttings. **3)** 4 himuro cypresses, 7 yrs., cuttings. **4)** Japanese grey-bark elm, 10 yrs., seedling. **5)** Dwarf cryptomeria, 6 yrs., cutting. **6)** Pyracantha, 7 yrs., cutting. **7)** Japanese spiraea, 6 yrs., cutting. **8)** Lycopodium, 5 yrs., dividing. **9)** Golden fern, 5 yrs., dividing. **10)** 2 rock cotoneasters, 8 yrs., cuttings. **11)** Dwarf flowering quince, 7 yrs., cutting. **12)** Dwarf wild thyme, dividing. **13)** Wild-thyme azalea, 5 yrs., dividing. **14)** Small rocks. **15)** Gravel, No. 5 size.

Plate 158. Tray landscape of cactuses. Just made. Reddish-grey Japanese pot of Tokoname ware.

Plate 159. Tray landscape. Pale-green glazed Chinese pot, 3′ long.

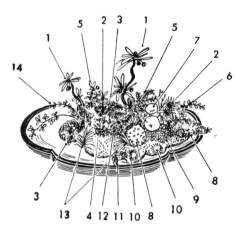

Key to Plate 159. 1) 2 pyracanthas, 5 yrs., cuttings. 2) 5 five-needle pines, 5 yrs., natural. 3) Golden fern, 2 yrs., dividing. 4) U-tricularia bifida. 5) Dwarf smilax china, 4 yrs., dividing. 6) 3 rock cotoneasters, 3 yrs., cuttings. 7) Flowering quince, 6 yrs., cutting. 8) 4 star jasmines, 5 yrs., cuttings. 9) 3 wild-thyme azaleas, 3 yrs., cuttings. 10) 2 lyco-podiums, 2 yrs., cuttings. 11) Ornamental bronze crab. 12) Chrysanthemum arcticum, 4 yrs., dividing. 13) 10 dwarf sweet-rushes, 4 yrs., dividing. 14) 5 dwarf dog-roses, 2 yrs., cuttings.

Plate 160. Planting of herbs clinging to a rock: dwarf sweet-rush. 10″. Planted on rock 4 yrs.

Plate 161. Planting of grasses. 1′5″. Planted in a concave Kurama stone 2 yrs. ago. Particularly enjoyable in summer.

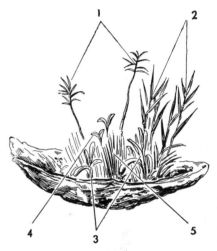

Key to Plate 161. 1) 3 weeping willows, 4 yrs., cuttings. 2) Dwarf common reed, 3 yrs., dividing. 3) 30 pecteilis, 2 yrs., natural. 4) 10 violets, 2 yrs., natural. 5) Dwarf scouring rush, 2 yrs., dividing.

Plate 162. Planting of grasses: *Pleioblastus gramioeus* bamboo. 11″. By dividing. Planted on flat Kurama stone 4 yrs. ago.

Plate 163. Planting of cycad. 1'10". About 100 yrs. From a natural plant, trained about 80 yrs. Cobalt-blue glazed Chinese pot.

MINIATURE BONSAI

Plate 164. From left to right and top to bottom: 1) Needle juniper; about 25 yrs.; from a natural tree, trained 10 yrs. 2) Dwarf hypericum; 2 yrs.; by dividing. 3) Dwarf azalea; 2 yrs.; from a cutting. 4) Dwarf needle juniper; 10 yrs.; from a cutting. 5) Stone in shape of a thatched-roof farmhouse. 6) Dwarf star jasmine; 5 yrs.; from a cutting. 7) Japanese black pine; about 35 yrs.; from a natural tree, trained 15 yrs. 8) Stones and fine gravel in a bronze container.

Plate 165. Five-needle pine. 3 yrs. From a seedling. Such miniature plants need repotting every 3 yrs. and must be moved to a larger pot after 10 yrs.

Because of its very smallness, the so-called "miniature" bonsai (less than two inches in height) is often regarded as a separate category (see Color Plate 25 & Plates 164–65), but it is properly classified under one of the foregoing categories.

In the case of multiple trunks and group plantings it should be noted that the Japanese have a strong dislike for even numbers. Only the number two is used; four and six in particular are avoided, both in bonsai training and in flower arrangement, as being clumsy, difficult to arrange, and unlucky.

As a result of three centuries of experience the Japanese have drawn up fairly definite rules as to which styles best suit the various species of trees growing in Japan. As has been said, a bonsai must look natural. Therefore, to attempt to train an essentially upright tree such as the fir, cypress, or cryptomeria into a "cascading" bonsai would be wrong by Japanese, or indeed by any standards. Western people experimenting with new types of trees should always bear in mind the way these trees grow in their native habitat, and it would be well to collect photographs or sketches of fine specimens of the full-grown tree before starting to experiment with the training of such a bonsai.

Indications of the styles best suited to the various species of trees will be found in the table given in Appendix 3. In that table it will be noticed that the red pine is not among the trees recommended for bonsai. Although red-pine bonsai do exist and the species is in many ways suitable, it is so delicate that it cannot survive if there is the least pollution in the air, even if the trunk and branches are constantly washed. It can, however, be grown in pure country air.

METHODS

Some of the same tools and also the table, stool, and revolving stand used for repotting will be required for wiring and pruning (see Appendix 1). The work is best done in a shed. The rewiring of a fully matured tree may take several hours, which can be split up into two or more mornings' or afternoons' work, as the amateur will find at first that his fingers quickly grow tired, sore, and clumsy. The trunk and heavy branches are wired first to give the tree its basic shape. Then the smaller branches are wired, beginning with the lowest.

1. *Wiring* (Figs. 23–29 & Plates 166–82). Wiring is never done in the budding

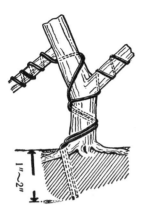

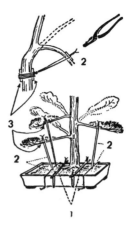

Fig. 23.—Wiring trunk. Note how double wires are inserted in ground and lie close together.

Fig. 24.—Pulling down heavy branches, 2 methods. 1) Sticks and wires to hold tree firmly in place. 2) Wires arranged for pulling down branches. 3) Bits of rubber to protect bark.

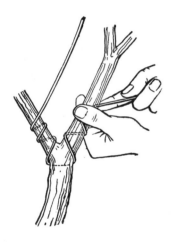

Fig. 25.—Hand positions in wiring. *Right hand:* grasps wire very close to branch, but does not hold branch and wire together; index finger guides wire. *Left hand:* holds bottom of wire firmly, moving up to follow right hand.

season as the young buds and shoots might be damaged. Shoots less than one to two inches long are never wired. The best season for deciduous trees is the growing season as soon as possible after the leaves are grown to their full size, but while the branches are still supple. Deciduous branches break easily, especially those of the azalea and maple, so it is advisable not to water such trees for about six hours before beginning wiring. Evergreens should be wired in autumn; they can also be wired in winter without doing harm. Pine branches tend to split easily at a fork, so when a branch is being bent, the nearest fork should be protected by grasping it firmly with the thumb and two fingers of one hand.

The wire used is copper wire, which must first be annealed in a low-temperature fire. In Japan it is customary to use rice straw, which is allowed to burn to embers, the wire

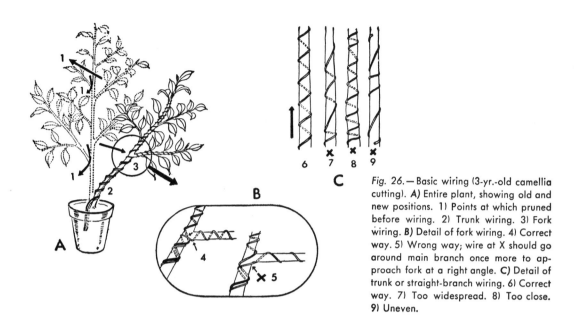

Fig. 26.— Basic wiring (3-yr.-old camellia cutting). **A)** Entire plant, showing old and new positions. 1) Points at which pruned before wiring. 2) Trunk wiring. 3) Fork wiring. **B)** Detail of fork wiring. 4) Correct way. 5) Wrong way; wire at X should go around main branch once more to approach fork at a right angle. **C)** Detail of trunk or straight-branch wiring. 6) Correct way. 7) Too widespread. 8) Too close. 9) Uneven.

being annealed in the latter. Wheat straw can be substituted when rice straw is not available. Iron wire must never be used as it causes the wood to rot. The same piece of copper wire may be used many times by straightening and annealing it each time.

Wires of different thicknesses should be prepared in advance, as the thickness of each branch will determine the proper size of wire to use on it. The ideal size of wire in a given case is one just thick enough to hold the branch in position, but not so thick as to cause the branch to bend in and out under the pressure of the spirals of the wire. In the case of soft-barked trees such as cherry, maple, pomegranate, willow, etc., the bark should be protected by wrapping all but the thinnest wires in spirals of rolled paper.

When it is necessary to bend the trunk, the lower end of the wire is inserted in the

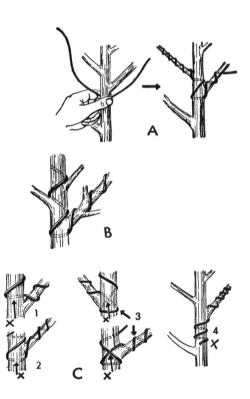

Fig. 27.— Details of fork wiring. **A)** Correct way for two branches. **B)** Correct way for trunk and 1 branch. **C)** Mistakes. 1) Too high 2) Too low. 3) Crossed wires. 4) Lower portion will not hold.

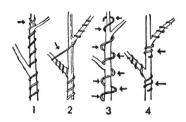

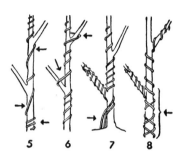

Fig. 28.—Wiring mistakes. 1) End of wire should not be bent down. 2) Wire should not continue through open air. 3) Wire is too loose. 4) Lower portions of wires do not provide enough support for upper portions. 5) Spirals too wide apart. 6) Bad fork wiring. 7) Spiral at base should be more parallel with earth. 8) Wires should not cross.

earth to hold it firm. A thick wire is used, but if this is not strong enough to control the trunk, double wire may be used, the two wires being laid very close together so that they look like one broad wire. They should, however, be put on separately. When wiring branches, the two ends of the wire are best used on separate branches as this prevents slipping. The wire is wound round the trunk or branch at an angle of about forty-five degrees. It is pushed round the underside of the branch with the forefinger of the right hand. It should not be too loose, but neither should it be too tight for that might damage the bark as the tree grows. The bands are placed about a quarter to half an inch apart and, in the case of young to middle-aged deciduous trees, are left on the tree for from three to six months; pines and other slow-growing trees, which include all

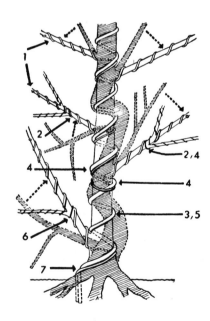

Fig. 29.—Correcting mistakes as numbered in Fig. 28.

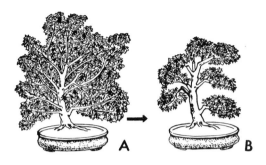

Fig. 30.—Drastic pruning (mountain maple).
A) Before. B) After.

Fig. 31.—Drastic pruning (satsuki azalea).

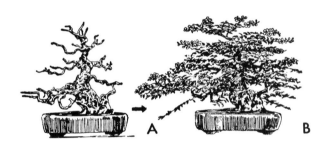

Fig. 32. — Drastic pruning (crape myrtle).
A) As pruned in early spring or late autumn. B) Next flowering, in summer.

very old trees, can be left wired for a year. It is advisable to bend the branch firmly in the desired direction while the wire is being put on. If the branch needs to be twisted forward or pushed back, the wire must follow the direction of the twist. The end of the wire is cut off straight and does not need to be turned back. When the wires are removed, the tree should be left for a year or longer before rewiring.

2. *Pruning.* Once they are full grown, evergreens, such as juniper, pine, cryptomeria, spruce, and cypress, cannot stand drastic pruning. Any alteration to their shape must be done by wiring and trimming only. Deciduous trees, on the other hand, will survive very drastic treatment (Figs. 30–32). If a tree has a fine trunk but poor, misshapen branches, all the branches can be cut right back and new shoots trained in their place. A tree may have a few well-shaped branches which give it a handsome form, but may be marred by long-neglected secondary branches. These should be cut off close to the parent branch and, if necessary, the parent branch itself pruned back to a more suitable length. When heavy branches, over one-eighth of an inch in diameter, are removed, the stump must be whittled off flush with the parent branch or trunk. Later the scar can be hollowed

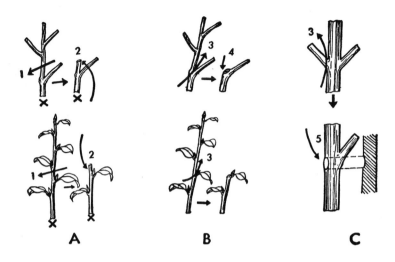

Fig. 33.— Pruning details. **A)** Bad examples. 1) Scissor-cut direction downward. 2) Stump remains. **B)** Good examples. 3) Scissor-cut upward. 4) Knife-cut stump smoothly. **C)** Heavy-branch method. 5) Hollowed-out stump.

out slightly with wood-carving tools. This hollow will heal flat and obviate an unsightly blemish (Fig. 33). The willow is a particularly quick-growing tree. Provided the tree has a good shape, all the small secondary branches can be cut right back every autumn, leaving only the thick main branches. The long new shoots which appear in springtime should, however, never be touched until the autumn pruning. The opposite is the case with the crape myrtle, which produces its flowers in summer upon that year's new shoots. If these shoots are cut back in spring the second burgeoning will give more and better flowers (Fig. 32).

When altering the shape of a deciduous tree it is often necessary to encourage the formation of a new branch. The appropriate shoot is allowed to grow without pruning until it is about the thickness of an ordinary pencil; then it is cut off at the required length.

A branch is always pruned just above a node and is cut on the slant upwards toward the node (Fig. 33). Trees which require pruning and do not yet require repotting must be heavily manured for at least a month beforehand so that they are in good condition and able to stand drastic treatment. If the earth in the pot is hard, however, the bonsai should be repotted at the proper time, after which it may be pruned immediately.

3. Correcting Defects. When choosing a potential bonsai it is extremely important

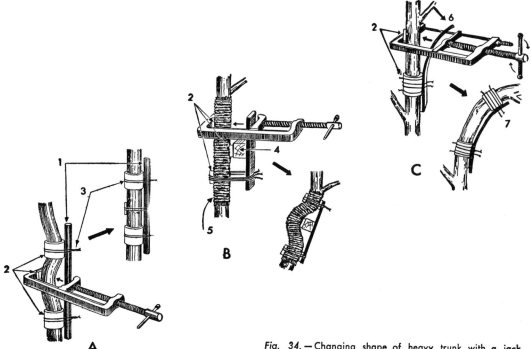

Fig. 34. — Changing shape of heavy trunk with a jack.
A) Straightening trunk. 1) Iron rod. 2) Rubber pieces. 3)
Heavy copper wire. B) Making a double curve. 4) Wooden
block. 5) Hemp-cord wrapping to avoid breaking or splitting.
C) Making a single curve. 6) Curved iron rod. 7) Iron rod
fastened with copper wire and left 2-3 yrs.

to find a tree with the fewest possible basic defects. Certain defects can never be corrected and trees which have these malformations must be discarded; but less serious faults can often be corrected with careful training as has already been shown in the section on pruning. Defects may be in the root formation, the trunk, or the branches.

Roots. A bonsai must have roots all round the base of the trunk; a one-sided tree is unsuitable. This defect cannot be corrected in pines, but in deciduous trees, if a fine natural bonsai lacks roots at one side, they may be produced artificially by layering. In all bonsai the surface roots are extremely important as they add to the

beauty of the tree. To encourage handsome surface roots, the taproot and the roots below the surface must be cut as short as possible. If a natural bonsai has the roots at one side twisted back upon themselves, they should usually be carefully straightened out and encouraged to grow in the right direction.

Trunk. A tree with ugly malformations on the trunk should never be chosen for making into a bonsai. A trunk which has been sawn off at the top is unsightly and should not be used. If a tree of the pine family is too tall, the top must almost never be cut off. The bark is peeled from the top section, which will then wither in a natural

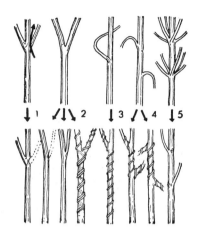

Fig. 35. — Correcting branch defects by wiring. 1) Two branches at exactly the same height. 2) Even-forked branches. 3) Trunk-crossing branch. 4) Half-moon branches. 5) Wheel branches.

way so that the dead wood can be used to form part of the pattern of the tree (see Plate 183). A curve in the trunk (called in Japanese a "curved breast") is beautiful and should be displayed to the best advantage. Scars where branches have been cut off must be eliminated by paring the stumps flat with the trunk and then scooping the scar out slightly with wood-carving tools. This little hollow will gradually grow flat and the scar will be hardly noticeable. One reason why grafted trees are not considered good bonsai is because the graft leaves an ugly malformation which cannot be disguised.

Branches (Figs. 35 & 36). A tree with branches on one side only is not a good choice for a bonsai, although it may be transformed into a semicascade, a cascade, a wind-swept, or a multiple-trunk tree if the trunk is a fine one. Parallel branches are considered ugly and one branch is best removed. A branch which grows across the trunk, spoiling the line, or two crossing branches must be corrected by wiring. A branch which sticks straight out from the front of the trunk must either be cut off or trained to curve to one side; if it is more than two-thirds of the way up the trunk, it can be left alone as it will not spoil the line of the tree. When a number of branches spring from one place (a common condition in young pines) all the branches except one must be removed. A branch which grows in a half-moon without any small side-branches to break the line is unsightly and should be trained straight, willows of course excepted. A branch which divides at the end to form a U can be corrected by making the two ends grow

CHAPTER 4

Plate 166. Wiring a naturally stunted five-needle pine. Note the position of the hands and fingers. The copper wire has been wrapped in paper for photographing; actually, such wrapping is not necessary in the case of five-needle pines.

Plates 167-78. Three stages of the wiring process on four different trees. *1st stage:* the unwired tree. *2nd stage:* the basic shape decided upon begins to emerge. *3rd stage:* the finished wiring.

Plate 179. Shaping a chabo cypress, 2' high, grown un-potted for 5 yrs. from a cutting. **Left:** The tree is planted in a training pot with sphagnum moss. **Right:** After only 30 minutes the tree emerges as a bonsai in the formal up-right style. Its top has been cut off, it has been pruned and given shape by wiring, and the sphagnum moss **has** been replaced with soil.

Plate 180. An example of a fully wired bonsai. Five-needle pine, 2'4", twin-trunk style, from a natural tree.

Plate 181. Two methods of straightening copper wire so it can be used again: by stretching with pliers or by pounding with mallet.

Plate 184. Leaf trimming. **Left to right:** 1) untrimmed branch of mountain maple, 2) same, after full trimming, 3) untrimmed branch of grey-bark elm, 4) same, after full trimming. **Below:** 5) grey-bark elm, after safe trimming meth-od, 6) trimming scissors.

Plate 182. Straightening the trunk of a naturally stunted five-needle pine by using an iron rod and wires.

Plate 183. A stripped and silvered top of a naturally stunted needle ju-niper, 2' high, adds a striking deco-rative element.

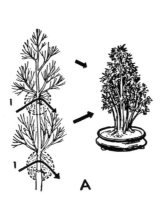

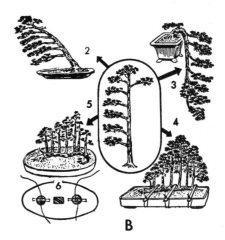

Fig. 36. — Correcting branch defects by changing style of tree. *A)* Wheel-branches changed into a multiple-trunk bonsai by layering. 1) The two layering points. *B)* One-sided upright tree changed into a 2) wind-swept, 3) cascade, 4) straight-line, or 5) sinuous style. 6) Method of wiring 4 and 5 into pot, showing the outer holes of a 3-hole pot with sticks beneath them holding copper wires; this method is an alternate to that shown on 4.

in different directions or by tying them close together while the wood is still young and soft.

4. *Leaf Trimming* (Plate 184). Elm, maple, zelkova, and ivy should have their leaves cut off during late spring or early summer. A new crop of leaves will grow which will be smaller and more beautiful. If the tree is in poor condition, each leaf should be cut so that the stalk with a quarter of the leaf attached remains on the tree. The tree will require manuring for a month before leaf cutting so that it may have the strength to form new leaves, and after the cutting it must be protected for a fortnight from heavy rain. It should, however, be allowed as much sunshine as

possible as this assists the growth of the new leaves. The leaves of evergreens must never be cut. In the case of the five-needle pine, however, the still-soft new needles may be pulled out in the spring just before they begin to harden; the following spring very short, bunched needles will appear, thus enhancing the tree's beauty.

5. *Trimming.* When a bonsai has become established and has been given a handsome shape, this shape must be retained by trimming. That is to say, the new leaf buds are removed as they appear in the spring so that the twig or branch does not grow. Following are some general remarks on trimming; more specific methods, designated by the letters A through G, are

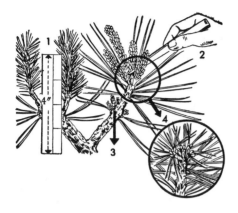

Fig. 37.—Trimming Method **A** (black pine, spring).
1) Shoots developed 2 wks. beyond time for trimming.
2) Shoots ready for trimming by being broken or
pinched off. 3) Shoots which will require trimming in
about 1 wk. 4) 1 mo. after trimming.

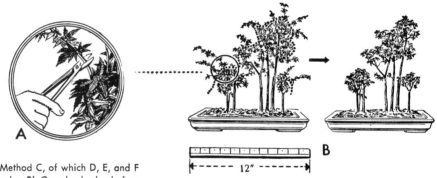

Fig. 39.—Trimming Method C, of which D, E, and F
are variants. *A)* Maple. *B)* Grey-bark elm before
and after trimming on dotted lines.

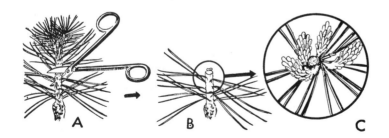

Fig. 40.—Trimming Method G (black pine, autumn).
A) Using pruning scissors. *B)* Branch tip after trimming.
C) After 3 mos.

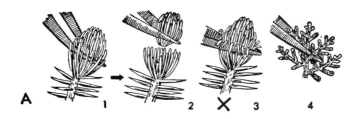

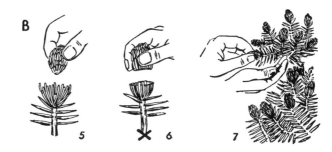

Fig. 38. — Trimming Method B. **A)** With pincettes. 1 & 2) Correct way of trimming needle juniper, spruce, cryptomeria. 3) Wrong way, as the needles whose tops are broken off will later turn brown. 4) Correct trimming of Sargent juniper, cypress. **B)** With fingers. 5) Correct. 6) Wrong. 7) Hand inserted from below to hold branch.

described in Appendix 3 and illustrated in Figs. 37–40.

Trimming is done with pincers or pruning scissors or sometimes with the fingers. The greatest care must be taken never to touch new leaves or needles, other than those to be removed, as this will make them turn brown. If it is necessary to hold the branch firm so as to pull off the new shoot, the hand must be inserted from below so as not to come in contact with the fresh growth. In the case of needle trees particular care must be taken not to cut through any part of the needles which are to remain on the tree; the pincers, scissors, or the fingers must be inserted at the angle necessary to cut only the twig itself.

Sargent and needle juniper, cryptomeria, cypress, and so forth require frequent trim-

ming as they are very prolific. When trimming Sargent juniper or cypress the branch is held firmly and the new shoot (easily recognizable by its fresh color) is twisted off with pincers, care being taken not to damage the shoots which do not require trimming. Both these species will, with time and the constant nipping off of ragged sprays, produce close, smooth balls of foliage. When treating cypress, needle juniper, and cryptomeria it is not necessary to twist the shoot; it can be pulled out. Spruces and five-needle pines need not be trimmed more than once a year in the spring. The new needles are pinched off with pincers, leaving the base of the shoot with several needles adhering to it. This must be done before the new wood hardens.

Deciduous trees may be trimmed any

time during the growing season. In this operation, all new shoots are cut back to within an inch of the parent branch, leaving one or two nodes intact. At the top of the tree the twigs are cut very short leaving only one node. Flowering trees and fruit trees are trimmed after they have flowered, but by midsummer. Trees such as crape myrtle, privet, Spanish jasmine, roses, and pomegranate, which produce flowers on new shoots, may be trimmed in early spring to increase flowering, but must then be left alone until after the blossoms appear in summer. If, however, an unsightly new shoot grows too long and spoils the shape of the tree, it should be cut off.

6. *Manuring.* Manuring is of the utmost importance in the training and care of bonsai. An adequate supply of suitable manure should always be kept handy from spring to autumn, and during spring and summer it is as well to fix a weekly "manuring day" so that regular applications are not forgotten. Trees which are not properly manured have pale, anemic-looking leaves and, in the case of fruit or flowering trees, the blossoms are sparse and small.

Farmyard manure is too coarse and heavy for bonsai and should never be used. Various light natural manures are, however, suitable, although they tend to have an unpleasant smell. This does not matter as long as the bonsai is kept out of doors or if the manure is to be buried in the pot, but for bonsai which are brought fairly regularly into the house an odorless artificial manure is recommended. No matter what type of manure is used, the important thing to remember is that all bonsai require nitrogen, phosphorous, and potassium in appropriate quantities. All the following manuring systems are designed to fulfill these needs.

Natural manures can be divided into two main categories: (1) vegetable manures such as cottonseed, rapeseed, or soya beans, and (2) animal manures such as bone meal, fish meal, or chicken manure. Wood ash is used in combination with all these types of natural manures, but more as a soil conditioner than as a manure itself. It keeps the soil from becoming too acid. It is well to add about ten percent wood ash

Color Plate 12. Nagasaki crab-apple. "Small" bonsai in the informal upright style. 5″. 5 yrs. Produced by grafting onto a wild crab-apple stock. Glazed Japanese pot of Seto ware.

Color Plate 13. Dwarf needle juniper. Sinuous 9-trunk style. 1′6″. About 20 yrs. Produced from a cutting, the trunk of the former tree forming the twisting root of this. Glazed Japanese pot of Ichiyo ware.

Color Plate 14. Sargent juniper. Driftwood style. 2′ 10″. About 150 yrs. Produced from a naturally stunted tree and potted about 85 yrs. ago. Unglazed antique Chinese pot.

Color Plate 12

Color Plate 13

Color Plate 14

to any natural manure. Wood ash may also be used in a weak solution (1 teaspoonful to 2 quarts of water) by itself in a single application when the condition of the soil requires it. Vegetable manures, used either separately or in mixtures, may be used in powdered, liquid, or paste form. The same is true of the animal manures. Artificial manures may be used in either powdered or liquid form, but wood ash should never be mixed with them. An artificial manure for flowering and fruit trees should contain a high percentage of phosphorous; that required to encourage quick growth, of nitrogen. Any reliable nurseryman will be able to recommend a good brand of artificial manure.

Powdered manure, either artificial or natural (if the latter, first dry the material and then pound it to a powder), is sprinkled over the earth at the edge of the pot. The exact amount will vary according to the type and condition of the tree, but in no case should it exceed five teaspoonfuls for every six square inches of soil surface. The powder must be brushed off after about one month. This form of manure is not recommended except for trees in training pots or in the ground as it spoils the appearance of the bonsai.

Paste manure, either vegetable or animal, is made by adding water to powdered manure. The paste is best if left to mature for a month in cool weather or a week in hot weather; it then becomes rather strong smelling, but is more beneficial. The paste is made into small balls about an inch across. This can be done with the help of an old tablespoon. The balls are placed at the outer edge of the pot away from the trunk. They should be used in a ratio of about four balls to a pot six inches in diameter. This type of manure is excellent for rock plantings as it will adhere to the soil. To avoid the development of insect pests, paste manure should be sprayed once every two weeks with pyrethrum or nicotine and should be brushed away after six or eight weeks.

Liquid manure may be either natural or artificial. It may be made from powder by mixing one part of powder with ten parts of water and the liquid allowed to stand in the same way as in the case of paste. The solution is then poured off, the residue in the bottom of the receptacle being discarded. The liquid manure is bottled or placed in a container and used in the proportion of one part solution to ten parts water. Bonsai can be watered with this mixture once a week from spring to autumn. A weak mixture in the propor-

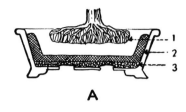
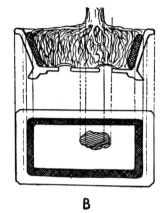
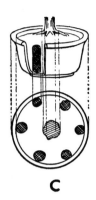

Fig. 41.—Applying basic-mixture manure. *A)* Upon repotting. 1) Main soil. 2) Basic mixture lining 4 sides. 3) Bottom soil. *B)* Without repotting. *C)* Alternate for B, used for pots under 4″ in diameter.

tion of one part solution to ten parts water may be used on trees for the first month after repotting.

Basic mixture. In addition to these various forms of animal, vegetable, or artificial manures, a basic mixture of manures is required for certain occasions. A very good mixture can be made as follows:

Cottonseed	3 parts
Fish meal	2 parts
Sulphur phosphate of lime	1 part
Soya beans	3 parts
Wood ash	1 part

This mixture must be set aside for about one month in summer or three months in winter, and not used until it is through fermenting. It should be applied once every year to flowering and fruit trees; it may also be used on other trees when they are in unhealthy condition or when it is desired to force their growth (Fig. 41). If the tree is being repotted, the basic mixture is put in the pot between the bottom soil and the main soil, covering the bottom and curving up the sides of the pot toward the top. In an ordinary six-inch pot the layer should be about half an inch thick, but if the pot is tall and narrow a thicker layer will be necessary. There must be at least half an inch of main soil between the roots and the manure. If the tree is not being repotted, then the basic mixture is applied by burying it in the soil. This is done by digging a trench against all four sides of the pot, extending to the bottom of the pot—the trench should be about half an inch wide for the average pot or up to an inch wide if the distance between the trench and the trunk of the tree is over five inches—filling the trench with the basic mixture almost up to the level of the soil, and then covering with topsoil. If the pot is very small, bury shafts of basic mixture at regular intervals around the rim.

Summary of manuring requirements. The basic mixture should be used once a year on flowering and fruit trees. All trees require the following seasonal manures, whether vegetable, animal, or artificial, in the form of powder, paste, or liquid. *Spring:* When the new buds first appear, two or three applications of a strong solution are made at intervals of a few days. Artificial or liquid manure is best as it acts quickly. As soon as the leaves begin to open, the tree is watered once a week with a normal solution of liquid or artificial manure; or paste balls are applied. Paste may be used three times during the growing season, i.e., during spring and summer. *Summer:* The tree is watered with liquid manure once a week as in spring, or paste is applied. *Autumn:* Two or three strong applications of liquid manure (artificial or natural) are made at a few days' interval before the tree becomes dormant. *Winter:* No manure is required.

7. *Dead Wood.* Dead wood is unsightly and as a rule should be cut away, certainly so when there is only a little of it, say small twigs or branches. In certain cases, however, when an entire branch or part of the tree dies (particularly in the case of a tree such as the Sargent juniper, half of which may sometimes suddenly die), the dead wood may be turned to advantage and the tree transformed into the "driftwood" style, with the silver-colored dead wood used as an effective decoration. To achieve this color, the bark of the dead wood is peeled off, the wood scraped with a piece of glass (wood-carving tools may also be used to achieve a desired shape) and painted with the strong lime-and-sulphur solution described on page 159. After six months, the surface of the "driftwood" is washed with a brush and water and the solution applied again. This should be repeated twice every year.

8. *Choosing the Pot.* The pot of a bonsai is like the frame of a picture: it should be chosen to show off the subject to the greatest advantage. When the training of a bonsai is sufficiently far advanced, a pot is chosen in which to display it, the size and shape depending on the size and shape of the tree. Examples of pots which harmonize excellently with the bonsai they contain will be found in the illustrations. Trees trained in slanting styles, such as the cascade and the wind-swept, look best in a round or equilateral pot, the trunk planted in the center and the branches sweeping down over the side. Upright trees show to advantage in oval or rectangular pots and are placed slightly off-center. A tall tree with a slim trunk and delicate foliage should never be planted in a deep, heavy pot, but such a pot is excellent for a tree with a thick trunk

and dense foliage. Care must be taken to plant the bonsai with its best side to the front and in such a way that the branches harmonize with the shape of the pot. If the branches are longer at one side than the other, the trunk is placed off-center, giving the longer branches the greater area of earth to spread over. Following the same principle, the highest point in a group planting should be about one-third from one edge of the pot.

The color of the pot ought to contrast with the tree. For this reason green pots are only used for trees with brightly colored flowers, foliage, or fruits. The pots of flowering or fruit trees are chosen to display the blossoms rather than the leaves, since it is then that the bonsai is enjoyed; con-

sequently, colored pots and pots with a high glaze are often used. Pines and deciduous trees require less showy pots, those which will not distract the eye from the beauty of the tree itself. Unglazed pots of a neutral color, reddish, grey, or brown, are best. The color of the pot must suit the type of tree. A heavy tree with dark-green leaves requires a dark, rich-colored pot, but a delicate, silvery trunk with light-green leaves requires a light, delicately colored pot. If the pot has three feet, the bonsai is placed so that one foot is in the middle of the front of the pot, giving symmetry to the whole; in the case of a cascade style, however, one foot must be directly under the cascading trunk in order to steady the pot.

5 ❖ ROCK AND GROUP PLANTINGS

ROCK PLANTINGS AND GROUP plantings have the particular charm of the miniature landscape and the advantage that they can both be made at home without too great expense and enjoyed immediately. Many of the ingredients can be collected on expeditions into the country, and these kinds of bonsai are particularly suited to the "town gardener" with limited space. Low troughs set round a balcony or a terrace or in a paved courtyard are excellent for the display of rock and group plantings. They can also be arranged as window boxes; not, of course, in the wooden boxes we associate with this kind of decoration, but in oblong earthenware pots supported on metal brackets.

ROCK PLANTINGS

1. Styles. Rock plantings can be of two kinds: (1) Root-over-rock style, meaning trees and plants grown on a rock standing upon a bed of soil. In this case the roots are trained down over the rock into the soil. (2) Clinging-to-a-rock style, meaning trees and plants grown in peat and adhering to the rock, the roots being contained in the peat. This type does not require a bed of soil, but should stand on a tray of moist sand.

Rock plantings may also be distinguished by two different perspectives: (1) The distant view. Here it is best to use small trees with very small leaves so as to give the effect of trees among mountains. The trees should be arranged to give a natural effect, clinging to the rock. (2) The near-at-hand woodland or garden scene. Here larger trees and smaller rocks can be used, the tree clasping the rock with its roots. The effect of a woodland glade can be achieved by the use of miniature shrubs such as dwarf azaleas or dwarf bamboo planted at the base of the rock.

2. *Methods* (Plates 193–204). The best rocks for rock plantings are those with a rough surface. Volcanic rocks with cavities in them are particularly suitable as they can hold pockets of soil. The size of the rock depends on the proportions of the miniature landscape envisaged by the maker, but, on the whole, fairly large ones are best, small rocks and stones being kept for use in group plantings. A tall rock can be made to look like a cliff, with trees hanging over the crest and the steep front face left bare; a flat, stratified rock can have groups of small trees on the upper surface. The former could be treated as a rock on a bed of soil, the roots of the trees being trained down the back of the rock; the latter, as an "unattached" rock so that the pattern of the stratification can be seen to advantage. The color and veining of the rocks are of importance and trees which blend with them should be chosen. Anyone can collect his own rocks (see Plates 185–92). Those found on the seashore must be soaked in water for several months to remove the salt as this will kill any plants which come in contact with it. Apart from the fact that they look more decorative, rocks with rough knobs on them are convenient because the peat which attaches the plants to the rock needs to be held in place with wires until it is firmly established and overgrown with moss; the wires can be attached inconspicuously to a couple of knobs. A rock which is roughly triangular is excellent as the planting can be made along the longest side, the wires being held by the two angles and the third angle forming a focal point in front. If the rock has no natural holes or knobs, small holes can be chipped in the surface, wires cemented into them, the place being hidden with peat or soil, and the wires fastened round the planting. If the wires are cleverly concealed they can be left in place permanently and lessen the danger of the tree's being torn or washed off the rock.

Pines and spruces are well suited for rock plantings as they require little moisture and also look particularly appropriate in a rocky setting; maples can also be used successfully as their roots attach easily (for other suitable species, see Appendix 3). A single pine or maple of considerable age looks magnificent when planted on a rock, but for those who want quicker results, groups of seedlings from three to five years old can be arranged very effectively. These seedlings will one day become an ancient bonsai forest, but there is no need to wait till then to enjoy them. Natural seedlings can often be found when one is on a rock-hunting expedition, and it is as well to go provided with the necessary paraphernalia for collecting them. Ferns, moss, and small rock-plants can also be found. Some of these may need to be renewed annually, but that is easily done. Seedlings and plants of this kind can, of course, be grown at home or bought from a nursery.

Rock plantings should be made in the repotting season. The rock is placed on the revolving table. In addition to the usual repotting tools and soil, a quantity of peat is kneaded in water until it is sticky. Pieces of fresh green moss will also be needed and are best laid out on a board or tray.

The first thing to decide is where to place the tree or trees on the rock. They can be held in place by hand or lightly stuck to the rock with a little peat to get the general effect before work begins. In this way the gardener knows what he is aiming at and, if necessary, can draw a rough sketch for reference.

The soil is washed from the roots of the plants, but the roots are not pruned. A thin film of peat is smeared onto the rock at the place where the principal tree is to be attached; the tree is placed against it; and the roots are covered with a lump of peat. The other plants are arranged in the same way, and the mass of peat is tied into place with wire. The peat is covered with pieces of growing moss, dipped into water and then pressed on with the fingers.

If the rock is to be planted in a pot, the long roots are arranged round the rock so that they end up underneath it, the peat covering only the upper, exposed part. The pot is filled three-quarters full of soil as described in the section on repotting. The rock, which must be chosen to allow for about a quarter of its height being buried, is then placed in position and the pot filled with main soil which is made firm with a chopstick. The surplus main soil is brushed off and the surface is finished with topsoil and dried powdered moss. If it is desired to arrange the rock so that it looks as if it were at the edge of a pool or stream, a part of the pot surface can be left bare of moss and sprinkled with fine sand. If the root formation on the rock is to be exposed, the peat may be removed at the end of a year. Potted rock plantings must have the earth renewed in the ordinary way, but the tree is not removed from the rock, only the soil in the pot is changed.

If the rock is to be set on a tray with no roots in the soil, the roots of the trees must be curled up inside the peat and the whole mass of rock, soil, and moss bound round with hemp string. When the moss starts growing, the string can be taken off and

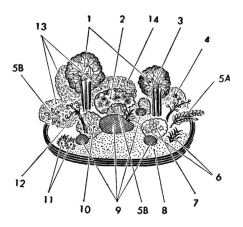

Key to Color Plate 15. *1)* Trident maple, 3 yrs., seedling. *2)* Five-needle pine, 6 yrs., grafting. *3)* Star jasmine, 3 yrs., cutting. *4)* Rock cotoneaster, 3 yrs., cutting. *5)* Satsuki azalea, 5 yrs., cutting, *a)* with white flowers and *b)* with pink. *6)* Dwarf sweet-rush, 3 yrs., dividing. *7)* Japanese serissa, 3 yrs., cutting. *8)* River sand, No. 5 size. *9)* Stones. *10)* Japanese box, 3 yrs., cutting. *11)* Golden fern, 1 yr., dividing. *12)* English holly, 2 yrs., layering. *13)* Sargent juniper, 4-5 yrs., cutting. *14)* Himuro cypress, 4 yrs., cutting.

the rock arranged on a tray of damp sand. The sand will get dirty after a while and must be renewed or washed. When lifting the rock it should always be held where the bare rock is exposed. This type of rock planting can be left for a very long time without repotting, or rather without being taken to pieces; as there is no pot, the roots cannot become constricted. It must be watered frequently.

Rock plantings need special care during the first two years because of the drastic washing given to the roots. Especially during the first month or so they must be kept moist and must not be exposed to heavy rain or strong wind. When watering them, it is important to spray not only on top, but the underside as well. After the second year the plants will be established and will need less attention. Paste manure should be used, as inconspicuously as possible. When caring for rock plantings, the moss on the surface should not be touched as this damages the color and texture.

GROUP PLANTINGS

Group plantings, although less exotic than rock plantings, are also hardier as the trees do not require such drastic root cleansing. The object is to create a miniature wood, and here again seedlings can be used effectively. Any kind of tree or shrub can be used in group plantings, but the Japanese

Color Plate 15. Group planting in the tray-landscape style. 1′9″ by 1′. See planting chart above for make-up and Plates 214–18 for methods of making. Unglazed Japanese pot of Tokoname ware.

Color Plate 16. Five-needle pine. Twin-trunk style. 3′. About 100 yrs. Produced from a naturally stunted tree and potted about 80 yrs. ago. Unglazed Chinese pot. A very famous bonsai, its well-proportioned shape producing a feeling of great strength.

Color Plate 17. Rock planting in the clinging-to-a-rock style. 1′5″. Glazed Chinese pot of Nanking ware. Consists of five-needle pine at top (about 25 yrs., natural), dwarf needle juniper at left (15 yrs., cutting), dwarf azalea at right (about 10 yrs., made from natural dwarf about 5 yrs. ago), and golden fern at the front. The formation of the rock suggests a waterfall. This planting was made 2 yrs. ago, using very little peat muck in order to hurry it, but it was very delicate during the first year.

Color Plate 15

Color Plate 16

Color Plate 17

consider that the most effective are those made with one species of tree only and prefer varieties with very small leaves such as pines, spruces, cryptomeria, larches, and maples. Large flowering trees are not recommended, for when the leaves are fully grown they throw the whole landscape out of proportion. An exception is made for the Japanese flowering apricot, the *ume*, often incorrectly called plum as will be explained further on. Flowering shrubs such as the dwarf azalea and lilac or the miniature rose can be used with great success as can also the cotoneaster, whose tiny leaves and flowers are particularly suitable.

As set forth in the classification of styles in Chapter 4, there are eight group-planting styles which pertain to true bonsai, together with three additional styles which, though not bonsai strictly speaking, are deserving of mention.

1. Bonsai Styles of Group Plantings (Fig. 42 & Plates 205–13). Here the pattern of the trees themselves is the focus of interest, with little if any other ornamentation. A group planting in any of the eight bonsai styles makes use of only one species of tree, as a mixed group might spoil the neat, studied, and sometimes even "artificial" effect which characterizes the usual ex-

amples of group plantings. The special category known as the natural-group style is much more "natural" in feeling, seeking to re-create a group of trees such as might be found growing in nature, with the roots of the trees negligently arranged. The clustered-group style, on the other hand, is much more "formal" in appearance, the trunks being much more closely grouped, as though gathered up in the fist and thrust into the soil, sometimes so much so that they resemble a single tree. These terms "natural" and "formal" and "artificial" are, of course, only relative, and in a sense all examples of the bonsai styles of group plantings seek to re-create a single important element of a landscape rather than to reproduce an entire landscape on the scale of the tray-landscape style treated below. For the clustered-group style a circular clump looks well in a rather ornate hexagonal or petal-shaped dish, which emphasizes the artificial quality; it can also be planted at the highest point of a gentle slope in an oval dish. A long, narrow clump of trees in a narrow, rectangular pot should be so arranged that the tallest tree comes at the focal point. Maple, zelkova, beech, and cryptomeria lend themselves particularly well to this style of group planting.

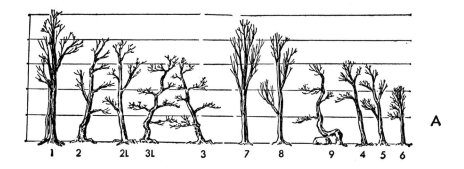

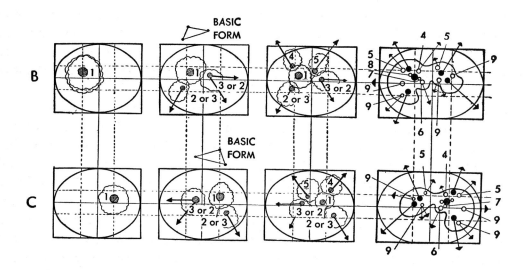

Fig. 42. Natural-group styles of group plantings, in either rectangular or oval pots. (The lower edge of each diagram is the front; arrows indicate directions in which trees slant.) See also Plates 205-13. *A)* Suitable shapes and relative heights of trees used at positions numbered in diagrams, "L" indicating that a tree is used only in a left-side arrangement. *B)* Left-side arrangements showing 3-tree, 5-tree, and multiple-tree plantings, together with the beginning of the planting. (In the multiple-tree planting the waving line indicates the limits of a slight hillock; the numbers of the first 5 trees are not repeated.) *C)* Right-side arrangements showing same.

2. *Bonkei or Tray-Landscape Style* (Plates 214–18). Here the aim is to create a realistic landscape seen through the wrong end of a telescope. Various materials are used—trees, grasses, rocks, sand, and the like, as found in nature, and some persons go on to add tiny figures of people, animals, houses, bridges, waterfalls, and the like, though it is our opinion that these frills are not needed with a good bonkei; in fact they

detract from its effectiveness. The trees, always in uneven numbers, are scattered over the surface of a large, shallow container and bunched together slightly about a third of the width across to make a focal point. The point can also be built up to form the apex of a slope, or rocks can be used to give it emphasis, trees or shrubs being planted on a nucleus of peat behind the rocks. This focal point is extremely important as it prevents the group planting from looking dull and top-heavy. A level stretch of sand or fine gravel, to simulate a pool or a stream, balances the trees effectively; the stream can be made to issue from between two crags or from under overhanging bushes, but it cannot be made to trickle down a slope as constant watering will wash away the gravel. A beautiful bonkei, very suitable for a terrace, can be made in a long, narrow trough; two-thirds of the surface is taken up by an uneven bank of soil and rocks closely planted with trees and shrubs, while the remaining third, in the foreground, is a level "river" of sand.

3. *Seasonal Group Plantings.* There are certain groups of plants which the Japanese traditionally associate with the New Year and the autumn season, at which time effective group plantings are created with them. These groups are displayed for a short time only, and any lack of proportion or symmetry in the elements is overlooked because of the significance. The same plantings, or variations of them which will readily come to mind, can be the source of much pleasure in the West as well.

The New Year planting may also be made in time for Christmas. It must include the three plants representing happiness, long life, and virtue: *shô-chiku-bai,* i.e., pine, bamboo, and Japanese flowering apricot. The last must be in full flower: under the old lunar calendar New Year came in February, the *ume*'s true flowering season, so now its flowering must be forced to meet the modern calendar. This is done by bringing the tree into a greenhouse from 15 to 20 days before it will be needed, keeping it at a temperature of between 70 and 80 degrees, and spraying it twice a day with water at greenhouse temperature. To these three basic plants are often added fern fronds, yellow aconites, or the red-berried *manryô* ("ten thousand coins") to represent wealth. Other plants are also often combined with the basic three, but some of them require special forcing or propagation to meet the season. They are miniature bamboo *(sasa)*; the red-berried ardisia *(yabukôji)*; nandina *(nanten)*, whose red winter leaves harmonize well with green leaves; adonis *(fukuji-sô)*;

hepatica *(yukiwari-sô)*; and the Japanese wild orchid *(shunran)*.

The autumn planting is made up principally of the traditional "seven grasses of autumn": (1) *kikyô* (Chinese bellflower), which has a purple flower, (2) *hagi* (bush clover), mixed white and pink flowers, (3) *ominaeshi*, yellow flowers, (4) *nade-shiko*, pink flowers, (5) *susuki* or *kaya*, the kind with thin, green blades, (6) *fuji-bakama*, light-colored reddish-purple flowers, and (7) *kuzu*, purple flowers. Two of these, however, are unsuitable for a group planting—the sixth is too tall and the seventh is a vine with overlarge leaves—and can be replaced by one or more of the following: (a) *kakkô-azami*, with light-purple flowers, (b) *hyakunichi-sô*, the dwarf variety, with red or pink flowers, (c) *sennichi-sô*, with reddish-purple flowers, (d) *kata-hiba*, golden, tiny-leaved fern and (e) *kujaku-sô* (French marigold), with yellow flowers. All of these grasses are prepared the preceding spring and kept in small training pots (3 to 4 inches in diameter) until needed.

4. Plantings of Herbs, Grasses, and Shrubs. There is almost no combination of plants which, with inventiveness, cannot be made into an interesting and effective group planting. Under this category the gardener is limited only by the bounds of his own imagination—and a few practical, common-sense considerations. For instance, it is impractical to combine plants which require too dissimilar soils or care, such as cactus and alpine plants. One should likewise avoid any feeling of heaviness by choosing plants with small leaves and light, delicate flowers. The more effective arrangements usually reproduce a small scene from nature and frequently make use of rocks and water (either as an actual pool among the rocks or as sand to simulate a stream). There should always be some one focal point or main plant, perhaps even an actual bonsai, while the rest of the planting, consisting of subsidiary plants and ground cover, will be chosen to complement this keynote. Particularly popular in Japan are plantings representative of the season in which they are displayed. A safe rule to follow in choosing the soil for one of these plantings is to reproduce as closely as possible the soil found in the plants' native habitat. The plantings will need repotting about every two or three years, at which time it may be necessary to separate and rearrange the different plants.

5. Methods. The pot for a group planting should always be less than two inches deep, and care should be taken not to try to work

Plate 185. Rock in shape of distant mountains.

Plate 186. Rock in shape of a jutting island.

Plate 187. Rock in shape of a cape, with a bronze ornament.

Plate 188. Natural rock formation suggesting a waterfall.

Plate 189. Naturally formed rock basin.

Plate 190. Natural formation suggesting an old man staring out into space.

Plate 192. Another use for the house-shaped rock

Plate 191. Rock in shape of a thatched-roof hut, set amid moss and dwarf gentians, in a cobalt-blue glazed Chinese container of Nanking ware.

MAKING A ROCK PLANTING

Plate 193. Peat muck is smeared over portions of rock to be planted. Note that, as the rock is hard and smooth surfaced, copper wires have already been cemented into place.

Plate 194. Placing the plants on the muck.

Plate 195. Securing the plants with the copper wires.

Plate 196. Covering all the roots with muck.

Plates 197-200. Four views of the planting after the muck has been covered with moss and the whole tied firmly with hemp strings.

Plates 201-2. Front and back views of the planting after given final shape by wiring. *a)* Golden fern, 2 yrs., by dividing. *b)* Dwarf star jasmine, 4 yrs., from a cutting. *c)* Wild-thyme azalea, 5 yrs., from a cutting. *d)* Five-needle pines, 20 yrs., from natural trees. *e)* English holly, 3 yrs., by layering. *f)* Wild thyme, 2 yrs., by dividing.

Plates 203-4. Side views of the same rock planting.

MAKING A BONSAI-STYLE GROUP PLANTING

*Plate 205. Materials assembled. **Left to right:** 1)* White beeches, natural trees aged 15-20 yrs., trained in pot 5 yrs.; primary roots have been trimmed. 2) Container of main soil, No. 5 size, and small pots of golden fern for ground cover. 3) Pot, on revolving table, with pieces of coconut fiber for hole covers. 4) Container of bottom soil, No. 4 size, and various tools. 5) More white beeches.

Plates 206-9. Successive stages in planting a left-hand arrangement.

Plates 210-13. Successive stages in planting a right-hand arrangement. Note that the arrangements of Plates 209 and 213 are finished except for top soil and dry moss.

MAKING A TRAY LANDSCAPE

For finished planting see Color Plate 15, page 134.

Plate 214. Materials assembled. *Left to right:* 1) Tools and plant materials. 2) Stones and soils. 3) Pot and hole covers on revolving stand. 4) Water for moistening moss. 5) Moss on board and more plant materials. 6) Container of peat muck.

Plate 215. Placing stones above successive layers of bottom soil, main soil, and peat muck.

Plate 216. Viewing from opposite side, to make sure both sides are equally well arranged.

Plate 218. Arranging fine gravel after moss has been planted.

Plate 217. Arranging the plants with muck. ***Left to right:*** 1) English holly. 2) Main tree: five-needle pine 3) Subordinate tree: himuro cypress. 4) Japanese serissa.

in too much material just because it is attractive in itself. It is better to discard an interesting piece of rock in favor of a smaller, duller piece if the former would overload the pot and make the trees look cramped. In the same way the temptation to make use of a decorative tree which is really too large must be resisted, as the resulting lack of proportion will grow more and more irritating as time goes on. In this as in all bonsai work it must never be forgotten that empty spaces form part of the pattern. A pot with a wide rim, rather like a soup plate, is suitable for the display of a group planting although it would look too "fussy" if used for a one-tree type of bonsai.

All the material for a group planting must be collected beforehand; the same tools, soil, sticky peat mixture, and growing moss will be needed as for a rock planting. The pot is filled three-quarters full of soil in the proportions used in repotting. If rocks are to be used, they are arranged at this point, each stuck firmly onto a pad of peat; if a slope or hill is needed, this is made of a lump of peat and the trees are planted on top. When the rocks and plants are all arranged, main soil

is poured in to fill the pot and is made firm round the roots with a chopstick. A long wire is wound round the trunk and the two ends attached to a second wire running round the pot beneath the lip. When the planting is finished the surplus main soil is brushed off and the surface finished with topsoil and dried moss or sand, to represent water. Natural-colored sand or fine gravel should be used in preference to white. White gravel does not blend with the rest of the planting and, in Japan, is associated only with the vulgar, ill-made little "Japanese gardens" displayed in flower shops to catch the eye of the inexperienced tourist. Exposed lumps of peat are covered with pieces of green moss, dampened and pressed into place with the fingers. When the planting is complete it is watered carefully both from above and below. It must be repotted in the same way as an ordinary bonsai and for this reason it is as well, in a planting of mixed trees, to choose those which require new soil after about the same interval. Evergreens and deciduous trees can be mixed successfully and repotted at the end of three years. Great care must be taken when repotting to keep the roots of the different trees separate.

6 ◈ CARE OF BONSAI

No ONE SHOULD OWN A BONSAI unless he is prepared to give a certain amount of time every day to its care. As the reader will have gathered, a bonsai is much more like a pet than a plant and needs quite as much attention as a cat or a dog. In fact, there is a great deal in common between the care of a prize poodle and the care of a prize bonsai. Both require daily grooming, regular clipping, constant attention to health, and a good tonic from time to time. A bonsai cannot be left to look after itself if the owner goes away; to bury the pot in the garden and hope for the best is no solution. If it must be left for the weekend, it is important to arrange for someone trustworthy to water it regularly at the correct times. It is as well to leave it in a shelter so that a sudden storm will not damage it. If the owner intends to be absent for some time, the best plan is to board the bonsai out with a good nursery which will take an interest in it. If the nurseryman is not accustomed to the care of bonsai, clear instructions should be left with him.

PLACEMENT

The everyday essentials for a healthy bonsai are sun, air, water, and a temperature which avoids extremes. A bonsai is a miniature forest tree, not a hothouse plant, and it must live out of doors all the time, being brought into the house only on special occasions. The more beautiful the bonsai, the more temptation there is to keep it in the house too much. But this temptation must be firmly resisted. A bonsai will die if kept too much indoors, particularly in overheated rooms. It should be brought inside as little as possible, and never for too many hours at a time. It may safely be brought in once or twice a week—perhaps a bit oftener if for only two or three hours at

a time—during winter (provided the room has very little heat), spring (except while the new shoots are soft), and autumn; but almost never in summer unless the room is to all intents and purposes as well ventilated as the outdoors.

Two practical ways to avoid the temptation to bring the bonsai inside too often are to have several trees, which can be displayed in rotation, and to arrange them outside in such a way that they can be seen and enjoyed there. If the owner has a garden, the bonsai are best kept in a sunny, sheltered spot, not standing on the ground but on a wooden stand or table (see Plates 219–23). They should never be kept on a glass-covered veranda or under trees or shrubs, and the table should be set at least six feet away from a wall.

Breezes and gentle rain are essential to the good health of a bonsai, but it must be taken under cover if very heavy rain falls or if there is a gale or strong wind which might upset the pot or uproot the tree. One pot should not sit too close to another and should be turned about once a week so that all sides are exposed equally to the elements and the foliage can develop evenly; failure to observe these precautions may even result in dead branches.

WATERING

Bonsai experts say that it takes three years to learn to water a tree properly, but fortunately most trees will flourish even with less experienced care. The best water for bonsai, as for any plant, comes from a spring, well, or rain cistern. Chlorinated water directly from the tap is not good for any bonsai and will quickly kill the less hardy varieties; if no other water is available, however, tap water may be used by putting it in a large receptacle and leaving it in the open air for at least twenty-four hours. If goldfish or some other living creatures can be kept in it, so much the better; this should be possible for anyone with a garden, balcony, terrace, or fire escape.

The best watering can is one with a fine spray and a long spout. The spray should be held above the surface of the soil and waved up and down so that the water falls evenly like rain. If the surface soil is dry, the bonsai must be watered thoroughly from all sides, not from the front only. The water should be sufficient to saturate the soil and drip out at the drainage hole in the bottom of the pot; if necessary, it is as well to lift the pot to make sure of this.

The amount of water needed must be judged by the waterer; it depends on the species, the condition of the tree, the size of the pot, and the weather. As a general rule in dry weather, if the water space at the top of the pot is filled to overflowing and the moisture allowed to sink in five times, it is enough. A deep pot holds moisture longer than a shallow one and needs less watering. Trees with large leaves, such as maple, beech, ivy, and all the fruit trees require more water than those of the pine family. Young, growing trees require more than trees which have reached maturity. Rock plantings are particularly liable to get dry and need frequent, careful watering.

If the whole of the soil of the pot is so dry that, in the case of a deciduous tree, the leaves curl up and droop, it is dangerous to drench the tree with water immediately. The tree should be removed to a shady place and the leaves sprayed with a syringe. When the sun has set, the pot can be watered sparingly and the leaves sprayed again. Next morning rather more water is given. The tree is kept in the shade for another three days, the amount of water being increased gradually until normal conditions are re-established and the tree looks healthy again.

The following chart for seasonal watering will be found useful:

Early spring (budding season). Unless rain has fallen, the bonsai needs water once or twice a day. The principal watering is given between 9 and 10 a.m. If the weather is unusually warm and dry, the tree may need to be watered again before 3 p.m. It should never be watered in the evening as a slight frost might freeze the water, thus damaging the tree or loosening the soil.

Late spring. Water must be given twice or three times a day if necessary. If the bonsai is watered twice, it should be at

Color Plate 18. Needle juniper. Driftwood style. 2'. About 100 yrs. Produced from a naturally stunted tree and potted about 20 yrs. ago. Unglazed Chinese pot. The scroll painting of monkeys emphasizes the feeling that this is a tree growing far in the mountains, from which the viewer turns to see, in the distant plains below, but a single trace of humanity, represented by the tiny bronze pagoda on the ornamental rock.

Color Plate 19. Japanese ·mountain maple (dwarf variety "Yatsubusa"). Slanting style. 2'3". About 30 yrs. Produced by layering or grafting. Glazed Chinese pot of Nanking ware. The arrangement with a red stone in a pool of water is in the cooling summer style.

Color Plate 20. Trident maple. Nine-tree style. 2'. About 30 yrs. Produced from a seedling. Made about 25 yrs. ago and now roots have grown together so they almost seem a single root. An exquisite group planting, looking so much like a forest in Lilliput that one almost expects to hear birds singing and a brook rippling. Glazed Chinese pot of Kuang-tung ware.

Color Plate 18

Color Plate 19

Color Plate 20

9 a.m. and 3 p.m.; if three times, at 9 a.m., 12 noon, and 3 p.m.

Summer (hot weather; that is to say, a temperature up to between 90° and 100°, or conditions with a strong, dry wind). The tree must be watered from three to five times a day, the number of times depending on the dryness of the soil. The leaves should never be moistened in the middle of the day when the sun is on them as they will be burned. The first watering can be given at between 8 and 9 a.m. and the last at about 4 p.m.

Early autumn. As for late spring.

Late autumn. As for early spring.

Winter. Trees kept under cover but exposed to the air on one or more sides are watered every second day at about 10 a.m. In a normal winter climate a bonsai can be brought out to enjoy any sunshine and can be watered then, but not after 1 p.m.

SPRAYING

In addition to watering the roots, it is also essential that the leaves be well sprayed each day. This operation may be combined with the watering if the time of day is right, using the same watering can. In great heat, spraying must only be done in the early morning (7 to 8 a.m.) or the evening (4 to 5 p.m.). A syringe instead of a can should be used in certain conditions already mentioned, i.e., to keep the leaves of a newly transplanted natural bonsai fresh and when a tree is suffering from acute lack of water. This syringe-spraying is done with cool water. If the day is very hot so that water exposed to the sun is warm, the water to be used for spraying must be kept in a cellar or some other cool place. This does not, of course, apply to well water.

WEEDING AND CLEANING

Bonsai must be kept carefully weeded as weeds take nourishment from the soil. They should be removed with pincers, root and all. If the weed is a very large one, so that when it is uprooted there is danger that the soil will be disturbed, the soil should be held down with the palm of the hand with the weed coming up between the fingers. Fallen leaves must be removed and any dead foliage on the tree picked off; this is especially necessary for pines and junipers in the late spring.

Special Winter Care

Cold weather will not harm bonsai and they should on no account be put into a greenhouse or brought permanently indoors in winter. They do, however, require some protection (see Plates 224–32). In Japan the commonest procedure is to erect a wooden frame over the bonsai-stands; the top and three sides of this frame are then covered with straw matting, one side (preferably that facing south) being left open. This will protect the trees from frost, but still give them plenty of fresh air. Boards or canvas could easily be substituted for matting and a good shelter can be improvised from a large packing case stood on its side. A single tree can be placed in a smaller box, provided the box is large enough not to bend or damage the branches. The tree must be turned round periodically. Snow or rain blowing into the shelter does no harm; frost is the only real enemy. In extremely cold countries where the temperature is below freezing almost all the time in winter, bonsai are best kept in a wooden shed or shelter enclosed on all sides. The shelter must be of boards and not of glass or corrugated iron as it is essential for air to penetrate freely. The bonsai can be enclosed in the shelter and left without watering until the spring.

Soil Conditions

If a bonsai becomes loose in the pot through being transported in a car or truck or because it has been left exposed to very strong wind, the soil should never be pressed firm about the trunk with the hands. This can cause air pockets below the surface where rot generates. Fresh earth is added on the surface and worked in round the trunk with a stick in the same way as for repotting.

Pine trees and hornbeams often produce a sort of benevolent white mould in the soil. This is not a disease, but the sign of a healthy plant and should not be touched. Care, however, must be taken not to mistake white grubs for this mould.

Damage to Bonsai

Below are listed three of the main sources of damage to which bonsai are prone, together with ways to prevent or correct them. Pests will be the subject of the following chapter.

Damaged leaf buds. New leaf buds are sometimes found to have turned brown and shriveled on top. This is due to one of the following causes:

1. Sudden change of temperature if the tree has been kept in a warm room for several hours and is then exposed to outdoor cold. To prevent this it is best to place the tree in a cool, protected spot, such as a shed or garage, for the night, before returning it to its stand outside.
2. Strong sunlight on overtender leaves. This can occur if the tree has been kept in a shady place and is then suddenly exposed to the sun.
3. Strong wind when the tree is not adequately protected.
4. Touching of the buds or their contact with a doorframe or some piece of furniture when being carried into the house.
5. Insects. (See the following chapter.)
6. Insufficient watering. This is particularly common among deciduous trees; its treatment will be found in the section on watering.
7. The use of too strong an insect spray. Particular care is needed with sprays containing oil.

Once the damage has occurred, there is no remedy for the ugly leaves which will subsequently appear except that, in the case of certain deciduous trees, the leaves can be cut off and the tree encouraged to produce a new crop.

Damaged leaves may result from any of a number of causes:

1. As pointed out above, damaged leaf buds will result in damaged leaves.
2. Root damage can affect the leaves; it may be due to: (a) insufficient or too much water, (b) too strong manure, (c) manuring too soon after repotting. If the damage is serious, the soil must all be washed away clean, the roots trimmed of dead wood, and the tree repotted.
3. Strong sunshine after a long period of rain and cloud can damage young leaves. It is as well to keep bonsai in the shade between 10 a.m. and 3 p.m. in these conditions.
4. Strong wind can shrivel young leaves, and bonsai should be given proper shelter to prevent this.
5. The spraying of young leaves with cold water while they are exposed to strong sunshine will cause them to shrivel.

6. Too strong insect spray as described above.
7. The urine of pets will turn leaves brown and in time damage the roots.

The only remedy for damaged leaves is to cut them off, but if more than a few leaves here and there are affected, this can only be done to certain deciduous trees.

Damaged Branches. If a branch dies suddenly, it may be due to disease or to being cracked or broken through rough treatment. In the former case the cause of the disease must be identified and the correct treatment given (see the following chapter). Whether the damage is due to disease or to carelessness, the dead branch should be cut off and the stump treated as described in the section on pruning. Another cause of damaged branches, as well as damaged leaf buds and leaves, is leaving bonsai placed too close together, as this prevents the free circulation of sun and air. Branches left continually in the shade will weaken and finally die from no other cause.

Plate 219. Ordinary table of wood and iron.

Plate 220. Two-level table for small-size bonsai.

Plate 221. Stands for cascade-style bonsai. Note that the trees are tied firmly to the stands.

Plate 222. View of training tables at Mr. Yoshimura's nursery, the Kofu-en, Tamagawa, Tokyo.

Plate 223. Display tables in Mr. Yoshitake Yamana's Japanese-style garden.

Plate 224. Ordinary shed with protection on three sides.

Plate 225. Protection for small bonsai.

Plate 226. For semitropical plants.

Plate 227. Cold frame of rice straw and glass panels.

Plate 228. Cold room made by excavating 3′ of earth. Suitable for ordinary plants and particularly for those just grafted in cold weather.

Plate 229. Protection for cuttings and seedlings planted in the earth.

Plate 230. Another form of protection for outdoor cuttings and seedlings.

Plate 231. Winter protection around table shown in Plate 220.

Plate 232. The easiest way: bury the bonsai, pot and all, in the ground until spring.

7 PESTS

BONSAI ARE AS MUCH SUBJECT to pests as other plants and, because of their size, are easily damaged. The whole symmetry of a bonsai can be destroyed by the withering of a branch or even a few twigs, and its beauty can be impaired by the discoloration of the foliage. The best protection against disease is the use of new soil in repotting, soil taken from a depth of at least three feet where grubs are unlikely to be found, and the constant exposure of the tree to sun and breeze. Trees and bushes in the garden near the bonsai ought to be sprayed against insects during the winter with a strong lime-and-sulphur solution and at intervals during the rest of the year with a weak solution of the same. The leaves and soil of the bonsai must be examined frequently for insects or mildew and treated immediately if there are signs of disease. This is best done by spraying from a can fitted with a very fine spray.

INSECTICIDES

The insecticides recommended are solutions of pyrethrum and agricultural nicotine or sometimes pyrethrum and rotenone, all of which can be purchased at shops supplying garden requisites or at a chemist's. The amounts for making strong, medium, or weak solutions will be found in the directions on the bottles.

Powdered sulphur and lime can also be obtained easily and should be used in the following proportions. For a strong solution: 112 grams quicklime, 225 grams sulphur, and 1 liter water. For a weak solution: 22.5 grams quicklime, 25 grams sulphur, and 1 liter water. The lime and sulphur, in powdered form, are mixed separately, each in half the amount of water. They are then mixed together and boiled for fifty minutes. The solution turns brown.

When treating mildew a solution known as "Bordeaux mixture" (because it is used in the French vineyards) is the most effective. It can often be purchased ready prepared, but if not available it can be made as follows. For a strong solution: 6 grams copper sulphate, 1.5 grams quicklime, and 1 liter water. For a weak solution: 6 grams copper sulphate, 1 gram quicklime, and 2 liters water. The two ingredients are mixed separately, each in half the amount of water, and are then mixed together. The solution must never be kept in a metal container as the copper sulphate rots metal. It is best to use a wooden tub and do the mixing with a brush or wooden spoon.

COMMON PESTS

Ants. Ants appear from late spring to autumn in the soil and on the trunk and branches. On the tree they do no harm themselves, but they carry aphids and mealy bugs. They can be got rid of by spraying with a strong solution of pyrethrum and nicotine. If it is found that the ants have made a nest in the soil, the tree must be repotted immediately. The contaminated soil must be washed off the roots completely and the roots soaked in a weak pyrethrum solution for from five to ten minutes. New soil must be used for repotting and the old soil burned to purify it. This is done by sifting the earth onto a fire of embers. If the soil cannot be burned, it must be taken away and buried.

Aphids or plant lice. Aphids usually appear in spring and summer. They are found on the tops of new shoots and at the base of flower buds or on the backs of new leaves. Aphids look like tiny green or brown grains. They are easily killed off, but will return as easily and the tree must be examined constantly. They are treated with a medium solution of pyrethrum and nicotine. Ladybirds (the species, also called ladybugs, with seven spots on their backs) eat aphids and should be welcomed.

Boring insects. These insects appear from spring to autumn on the trunks and branches. Their presence can be recognized by the trails of slimy excretion they leave on the bark and by the holes they make. They bore into the wood and, if not dealt with immediately, may kill the tree. The best way to destroy them is to inject a very strong solution of pyrethrum or nicotine into the holes, using a clinical syringe with a heavy needle. The holes are then sealed up with clay or wax. If a hole is very

large, it may require more than one injection. When the slimy marks no longer appear on the bark, the insect is dead.

Caterpillars. Caterpillars appear in spring and early summer and eat the young leaves. Their presence is easily recognized by the trails of slime they leave on the soil and branches. They can be destroyed by spraying with a medium solution of pyrethrum or rotenone.

Earthworms. Earthworms appear in late spring and early summer. They develop in the soil and their presence can be detected from disturbances on the surface. Pots left standing on the ground are easily attacked by earthworms, which is one reason why it is better to keep bonsai on a raised stand. Earthworms can be got rid of by spraying the soil with medium pyrethrum solution.

May-beetle larvae. These appear in late spring and summer. They are found in the soil and are very hard to get rid of. They are whitish-yellow insects with hard heads and half-moon-shaped bodies, between a quarter of an inch to an inch in length. They make disturbances in the soil similar to those of earthworms and are very dangerous because they eat roots. The only way to get rid of them is to wash all the soil from the roots and then repot the tree in new soil. The old soil must be burned as described in the section on ants.

Mealy bugs. These may appear at any season on the trunk and branches of a five-needle pine. They resemble minute pieces of white cotton fluff. In winter the tree should be treated both with a lime-and-sulphur solution (one part solution to thirty parts water) and with a strong pyrethrum mixture. In summer the lime and sulphur should be half this strength, but the pyrethrum can be used with safety. These strong solutions must never be used in the budding season as they will damage the leaf buds.

Mildew. Mildew develops from spring to autumn on the branches and leaves. There are many kinds of mildew, all detrimental to the tree and all producing similar symptoms—curious colored patches or growths on the bark and flagging leaves. The condition is best treated with Bordeaux mixture, but, if this is unobtainable, a solution of lime and sulphur can also be used.

Red spiders. Red spiders appear from spring to autumn, usually on juniper, cryptomeria, and pines. They cause the foliage to take on a greyish tinge and later to turn brown. The spiders are very small, no larger than a pinhead, and may be seen by holding a white paper or the palm of the hand under the foliage and then shaking the branches. The tiny red insects can be seen moving about on the flat surface. They should be destroyed with dusting sulphur or a lime-and-sulphur solution sprayed on the branches. Pyrethrum and nicotine can also be used. Several treatments, once every three days for at least nine days, are necessary to get rid of the insects. The spiders spread easily and the affected tree must be isolated, while any trees near it should be sprayed as a precaution. It takes up to three years for a bonsai to regain its normal color after being attacked by red spiders.

Scale insects. These may appear at any season but are commonest in autumn and winter. They are found on the branches and leaves and look like small white or brown shells or lumps. When the tree is dormant in winter the branches can be treated with a strong lime-and-sulphur solution to which some nicotine and pyrethrum is added. Several sprayings may be necessary to get rid of scale insects.

Color Plate 21. Rock cotoneaster. Root-over-rock style. 1'6". About 25 yrs. Produced from a cutting and potted about 15 yrs. ago. Glazed Chinese pot.

Color Plate 22. Hornbeam. Root-over-rock style. 11". About 25 yrs. Produced from a naturally stunted tree and potted about 15 yrs. ago. The round-moss planted on the rock at the base of the tree produces the effect of a natural mountain scene. Glazed Chinese pot.

Color Plate 23. Japanese red maple, garden variety "Seigen." Informal upright style. 1'6". About 25 yrs. Produced by grafting about 20 yrs. ago. Glazed Japanese pot of Tofukuji ware. Photo taken in early spring; a little later leaves turn dark reddish-green, and then red again in autumn.

Color Plate 24. Satsuki azalea, garden variety "Matsunami." Sinuous, clinging-to-a-rock style. 1'. About 20 yrs. Produced by cutting or layering. Glazed Japanese pot of Tofukuji ware. Only in recent decades have azaleas been trained into bonsai shapes, having been appreciated previously merely for their blossoms.

Color Plate 25. Miniature bonsai, produced during the past 30 yrs. by Mr. and Mrs. Raiju Matsudaira. **Left stand,** reading left to right and top to bottom: 1) Bear bamboo. 2) Oriental arborvita, from an 80-yr.-old seedling. 3) *Ficus foveolata var. nipponica,* natural. 4) Trident maple, from a seedling. 5) Dwarf Thunberg barberry, cutting. 6) Quaker ladies. 7) Common Ezo spruce, natural. **Right stand:** 1) Five-needle pine, natural. 2) Needle juniper, natural. 3) *Ellisiophyllum pinnatum.* 4) Dwarf sweet-rush. 5) Group planting with common cryptomeria, from cuttings. 6) Japanese grey-bark elm, from a seedling. 7) Bronze ornament.

Color Plate 21

Color Plate 23

Color Plate 22

Color Plate 24

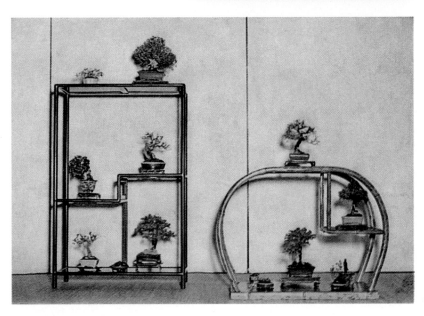

Color Plate 25

8 ❖ JUDGING AND EXHIBITING BONSAI

WE HAVE DESCRIBED IN THE preceding chapters the methods used in Japan for making and caring for bonsai. Not everyone, however, will wish to grow his own bonsai from seed or cuttings and not everyone has the opportunity to go into the countryside and look for natural ones. It is possible, not only in Japan but in many other countries, to buy matured bonsai from nurseries. For those who wish to do so, we give here some general rules for judging the condition and aesthetic value of a tree, as well as for exhibiting it.

It goes without saying that the "front" side of a bonsai is always the side which should be exhibited and by which its shape should be judged. But it is not always so easy to determine exactly which is the front, and mistakes are more frequent than one might think. There are, however, two tests which will serve in all but the most exceptional cases: (1) Applying the "rule of three" as described on page 63, look for that third branch and make sure it is at the back, where it belongs, leaving a generous portion of the lower trunk showing at the front. (2) Draw an imaginary line from the base of the trunk to the peak of the tree and observe the angle: the top should slant toward the front.

CHOOSING A BONSAI

A purchaser would do well to study a number of bonsai, or at any rate a number of photographs, before making his choice. Trees purchased from a garden where they can be seen in the open air generally prove a better bargain than those found at a florist's; the latter are often "quaint" and showy, and clever lighting can make their leaves turn a wonderful green, but careless shop assistants who forget to water and put them out of doors may already have done serious damage, particularly if an

unscrupulous gardener—for such do exist even in the world of bonsai—has been keeping the tree in the ground and has then potted it carelessly in poor soil. In Japan a reputable bonsai nurseryman can give the whole history of a tree, as a dog breeder gives a pedigree. If he has not bred it or collected it himself, he will say how long it has been in his possession.

There are two main characteristics essential to a bonsai; it must be in good condition and it must be beautiful.

Health. A healthy tree has rich, dark-green, shiny leaves and is free from any sign of disease. It must be well-established in its pot. A deciduous tree should have been in its pot at least four months since the last repotting. In the case of a pine, if purchased in winter, it should not have been repotted late the preceding autumn and should preferably have been in its pot over a year; if purchased after April, however, it will already have had at least seven or eight months in its pot, and the purchaser runs no risk of unpleasant surprises. Natural moss growing on the surface is a sure sign that a tree has been a good while in its pot undisturbed; so also is the presence of small, fine roots pushing through the drainage hole at the bottom of the pot. The soil should have a close-packed, solid look, although it must never

be hard, and, if the bonsai has been well tended, it will be free from weeds. In the growing season the tree will have strong new shoots and leaves on the branches; in winter, well developed leaf buds. A great many surface roots are a good sign, showing that the tree is well trained, has been well established in its pot, and that its heavy main roots have been properly cut. A poor bonsai has long, thick roots hidden in the pot and very few new surface roots, making root cutting very difficult at the next repotting.

Beauty. The beauty of a tree is judged in a number of ways. The shape of a bonsai should be suited to the species; it should have form and balance and be pleasing to the eye. Elegance of shape is the most important attribute. Overlong branches are unsightly and out of proportion. The branches of deciduous trees can, if necessary, be shortened, as has been described in the chapter on training, but those of a pine cannot. Inferior bonsai pines are sometimes found to have overlong branches, or long, spindly trunks, trained into S-bends to make them appear shorter. Ugly welts on the trunk where branches have been badly pruned spoil a bonsai, especially a pine. The knobby stumps of branches often left on fruit trees to give a gnarled, ancient effect are in this objectionable category; but the silvery-white dead wood found on junipers is a genuine sign of age, has no unhealthy significance, and is greatly admired. Trees which have weals on the bark, where wires have been carelessly put on and left too long in position, are to be avoided; naturally rough bark and lichen on the trunk are both considered beautiful. The bark is easily damaged so that fine bark is an indication of a well-cared-for tree. Anyone examining a bonsai with a view to purchase or for any other reason should never handle the trunk.

Unless the history of a bonsai has been documented, it is impossible to tell its exact age without destroying the tree and counting the annual rings. During training the sapling often changes hands several times. After it is twenty years old it is difficult to say whether it was grown from seed, from a cutting, or from a layering; a tree from seed and a layered tree may differ in age by as much as five years and look the same age. The age of a naturally stunted bonsai can only be guessed approximately when it is found on the mountainside. After fifteen or twenty years it will become indistinguishable from an artificial bonsai grown by any of the other methods, unless it has weather stains on the trunk or is of a very unusual shape.

There are certain bonsai—a wisteria, a five-needle pine grafted onto a red pine, a black pine, and a red pine—which have documented histories and are known to have been in pots for the last five hundred years and to have had their shapes improved by training during the seventeenth century. These trees are in the Imperial Garden in Tokyo and in the grounds of the Tokyo Horticultural School (see Plate 117). They are greatly treasured, but less because of their great age than because of their beauty. Age and historical association do not necessarily make a good bonsai, and once a tree is mature the Japanese do not require very exact data about its age. What they do require is a healthy plant, an exquisite shape, and a feeling of harmony between tree, form, and setting, for therein, not in its age, lies the value of a bonsai.

While we are on the subject, it should be pointed out that bonsai can in some cases still be imported from Japan. But import procedures are most exacting in the United States, and equally so in England. Some species are prohibited from importation altogether and others subject to special provisions. Even in the case of permitted species, the treatment necessary to free them of any possible contamination is often so drastic that only the hardiest trees can, with luck, survive. The would-be bonsai owner is therefore well advised to try to create his own dwarf trees but if he is impatient and determined to attempt importation despite all difficulties and risks, he should make a point of first ascertaining the latest regulations. Information can be had in the United States from the nearest Plant Quarantine Branch, Agricultural Research Service, Department of Agriculture, and in England from the Plant Health Branch, Ministry of Agriculture and Fisheries.

Exhibiting a Bonsai

We hope that we have by now impressed upon the reader the fact that a bonsai is a forest tree and must live out of doors. But on special occasions it is brought into the house, and in Japan the way in which a bonsai is placed on display is of great importance (see Color Plates 1, 18 & Plates 233–34). The Japanese, with their passion for tabulation, divide the method of presentation into three categories: formal, semi-formal, and informal. The three categories refer not only to the shapes and kinds of trees but to the color and shapes of their pots and the style of the room in which they are placed: all three elements—tree,

pot, room—must be in accord. The bonsai is placed in the alcove *(tokonoma)* of the principal room of the house and forms part of the only decoration in the room. A bonsai is never displayed alone in the alcove; it is always accompanied by a hanging scroll and a second, smaller bonsai or an ornament. This second bonsai should contrast with the first, e.g., a single tree offset by a small herb or rock planting. Often a piece of carving or a fine rock is substituted for the second bonsai. The principal bonsai always stands upon some form of base. If a number of miniature bonsai are used instead of a single tree they are displayed on a tiered stand. On the wall behind, midway between the bonsai and the subsidiary ornament, hangs a scroll *(kakemono)*, which is of great importance. The tree or trees and the scroll are chosen to form a harmonious whole, suitable to the season or the occasion (such as a wedding or other celebration). With a splendid, elaborate bonsai the scroll should be austere, possibly a single short poem written in a beautiful hand. If the scroll is the principal item on display the bonsai must blend with it but not detract from it.

The formal style. Evergreen trees such as pines and spruces are most suited to the formal style. An example of the perfect formal tree can be seen in Color Plate 11.

Plate 233. A formal summer arrangement for the tokonoma. *Left:* planting of dwarf common reed. *Right:* corticata pine, and beside it a bronze rabbit-shaped paperweight on a Chinese-style book.

Plate 234. Combining bronze figurines with bonsai. The fishermen combine with the cascade-style reed to create a lakeside scene.

Plate 235. A collection of typical bronze ornaments used with bonsai.

Plate 236. An example of the unobtrusive but effective use of a bronze ornament, in this case a small boat on the pebbles at the lower right.

It follows the rules for the placing of the branches exactly, and the trunk is straight and tapering. For this type of tree the pot ought to be austere in shape (rectangular, square, or round), without any pattern or other decoration, and of a natural brown or greyish-brown color. A bonsai of this kind is displayed on a formal, ceremonious occasion and looks its best in a classically simple room.

The semiformal style. When the trunk and branches of a bonsai have been trained into an artificial shape it is considered semiformal, even if the shape is not at all exaggerated. Referring to the classification on pages 65–66, such styles as the slanting, broom, split-trunk, driftwood, exposed-root, clump, straight-line, sinuous, and the like all fall into this semiformal category. Besides the usual rectangular and round pots, containers with more elaborate shapes —hexagonal, petal-shaped, and oval—are suitable for semiformal bonsai. The color of the pot should still be natural and discreet, but for maples and other deciduous trees with brilliant leaves a harmonizing color can be used. Semiformal trees adapt themselves to almost any occasion, but the more colorful ones are naturally better suited to gay festivities.

The informal style. The more extreme shapes of bonsai—such as the semicascade, cascade, "literati," coiled, wind-swept, rock-clinging, twisted-trunk, octopus, and the like—are classed as informal. They can be displayed in elaborate containers, and brightly glazed pots look well with flowering or fruit trees. Informal bonsai of the weeping variety are often placed on tall, carved stands. The scroll and subsidiary ornament or bonsai arranged to harmonize with an elaborate and informal tree must yield pride of place to the bonsai; otherwise the alcove will look overloaded.

In a Western house the Japanese alcove does not exist, but something of the same feeling should be aimed at when displaying a bonsai. The tree can be placed on a table in a corner of the room where its beauty can be isolated. If the table is large enough, a second bonsai or some other decoration can be added; if not, it is better to let the tree stand alone than for it to look cluttered up. Care must be taken to have the bonsai facing the right way; a tree with trunk and branches trained from left to right should stand on the left side of the table, not in the middle.

A plain, polished table is best, but the bonsai looks more complete as an ornament if it is raised on some kind of stand. A piece of polished or stained wood is quite sufficient—a rectangular board or a slice of a tree trunk taken across the grain and

left in its natural, irregular shape. Bamboo canes or other long, straight sticks can be made into a good stand by laying them side by side, like a raft, and weaving them together at either end with raffia. This mat is particularly suited to trees trained in the informal style and to the summer season, for it looks light and cool. The various weeping styles require, as has been said, high stands; otherwise the branches will get broken and distorted. In Japan special stands can be bought, but a carpenter could make something suitable. The tall, mahogany aspidistra stands, which can often be found in the attic or in a second-hand shop, are excellent for weeping bonsai, as are also the marble or stucco pillars upon which Victorian gentlemen liked to set a bust of Plato or Beethoven. Miniature bonsai can be displayed in groups. They look well on a mantelpiece with shelves or alcoves. A plain wall is best behind bonsai. In a room with patterned wallpaper a small, plain screen, either a folding screen or a flat screen with props at the back, should be placed behind. In Japan the screen is usually a plain white one, but gold or silver screens, without any decoration, are also used to give a luxurious effect, gold being best suited to pines and silver to flowering trees. A plain curtain would serve the same purpose as a screen. Bonsai do not

look their best on a window ledge where greenery outside detracts from their beauty.

True bonsai are never used in conjunction with the little ornaments used to make so-called "Japanese gardens." Red pagodas and bridges cheapen the beauty of the tree and are seldom seen except in shops which cater to the foreigner. Occasionally a small ornament can be used in conjunction with a rock or group planting if there is a wide, empty stretch of moss or sand (see Plates 234–36). The Japanese suit these ornaments to the season, and they are not left in place permanently. A figure of a boy riding a bullock and playing a flute represents spring and a little boat near a rock on a sea of sand looks pleasantly cool in summer. These little ornaments are of bronze or plain wood and are never painted in bright colors; their acquisition is one of the subsidiary pleasures of owning bonsai. When a flowering tree stands at one side of its base or table, a few petals can be scattered at the other side by way of decoration. Maple leaves are often used in the same way in autumn. A curiously shaped stone picked up in a river-bed can be placed among the moss at one side of the pot to give balance or, if the pot is a small one, can serve the same purpose on the stand. A small group of such stones arranged near a willow gives the illusion that the tree is standing at the edge of a pool.

All these small touches aim at creating the triangle which is fundamental in Japanese flower and tree design: the blending of Heaven and Earth by their reconciling factor, Man. This triangle is found in the shape of the bonsai, in the pattern it makes in the pot, and above all in the manner in which it is displayed. In the Japanese alcove the principal bonsai represents Man; the scroll, Heaven; and the subsidiary ornament, Earth. Without these three elements the whole display would be considered lacking in balance. A Westerner may not wish to follow this rule too closely, but he will find that, where bonsai are concerned, the principle of the triangle displays the tree to greatest advantage. A bonsai can blend with a water color or an oil painting as well as with a scroll, and the ornament which accompanies it need not be Oriental. The pattern created by the three elements is simple, but never fails to delight the eye.

TOOLS AND EQUIPMENT

The various bonsai tools and equipment actually used in Japan are illustrated in Plates 237–45. Although these exact items may not always be readily available elsewhere, satisfactory common-sense substitutes can generally be found. Nor are all these various items absolutely essential: the most common operations can be adequately performed with the eight basic tools listed on page 177.

In the following paragraphs there will be given first a description of the various tools shown in the plates, then a list of the eight basic tools, and finally a ready-reference outline of the tools required in any given operation. In each case the numbers and letters used to describe the items are the same as those superimposed upon the plates themselves.

DESCRIPTION OF TOOLS AND EQUIPMENT

1. Working tables. The arrangement shown has proven ideal in actual use. The height of all the tables is approximately 22 inches, with the center table slightly higher. **(a)** Main table is 23 by 30 inches in area. **(b)** Trash box has a removable cover ($7\frac{1}{2}$ by 22 inches) and stands open when in use. The inside is painted with a protective coating of tar and a whisk broom is hung on a hook near the top. **(c)** Side tables have an area of 18 by 22 inches each. **(d)** Revolving stand, a most important piece of equipment, is described in more detail under item 13.

2. Pincettes. **(a)** Pointed, used for trimming juniper, cryptomeria, and spruce. **(b)** Ordinary. These pincers are used for the same purposes as the foregoing and also for weeding, removing old leaves, and catching insects. The points can be used for removing hardened soil from roots when repotting, although the iron hook (7) is, in general, better for this purpose. The flat head is convenient for a number of purposes: for the final pressing down of the soil and dry, powdered moss after repotting, for loosening the soil from the pot before repotting, for handling moss either in powdered or living form.

3. Scissors, cutters, and shears. **(a)** For trimming leaves of all deciduous trees except flowering or fruit-bearing varieties. **(b)** For cutting the thinner types of wire. **(c)** For trimming and pruning thin branches and twigs and, when repotting, for cutting off exposed roots which cannot be pushed down into the soil. **(d)** The long handles make these scissors useful for trimming branches or shoots which are hard to reach,

but these are not strong enough for heavy branches or roots. **(e)** These scissors can be used for cutting branches up to the thickness of the thumb and are the standard scissors for flower arrangement. **(f)** For cutting heavy branches or roots these shears may be used, but in general it will be found that the knife 5b will make a flatter cut.

4. Brushes and whisks. **(a)** Animal-hair brush with bamboo handle, used in smoothing the top soil while repotting and in spreading sand in a group planting. **(b)** A smaller version of the same brush, for miniature bonsai. **(c)** Coconut-fiber whisk for smoothing soils while repotting, cleaning the inside of pots, and sweeping away excess soil. This particular brush has been considerably worn away by use, while an unused brush of the same variety is shown as item 4e. **(d)** Coconut-fiber whisk for cleaning inside of pots only, being too coarse for smoothing soil. **(e)** An unused version of item 4c.

5. Knives and razors. **(a)** Metal-and-ivory bud-grafting knife. The metal blade is used for cutting the bark and the ivory tip for holding the bark open while the bud is inserted. **(b)** Heavy-duty knife with wooden scabbard, used to cut wood and to pare away branches flat with the trunk. **(c)** Light-weight knife with leather scabbard, used only for cutting and grafting. The blade is very thin and sharp and must be used with great care to avoid cutting too deeply. **(d)** Razor with metal cover, used for grafting thin branches and particularly suitable for top-grafting of pines.

6. Whisk brooms. **(a)** Usually hangs inside the trash box (1b). **(b)** Heavy-duty whisk for general sweeping. This is particularly useful in sweeping under bonsai pots about once a week to avoid insects' making their nests there.

7. Iron hook with wooden handle. Used in removing hardened soil when repotting. Must be used with caution so as not to loosen too much soil or damage the root.

8. Trowels. **(a)** For pressing down the soil when repotting has been finished. **(b)** For same and for collecting moss.

9. Various sizes of bamboo chopsticks used in repotting for loosening old soil and for working new soil down into the roots.

10. Covers for holes in bottom of pot. **(a)** Specially made covers of clay. **(b)** Potsherd. This should be about twice the size of the hole to be covered and should be placed concavely above the hole. **(c)** Coconut fiber. **(d)** A hole drilled in a vase to make it a bonsai pot, and its specially made clay cover.

11. Shovels. **(a)** Sharpened shovel and leather sheath used for digging in hard earth. **(b)** For transplanting plants with their soil. **(c)** Small copper or brass shovel for use with miniature bonsai. **(d)** Shovel commonly used for repotting.

12. String. **(a)** Coconut-fiber string for tying down top-heavy pots. **(b)** Hemp string for tying plant in the pot after finishing repotting and for tying moss and peat in rock plantings.

13. Revolving stand for working tables (see 1d). **(a)** Top, $11\frac{1}{2}$ inches in diameter and $1\frac{1}{2}$ inches thick, made of hard wood. **(b)** Base with drawer and casters, 12 by 12 inches square, $4\frac{1}{4}$ inches high.

14. Nest of sieves. **(a)** Holder into which a sieve is placed when being used. This is tall enough to accommodate all seven sieves for storing. **(b)** Top for holder, used both for storing and to avoid dust when sieving. **(c-i)** Sieves in various sizes.

15. Hammers, used for tapping rocks or breaking pots.

16. Pliers. **(a-c)** Used for stripping off bark when making a driftwood-style bonsai and

for unbending training wire to remove it from branches. **(d-f)** Used for same purposes as foregoing and also for straightening the thinner gauges of used wire, for cutting wire, and for twisting wire when wiring a bonsai into its pot or making a rock planting.

17. Lever, used to bend large branches.

18. Jack, used to pull large branches toward trunk.

19. Small anvil and wooden mallet, used to straighten heavy wire.

20. Pincers. **(a-b)** For cutting heavy branches, trunks, roots, etc. **(c)** For cutting heavy wire. **(d)** For heavy-duty cutting of wood or wire.

21. Copper wire in various sizes. **(a-e)** Cut into short lengths for convenience in use by beginners. **(f-g)** Uncut.

22. Iron rods. **(a)** For bending heavy branches. **(b)** For straightening heavy trunk. **(c)** For straightening thinner trunk.

23. Tape. **(a)** Friction tape, for covering exposed surfaces after cutting off heavy branches. Also, if a branch is accidentally broken while wiring, the quick application of this tape around the break may save the branch by preventing the entry of air. **(b)** Paper tape, for wrapping wire to be used on tender bark.

24. Chisels and awls, used to make holes in rock to fix copper wires.

25. Wood-carving tools, used to carve designs on trunks, to carve out stumps of branches, and to peel the bark when layering.

26. Iron pick for removing scale from branches.

27. Saws, for cutting heavy trunks or roots.

28. Sprays of various sizes for watering can, made of copper or brass.

29. Sprayers. **(a)** Compression sprayer with fine nozzle; can also be used for watering foliage with a mist spray. **(b)** Ordinary type of insect sprayer. **(c)** Mouth sprayer.

30. Scales and measures. **(a)** For weighing solids. **(b-e)** Various sizes for measuring liquids.

31. Hypodermic syringe for injecting insect holes.

32. Toothbrush, for washing trunk when making driftwood styles.

33. Markers of wood, plastic, and light metal.

34. Watering cans of various sizes, made of copper, brass, or galvanized metal.

35. Compression sprayer.

36. Rucksack.

37. Shoulder bag.

38. Specimen case, of galvanized metal.

39. Tape and cord.

40. Sphagnum moss in plastic wrapper.

41. Cloth wrappers.

42. Mountaineer's pike.

43. Saw.

BASIC TOOLS

Following are the eight basic bonsai tools:
Ordinary pincettes (2b)
Cutters for thin wire (3b)
Long-handled scissors (3c)
Garden scissors (3e)
Animal-hair brushes (4a or 4b)
Whisk brush (4c)
Light-weight knife (5c)
Bamboo chopsticks (9)

TOOLS AND EQUIPMENT FOR VARIOUS OPERATIONS

For sowing: Training pot or box, soil, and the following: 1a–d, 2b, 3e, 4a–b, 4c, 5b, 6a, 8a–b, 10a–c, 11b, 11d, 13a–b, 14a–i, 28, 34, 40

Making cuttings: Training pot or box, soil, and the following: 1a–d, 2b, 3e, 4a–b, 4c, 5c, 6a, 10a–c, 11b, 11d, 13a–b, 14a–i, 28, 34

Grafting: Straw or raffia and the following: 3e, 3f, 5a–d, 6a, 11b, 28, 34

Layering: 3b. 3e. 5b. 11b. 16d–f. 21a or b, 25, 28, 34, 39, 40

Pruning and trimming: 1a–d, 2a–b. 3a–f, 4c. 5b, 6a, 13a–b, 23a. 25, 27, 28, 34

Repotting: Powdered moss and the following: 1a–d, 2b, 3b–f, 4a–e, 5b, 6a, 7, 8a–b, 9, 10a–d, 11b–d, 12b, 13a–b, 14a–i, 15, 16d–f, 21b or f, 27, 28, 34, 40

Shaping and wiring: 1a–d, 2b, 3b, 3d–f, 4c, 5b, 6a, 12a, 13a–b. 16–20, 21–23, 25, 27, 28, 34

Rock planting: Peat, soil, powdered moss or pieces of moss, and the following: 1a–d, 2b–e, 3b-f, 4c, 5b, 6a, 8, 10a–d, 11b, 11d, 12b. 13 a–b. 14a–i, 15, 16d–f, 21a–g, 24, 28. 34

Group plantings of trees: Small rocks, soil, powdered moss or pieces of moss, peat. pot, and the following: 1a–d, 2b, 3b–f, 4a–c, 5b, 6a, 8, 9, 10a–d. 11c–d. 13–14, 16d–f, 21a–g, 28. 34

Group plantings of grasses and herbs: Small rocks. soil. peat, sand, moss, pot, and the following: 1a–d, 2b, 3b–e, 4a–c, 6a. 8–10, 11c–d, 13–14, 28, 34

Daily care: Basic tools and the following: 1a–d, 3d, 6a–b, 12a, 13a–b, 26, 28–35

TOOLS AND EQUIPMENT

(The key numbers refer to the full descriptions given in the text.)

Plate 237. Working tables.

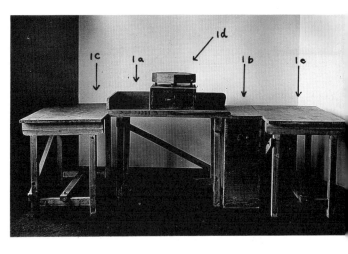

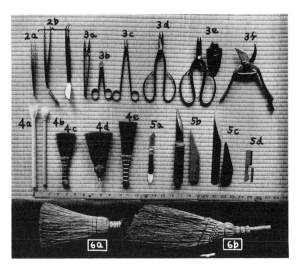

Plate 238. Pincettes, scissors, cutters, shears, brushes, knives, etc.

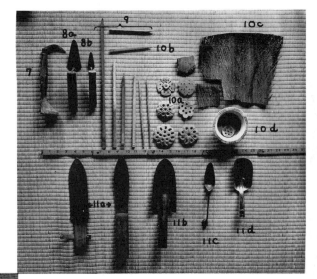

Plate 239. Hooks, trowels, chopsticks, hole covers, shovels.

Plate 240. Sieves, revolving stand, string.

Plate 241. Hammers, pliers, jacks, etc.

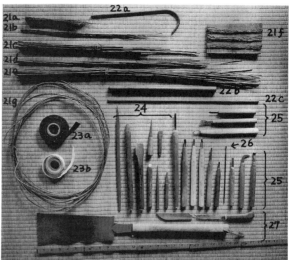

Plate 242. Wires, tapes, chisels, saw, etc.

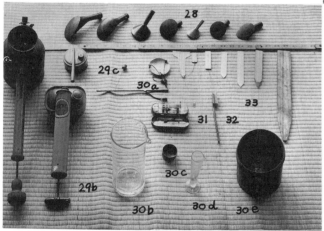

Plate 243. Sprayers, syringes, markers, etc.

Plate 244. Watering cans and sprayers.

Plate 245. Equipment for a collecting expedition.

APPENDIX 2

SOIL ANALYSES

Following are the results of soil analyses made on March 31, 1955, by the Japan Soil Association, Tokyo. The soils analyzed were samples taken from the following soils in daily use at the Kofu-en Bonsai Nursery, Tokyo:

Symbol	Japanese name	Description	Color
S$_1$	Tenjingawa-suna	River sand	Pale orange & light grey
S$_2$	Kiryu-suna	Sand-and-clay mixture	Pale yellowish-brown & grey
BS	Kuro-tsuchi	Black loam	Greyish black
C	Aka-tsuchi	Red loam	Reddish brown
K	Kanuma-tsuchi	Light clay and sand	Light reddish-yellow
P	Keto	Peat	Dark brown and grey
L	Fuyo-do	Leaf mould	Mineral grey
SM	Mizu-goke	Sphagnum moss	Greenish white
Mix	Kongo-do	Main soil used on deciduous trees while in training	Brown, greyish black, and corn-yellow

TABLE A

Soil	% Moisture after heating[1]	Acidity[2]	% Loss by burning[3]	% Humus (air-dry matter)	% Water-holding capacity	
					Max.	Min.
S_2	6.24	6.11	0	0.16	47.2	16.0
P	23.11	6.04	0	9.05	135.1	63.2
K	15.04	6.02	0	0.74	190.9	118.4
L	16.22	6.39	38.24	27.46	(400.0)	0
S_1	1.13	6.18	0	0.05	30.9	10.2
BS	21.71	5.83	0	14.78	160.1	68.3
C	22.14	5.93	0	3.37	148.8	67.0
SM	17.36	5.06	77.33	0	(4500.0)	0
Mix	15.95	5.86	0	5.26	119.7	52.4

[1]Percentage of moisture remaining after heating 1 hr. at 110° C.
[2]Glass electrode reading after dissolving sample in water; over 7 is alkaline; under 7 is acid.
[3]Percentage of loss after burning in fire of 400 to 500° C.

TABLE B
RESULTS OF MECHANICAL ANALYSIS BY ASK SOIL ELUTRIATOR

Soil	% Coarse sand (0.25 to 2.00 mm.)	% Fine sand (0.05 to 0.25 mm.)	% Silt (0.01 to 0.05 mm.)	Total % sand and silt	% Clay[1] under 0.01 mm.	% Gravel over 2 mm.
S_2	74.0	3.0	1.0	78.0	22.0	0
P	3.0	4.5	9.0	16.5	83.5	0
K	(24.5)[2]	(6.0)	(0.0)	(30.5)	(69.5)	0
S_1	93.5	1.0	0.5	94.5	5.5	0
BS	8.5	4.0	11.5	24.0	76.0	0
C	5.5	5.0	7.0	17.5	82.5	0
Mix	29.0	4.0	4.0	37.0	63.0	8.0

[1]Containing moisture and humus.
[2]Over 0.25 mm. and less than 4 mm.

BASIC DATA ON BONSAI PLANTS

This and the following two appendices attempt to assemble for the first time the basic essential information concerning the varieties of plants used for bonsai. About two hundred of the less frequently used varieties have been omitted from the list, leaving a total of 340.

Technically, this information should form one of the most useful parts of the book, and it represents an ambitious undertaking. Even in a single language, the confusion surrounding the nomenclature of plants is considerable; it becomes compounded when dealing with two such dissimilar languages as Japanese and English. The task, however, has long needed performing, and the following lists, based upon notes collected by Mr. Yoshimura over a long period of time, are offered as a beginning. Additions and corrections will be welcomed for incorporation in later editions : they may be addressed to the publisher.

As many of the plants are more or less peculiar to Japan and are commonly known, even outside Japan, by their Japanese names, this first and basic list has been arranged alphabetically according to the most common Japanese names. English and scientific names are indexed in Appendix 4, and the Chinese-Japanese characters for the names are arranged according to number of strokes in Appendix 5, each entry in the indexes being designated by a key number which permits immediate reference back to the fuller information contained in the basic list.

EXPLANATIONS AND SYMBOLS

The following items of information are given for each plant in the basic list, but only when applicable :

1. Key number.

2. Common Japanese names. Parentheses ( ) indicate alternate names. Brackets [ ] indicate names frequently but incorrectly used. References beginning *see also* refer to plants which are similar.

3. Chinese-Japanese characters used to designate the plant. The names of plants for which no characters are given are properly written in Japanese in *kana*, the Japanese syllabary.

4. Common English names. Parentheses and brackets are used as in the case of the Japanese names.

5. Scientific names.

6. *Type.* The nature of the plant is indicated by the following symbols :

T—tree, perennial
S—shrub, perennial
G—grass, including herbs, vegetables, & bamboo
V—vine
Dec—deciduous
Egr—evergreen
An—annual

Bi—biennial
Pe—perennial

AP—alpine plant
NE—needled
BL—broad leafed
DIO—dioecious

FL—flowering
FR—fruit bearing

Italicizing one of the last two symbols indicates whether the principal beauty of the plant lies in its flowers or its fruit.

7. *Use.* The uses to which a plant may be put are co-ordinated with the outline of styles given on pages 65–66, being indicated by the following symbols, the most suitable in italics:

1—formal upright style	22—two-tree
	23—three-tree
2—informal upright	24—five-tree
3—slanting	25—seven-tree
4—semicascade	26—nine-tree
5—cascade	27—multiple-tree
6—literati	28—natural-group
7—coiled	29—clustered-group
8—broom	group
9—split-trunk	30—tray-landscape
10—driftwood	31—seasonal group
11—wind-swept	planting
12—exposed-root	32—planting of
13—root-over-rock	herbs, etc.
14—clinging-to-a-rock	Gr—ground cover
	Min—suitable for
15—twisted-trunk	miniature bonsai
16—octopus	MinDw—dwarf of
17—twin-trunk	species suitable
18—clump	for miniature
19—stump	MinGr—suitable
20—straight-line	for miniature
21—sinuous	ground cover]

8. *Way.* The ways in which a plant may be propagated for bonsai use, as described in Chapter 2, are indicated by the following symbols, roughly in order of preferability:

Nat—from naturally stunted tree
Seed—from seed or seedling
Cut—from cutting
Grf—grafting, including (1) top, (2) side, (3) cleft, and (4) inarching.
Lay—layering, including (1) Method A, (2) Method B, and (3) Method C.
Div—dividing the following parts: (1) entire plant with roots, (2) shoots over 3 in., with roots, (3) buds under 3 in., with roots, (4) roots without buds, (5) roots, bulbs, or rootstock, with buds.

9. *Pot.* This heading indicates the time of year during which the plant may be repotted. The frequency of repotting is given only in cases which are exceptions to the general rules given in Chapter 3.

10. *Trim.* General remarks on trimming are given in Chapter 4. The symbols used hereunder refer to more specific methods as follows:

A—Trim several times in spring, breaking or pinching off the new shoots before they harden and leaving only a few needles adhering to the base of the shoot. Example: black pine.

B—Pinch or pull off the top of the new bud at any time during the growing season. Example: juniper.

C—After the new shoot has from 3 to 5 nodes during the growing season, trim with scissors, leaving from 1 to 2 nodes. Example: maple.

D—Trim with scissors after the blossoms wither and before the new buds harden in the latter part of summer. Example: crab apple.

E—After blossoms appear, trim as in C. Also in early spring or late autumn trim the shoots back to from 2 to 3 nodes. Example: crape myrtle.

F—Leave the new shoots until late summer and then trim as in C. Example:

Japanese flowering apricot.

G—Once every two years, in early autumn cut back the tip of each branch so that only about 5 clusters of needles remain at the base. Example: black pine.

LT—Trim the leaves (see page 121) during late spring or early summer. Example: maple.

11. *Wire.* This heading indicates the time of year during which the plant may be wired. the wires remaining thereafter as long as necessary.

12. *Note.* This heading includes miscellaneous notes on the plant, with particular reference to where it should be kept, how it should be watered, and the pests to which it is prone.

— A —

1. Abura-giri (Yama-giri, Dokue). 罌子桐, 油桐, 山桐. Tung. *Aleurites cordata* Muell. Arg. **Type:** T Dec BL FL FR. **Use:** *2 3* 4 17 *18* 22 23. **Way:** Nat, Seed. **Pot:** early sprg. **Trim:** D. **Wire:** late sprg to sumr. **Note:** Full sun; keep warm in wntr.

2. Ajisai; *see also* 56 Gaku-ajisai. 紫陽花. Hydrangea. *H. macrophylla* A.P. de Candolle var. *otaksa* Honda; *H. macrophylla* DC. f. *otaksa* Wilson. **Type:** S Dec BL FL. **Use:** 2–5 17 *18* 22 23. **Way:** Div(1), Lay(2), Cut. **Pot:** early sprg or immediately after finished blooming. **Trim:** D. **Wire:** late sprg to sumr. **Note:** In sumr half shade & water often.

3. Aka-ezomatsu; *see also* 174 Kuro-ezomatsu. 赤蝦夷松, 蝦夷松. Common Ezo spruce; fir; Edo spruce; Yedo or Yesso spruce. *Picea glehnii* Mast. **Type:** T Egr NE. **Use:** *1–7 9 10 13 14 17–30* 32 Min MinDw. **Way:** Nat, Cut, Seed, Lay(1). **Pot:** sprg or early autm. Keep in shade for a wk after repotting. **Trim:** B, once or twice in sprg, leaving a few needles at base. **Wire:** autm to wntr; do not twist too much. **Note:** Full sun; water-spray foliage sprg to autm.

4. Aka-matsu (Me-matsu). 赤松, 女松. Japanese red pine. *Pinus densiflora* Sieb. et Zucc. **Type:** T Egr NE. **Use:** 1 *2 3* 4 5 6 10 12–14 16 *17–19* 22–27. **Way:** Nat, Seed, Grf (1, 2). **Pot:** in sprg before new needles have opened or in autm. **Trim:** A; G. **Wire:** any time in growing season. **Note:** Full sun; keep soil somewhat dry. Do not expose to sea winds; watch for red spiders.

Akashia. *See* 217 Nise-akashia.

5. Aka-shide (Kana-shide, Soro); *see also* 115 Inu-shide, 169 Kuma-shide. 見風乾. Red-leafed hornbeam: loose-flower hornbeam. *Carpinus laxiflora* Blume; *Distegocarpus laxiflora* Sieb. et Zucc. **Type:** T Dec BL FL FR. **Use:** *2 3* 4–6 *13* 17 18 22 23 *24–27* 29 30. **Way:** Nat, Cut, Seed, Lay(2). **Pot:** early sprg. **Trim:** C; D. **Wire:** sprg to sumr. **Note:** In sumr half shade & water often.

6. Akebi (Akebi-kazura); *see also* 199 Mube. 野木瓜, 木通, 通草. Five-leaf akebia. *A. quinata* Decne. **Type:** V Dec BL FR. **Use:** *2 3* 4 5 13. **Way:** Cut, Lay (3, 2). **Pot:** early sprg. **Trim:** D. **Wire:** in growing season. **Note:** In sumr half shade & water often.

7. Aki-nire (Nire, Ishi-geyaki, Nire-geyaki). 楡, 楡欅, 紅鷄油. Chinese elm. *Ulmus parvifolia* Jacq. **Type:** T Dec BL. **Use:** 1 2 3–5 8 *13 14* 17 18 22 23 *30*. **Way:** Seed, Cut, Lay(2, 1). **Pot:** Early sprg to sumr. **Trim:** C; LT. **Wire:** when trimming leaves in late sprg. **Note:** Full sun.

Amendō. *See* 83 Hentō.

8. Amerika-fuji. 米藤. Wisteria. *Wistaria frutescens* Poir. **Type:** V Dec BL FL. **Use:** *4 5 13*. **Way:** Lay(3, 2), Cut, Grf(3), Div(4). **Pot:** early sprg. **Trim:** D. **Wire:** in growing season. **Note:** Water often in growing season; water basin in sumr.

9. Amerika-hanazuō. American redbud; Canadian redbud; Judas. *Cercis canadensis* L. **Type:** S Dec BL FL. **Use:** *2 3 13* 17 *18* 22–25. **Way:** Nat, Seed, Grf(1, 2). **Pot:** early sprg. **Trim:** D. **Wire:** in growing season.

10. Amerika-sanyōshō. 米國三葉松. Northern pitch-pine. *Pinus rigida* Mill. **Type:** T Egr NE. **Use:** *1–3* 4 5 7 9 12 *13* 17–19 22 23. **Way:** Nat, Seed, Grf(1, 2). **Pot:** sprg or early autm. **Trim:** A; G. **Wire:** autm to wntr. **Note:** Full sun; keep somewhat dry.

Amerika-suishō. *See* 233 Rakuushō.

11. Anzu. 杏, 杏子. Apricot. *Prunus armeniaca* L. var. *ansu* Maxim.; *P. ansu* Komar. **Type:** T Dec BL FR *FL*. **Use:** 2 3–5 17 18. **Way:** Grf(3), Lay(2), Seed. **Pot:** early sprg. **Trim:** F. **Wire:** in growing season. **Note:** Full sun; water often; manure well; watch for borers.

Araragi. *See* 110 Ichii.

12. Ao-giri. 梧桐, 青桐. Chinese parasol. *Firmiana platanifolia* Schott et Endl.; *F. simplex* W.F. Wight. **Type:** T Dec BL. **Use:** 2 3 17 18. **Way:** Lay(1), Seed. **Pot:** early sprg. **Trim:** D. **Wire:** late sprg to sumr, paper wrap. **Note:** Water often; full shade in sumr.

Asama-tsuge. *See* 311 Tsuge.

13. Asebi (Asebo). 梫木, 馬酔木. Japanese andromeda. *Pieris japonica* D.Don. **Type:** S Egr BL *FL* FR. **Use:** *2* 3–5 *13* 17 18. **Way:** Div(1), Lay(1). **Pot:** early sprg. **Trim:** D. **Wire:** late sprg to sumr. **Note:** Leaves poisonous to animals & insects.

14. Ashi (Seiko-no-ashi). 葦, 蘆. Seiko reed; common reed. *Phragmites communis* Trin.; *P. longivalvis* Sted.; *P. vulgaris* Trin.; *Arundo phragmites* L. **Type:** G Dec Pe. **Use:** *14 18 30–32*. **Way:** Cut, Div(5). **Pot:** every 2nd sprg except in style 14. **Trim:** pull out central bud when plant reaches desired height. **Note:** Always keep in water basin; half shade.

15. Asuhi-kazura. 地刷子. Licopodium. *L. complanatum* L. **Type:** G Egr Pe NE(soft). **Use:** *14 30 32* Gr Min. **Way:** Div(3). **Pot:** every 3rd to 5th sprg. **Trim:** pinch off top of shoot in sumr. **Note:** Always half shade; water-spray sprg to sumr.

16. Asunaro (Hiba). 羅漢柏, 椙, 檔. False arborvita. *Thujopsis dolabrata* Sieb. et Zucc.; *Biota orientalis* Endl. **Type:** T Egr NE. **Use:** *1–3* 4 5 7 9 10 12 *13 17 18* 20–29. **Way:** Cut, Lay(1). **Pot:** sprg to autm. **Trim:** B. **Wire:** any time. **Note:** Half shade; water-spray sprg to sumr; watch for red spiders.

17. Atsumorisō. 敦盛草. Lady's-slipper. *Cypripedium thunbergii* Blume. **Type:** G Dec Pe FL. **Use:** *32*. **Way:** Div(3). **Pot:** every 3rd sprg. **Trim:** in wntr when stem is dead cut off at base. **Note:** Always half shade.

18. Azuma-giku (Miyama-azumagiku). Alpine chrysanthemum. *Erigeron alpicola* Makino. **Type:** G Dec Pe AP BL FL. **Use:** *30 32*. **Way:** Div(3), Cut. **Pot:** every 2nd sprg. **Note:** Watch for aphids on new shoots; half shade in sumr, otherwise full sun.

— **B** —

Bakumontō. 麥門多. *See* 239 Ryū-no-hige.

Bara. 薔薇. Rose. *Rosa* genus. *See* 81 Hatoya-bara, 163 Kōshin-bara, 195 Mokkō-bara, 335 Yashōbi. **Pot:** early each sprg. **Trim:** E, particularly after blooming, cut all branches way back, with the exception of 335, which is cut back after the berry is finished. **Wire:** any time in growing season. **Note:** Full sun; manure well; water often; watch for aphids on new shoots & mildew on leaves.

Bara-momi. *See* 76 Hari-momi.

19. (a) Bashō. 芭蕉. Banana. *Musa basjoo* Sieb. (b) Bashō (Hime-bashō). 姫芭蕉. Dwarf banana. *M. uranoscopos* Lour.; *M. coccinea* Andr. **Type:** G Egr (Dec in temperate zones) BL. **Use:** *13 14 17 21* 22–29. **Way:** Div(3). **Pot:** late each sprg. **Note:** Half shade; protect from cold.

20. Beni-dōdan; *see also* 38 Dōdan-tsutsuji. Red enkianthus. *E. cernus* Benth. et Hook. fil. var. *rubens* Makino; *Meiseria cernua* Sieb. et Zucc.; *Tritomodon cernua* Honda var. *rubens* Honda. **Type:** S Dec BL FL. **Use:** 2 3 4 13 17 *18* 22 23. **Way:** Cut, Div(1), Lay(2). **Pot:** early sprg. **Trim:** D. **Wire:** sprg to autm. **Note:** Half shade in sumr, otherwise full sun.

Beni-kobushi. *See* 91 Hime-kobushi.

21. Beni-shitan; *see also* 40 Edauchi-sharintō, 262 Sharintō. 紅紫檀. Rock cotoneaster. *C. horizontalis*

Decn. **Type:** S Egr BL FL *FR*. **Use:** *2–5 12 13 14 17 18 20 21 30 32* Min. **Way:** Cut, Div(1), Lay(2, 3). **Pot:** any time in growing season. **Trim:** C. **Wire:** any time except wntr. **Note:** Full sun; water often; watch for aphids & scale.

22. Binan-kazura (Sane-kazura). 美男桂, 南五味子. Scarlet kadsura. *K. japonica* Don. **Type:** V Egr (Dec in temperate zones) BL FR. **Use:** *2–5 13 17 18*. **Way:** Cut, Lay(3). **Pot:** any time in growing season. **Trim:** C. **Wire:** any time except wntr. **Note:** Full sun; water often.

23. Biwa. 枇杷. Loquat. *Eriobotrya japonica* Lindl. **Type:** T Egr BL FR. **Use:** *2 3 17 18*. **Way:** Seed, Grf(3), Lay(1). **Pot:** any time in growing season. **Trim:** D. **Wire:** any time except wntr. **Note:** Full sun; water often.

24. Bodaiju. 菩提樹. Lime; linden. *Tilia miqueliana* Maxim. **Type:** T Dec BL FR. **Use:** *2 3 17 18 22 23*. **Way:** Div(2), Cut, Lay(2), Seed. **Pot:** late sprg. **Trim:** D. **Wire:** any time except wntr. **Note:** Half shade in sumr, otherwise full sun; water often.

25. (a) Boke (Kara-boke). 木瓜, 唐木瓜. Flowering quince; japonica. *Chaenomeles extus-coccine* Carr.; *C. lagenaria* Koidz. (b) Boke (Hi-boke). 緋木瓜. Flowering quince; japonica. *C. cardinalis* Carr. **Type:** S Dec BL *FL* FR. **Use:** *2–5 6 7 12–14 17–21 28–32*. **Way:** Div(1, 5, 2), Cut, Lay(3, 2). **Pot:** every 3rd yr, early sprg or autm. **Trim:** C. Let longer new shoots get 5–7 nodes before pruning, but cut off immediately any new shoots growing from base of trunk. **Wire:** any time except wntr. **Note:** Full sun; watch for aphids on new shoots & scale on bark.

26. Botan-zakura; *see also* Sakura. 牡丹櫻. Double flowering cherry. *Prunus donarium* Sieb. **Type:** T Dec BL FL. **Use:** *2–4 5 17–21*. **Way:** Div(2), Grf (3), Lay(1). **Pot:** early sprg or after blossoming or autm. **Trim:** D. **Wire:** late sprg to autm, paper wrap. **Note:** Half shade in sumr, otherwise full sun; water often; manure well; watch for caterpillars & borers.

27. Budō. 葡萄. Grape vine. *Vitis vinifera* L. **Type:** V Dec BL FR. **Use:** *2–5 13*. **Way:** Cut, Lay(2, 3), Grf(3). **Pot:** sprg. **Trim:** D. **Wire:** sprg to sumr. **Note:** Water & manure often; watch for borers & May beetles.

28. (a) Buna (Buna-no-ki, Shiro-buna, Hon-buna). 山毛欅, 椈. Crenata beech; white beech. *Fagus crenata* Blume; *F. sieboldi* Endl.; *F. sylvatica* L. var. *sieboldi* Maxim.; *F. sylvatica* L. var. *asiastica* DC. (b) Buna (Inu-buna). 山毛欅, 椈. Japanese beech; black beech. *F. japonica* Maxim. **Type:** T Dec(dead leaves remain until sprg) BL. **Use:** 1 *2 3 17 18* 19–21 22–29. **Way:** Nat, Cut, Lay(1), Seed. **Pot:** sprg. **Trim:** C; LT once in late sprg. **Wire:** sprg to autm, paper wrap. **Note:** Half shade in sumr, otherwise full sun; (a) preferable.

29. Bushukan. 佛手柑. Fingered citron; horned orange. *Citrus medica* L. var. *sarcodactylus* Swingl.

Type: T Egr BL FR. **Use:** 2 3 4 5. **Way:** Cut, Lay(2), Grf(3). **Pot:** late sprg. **Trim:** E. **Wire:** late sprg to sumr, paper wrap. **Note:** Keep indoors & warm in wntr, otherwise full sun but no strong winds; water often; watch for scale.

Byakushin. 柏槇. *See* 108 Ibuki, 269 Shimpaku.

— C —

30. Cha. 茶, 茗. Bohea tea. *Thea sinensis* L. var. *bohea* Szusz. **Type:** S Egr BL FL. **Use:** 2 3 6 13 17 18 19–21 22–29. **Way:** Cut, Div(1), Lay(2), Seed. **Pot:** sprg. **Trim:** C. **Wire:** any time except wntr. **Note:** Full sun; will not bloom until 3rd yr; watch for aphids on new shoots & scale on trunk.

31. Chabo-hiba (Kamakura-hiba); *see also* 101 Hinoki, 250 Sawara. 矮檜. Chabo cypress. *Chamaecyparis obtusa* Endl. var. *breviramea* Mast. **Type:** T Egr NE. **Use:** 1 2 7 12 13 14 16–18 20–29. **Way:** Cut, Lay(2). **Pot:** any time except wntr. **Trim:** B. **Wire:** any time; handle gently, as branches split easily at base. **Note:** Half shade in sumr & water-spray foliage; watch for red spiders in dry season.

32. Chigo-zasa; *see also* Sasa. 稚兒笹. Dwarf bamboo; whitish-striped bamboo. *Pleioblastus fortunei* Nakai. **Type:** G Egr Pe. **Use:** 14 30–32 Min. **Way:** Div(5). **Pot:** any time. **Trim:** pull out central shoot when plant reaches desired height; cut back all the stem in late sprg & sumr. **Note:** Half shade; keep damp; keep warm in wntr; watch for scale at base of leaves & for ants.

33. Chirimen-kaede; *see also* Kaede. 縮緬楓. Japanese red maple (fine, dark-red leaves). *Acer palmatum* Thunb. var. *dissectum* Maxim. **Type:** T Dec BL. **Use:** 2–5 13 17 18 20–29. **Way:** Seed, Grf(4, 3), Lay(1). **Pot:** early sprg. **Trim:** C; LT in late sprg to sumr. **Wire:** late sprg to sumr, paper wrap. Branches break easily. **Note:** Half shade in sumr, otherwise full sun; protect from strong winds especially while new shoots still soft; watch for aphids on new shoots in sprg & scale on trunk.

Chirimen-kazura. 縮緬葛. *See* 293 Teika-kazura.

Chisanoki (Chishanoki). *See* 42 Egonoki.

34. Chishio-momiji. 血潮楓. Japanese red maple. *Acer formosum* Carr. f. *chisio* Nemoto. Data same as that for No. 33. New shoots very soft and damage easily.

35. Chōji (Jin-chōge). 瑞香, 沈丁花. Daphne. *D. odora* Thunb. **Type:** S Egr BL FR. **Use:** 2 17 18. **Way:** Cut, Lay(2), Div(1). **Pot:** early sprg. **Trim:** D. **Wire:** any time except wntr.

Chōji-kazura. 丁字桂. *See* 293 Teika-kazura.

Chōjubai. 長壽梅. *See* 276 Shudome.

Chōsen-gaya. *See* 36 Chōsen-maki.

Chōsen-goyō. 朝鮮五葉. *See* 36 Chōsen-matsu.

Chōsen-hime. 朝鮮姫. *See* 95 Hime-sekiryū.

36. Chōsen-maki (Chōsen-gaya, Tō-gaya). 朝鮮槇. Korean podocarpus. *Cephalotaxus drupacea* Sieb. et Zucc. var. *koraiana* Sieb. **Type:** S Egr NE. **Use:** 1 2 17 18. **Way:** Cut, Div(1), Lay(2). **Pot:** sprg & autm. **Trim:** B. **Wire:** any time. **Note:** Full sun.

37. Chōsen-matsu (Chōsen-goyō). 朝鮮松, 海松, 朝鮮五葉, 新羅松. Korean pine. *Pinus koraiensis* Sieb. et Zucc. **Type:** T Egr NE. **Use:** 1–7 9–14 16–29. **Way:** Nat, Seed, Grf(1, 2), Lay(1). **Pot:** sprg or autm. **Trim:** A; G (healthy trees only); late every 2nd sprg pull out all new needles. **Wire:** autm or wntr. **Note:** Full sun; flourishes in wind; keep somewhat dry. Watch for mealy bugs.

Chōsen-sekiryū. 朝鮮石榴. *See* 95 Hime-sekiryū.

— D —

Dan-chōge. *See* 292 Tanchōboku.

38. Dōdan-tsutsuji; *see also* 20 Beni-dōdan. White enkianthus. *E. perulatus* C.K. Schn. **Type:** S Dec BL FL. **Use:** 2 3 4 13 17 18 22 23. **Way:** Cut, Div(1), Lay(2). **Pot:** early sprg. **Trim:** D. **Wire:** sprg to autm. **Note:** Half shade in sumr, otherwise full sun.

39. Doitsu-tōhi. 獨逸唐檜, 歐洲唐檜. Common spruce; Hondo spruce; Norway spruce. *Picea excelsa* Link.; *P. jezoensis* Carr. var. *hondoensis* Rehd.; *P. hondoensis* Mayr. **Type:** T Egr NE. **Use:** 1–7 9 10 13 17 18 20–29. **Way:** Nat, Cut, Seed, Lay(1). **Pot:** sprg or early autm. **Trim:** B, but only once a sprg and leave a few needles at the base. **Wire:** autm to wntr. **Note:** Full sun; water-spray foliage sprg to sumr.

Dokue. *See* 1 Abura-giri.

Doyō-fuji. 土用藤. *See* 208 Natsu-fuji.

— E —

40. Edauchi-sharintō; *see also* 21 Beni-shitan, 262 Sharintō. 枝打紫檀樹. Hupel cotoneaster. *C. hupehensis* Rehd. et Wils. **Type:** S Egr BL FL *FR*. **Use:** 2–5 12 13 14 17 18 20 21 30 32. **Way:** Cut, Div(1), Lay(2, 3). **Pot:** early sprg. **Trim:** C. **Wire:** any time except wntr. **Note:** Full sun; water often; watch for aphids & scale.

Edo-giku. 江戸菊. *See* 48 Ezo-giku.

41. Edo-higanzakura; *see also* Sakura. 江戸彼岸櫻. Flowering cherry. *Prunus itosakura* Sieb. var. *ascendens* Makino. **Type:** T Dec BL FL. **Use:** 2–5 17–21 22 23. **Way:** Div(2), Grf(3), Lay(1), Seed. **Pot:** early sprg or after blossoming or autm. **Trim:** D. **Wire:** late sprg to autm, paper wrap. **Note:** Full sun; water often; half shade in sumr; manure well; watch for caterpillars & borers.

42. Egonoki (Chishanoki, Chisanoki). 齊墩果. Styrax. *S. japonica* Sieb. et Zucc. **Type:** T Dec BL. **Use:** 2 3 13 17 18. **Way:** Nat, Seed, Cut, Lay(2). **Pot:** early sprg. **Trim:** D. **Wire:** in growing season. **Note:** Full sun.

Eizan-goke. *See* 171 Kurama-goke.

43. Eni-shida. **(a)** Common broom; Scotch broom. *Cytisus scoparius* Link. **(b)** White cytisus; Portuguese broom. *C. multiflorus* Sweet. **Type:** S Dec BL FL. **Use:** *2–5 7 13 17 18.* **Way:** Div(1), Cut, Lay(3). **Pot:** early sprg. **Trim:** E. **Wire:** in growing season. **Note:** Full sun.

44. Enju (Inu-enju, Shina-enju). 槐. Chinese scholar; Japanese pagoda. *Styphnolobium japonicum* Schott.; *Sophora japonica* L. **Type:** T Dec BL FL. **Use:** *2 17 18.* **Way:** Seed, Div(1). **Pot:** early sprg. **Trim:** E. **Wire:** in growing season. **Note:** Full sun.

45. Enkō-sugi. 猿猴杉. Monkey-tail cryptomeria. *C. japonica* D.Don var. *araucarioides* Henk. et Hochst. **Type:** T Egr NE. **Use:** *1 17 18 30.* **Way:** Cut, Lay(2). **Pot:** late sprg. **Trim:** B, but not in late autm. **Wire:** sprg to sumr. **Note:** Half shade; water often; water-spray foliage sprg to early autm; keep warm in wntr; watch for red spiders.

46. Enoki (Me-mukunoki). 榎, 朴樹, 朴仔樹. Chinese hackberry. *Celtis sinensis* Pers. var. *japonica* Nakai; *C. japonica* Planch. **Type:** T Dec BL. **Use:** *1 2 17 18 22–27.* **Way:** Seed, Cut, Lay(2). **Pot:** early sprg. **Trim:** C. **Wire:** sprg to sumr, paper wrap. **Note:** Full sun; branches get heavier with much manuring.

47. Enokorogusa; *see also* 141 Kin-enokorosō. 狗尾草. Foxtail. *Setaria viridis* Beauv.; *Panicum viride* L. **Type:** G An FL. **Use:** *32.* **Way:** Nat, Seed. **Note:** Full sun.

48. Ezo-giku (Edo-giku, Satsuma-kongiku). 蝦夷菊, 江戸菊. Chinese aster. *Callistephus chinensis* Nees. **Type:** G Dec Pe BL FL. **Use:** *30 32.* **Way:** Div (3), Cut. **Pot:** every 2nd sprg. **Note:** Full sun; half shade in sumr; watch for aphids on new shoots.

Ezo-matsu. 蝦夷松. *See* 3 Aka-ezomatsu, 175 Kuro-ezomatsu.

49. Ezo-no-chichikogusa. Cat's-ear. *Antennaria dioica* Gaertn. **Type:** G Egr Pe AP FL. **Use:** *14 30.* **Way:** Div(3), Nat. **Pot:** every 3rd sprg. **Note:** Half shade.

Ezo-ringo. 蝦夷苹果. *See* 94 Hime-ringo.

— **F** —

50. Fūchisō (Urahagusa). 知風草, 風知草. Hakone-chloa. *H. macra* Makino; *Phragmites macer* Munro. **Type:** G Dec Pe. **Use:** *14 30* MinDw. **Way:** Div (3). **Pot:** early every 3rd sprg. **Trim:** early sprg, cut stems off at base. **Note:** Full sun; half shade in sumr.

51. Fude-rindō. 筆龍膽. Dwarf gentian. *Gentiana zollingeri* Fawc. **Type:** G Bi BL FL. **Use:** *14 30 32.* **Way:** Nat. **Note:** Half shade.

52. Fuji (Noda-fuji); *see also* 208 Natsu-fuji, 153 Ko-fuji, 331 Yama-fuji. 藤, 紫藤, 野田藤. Japanese wisteria. *Wistaria floribunda* DC.; *Kuraunhia floribunda* Taub. **Type:** V Dec BL *FL* FR. **Use:** *3 4 5 7 13.*

Way: Cut, Div(4), Lay(2), Grf(3), Seed. **Pot** early sprg. **Trim:** D. **Wire:** sprg to sumr. **Note:** Full sun; manure well; water often even in wntr and in sumr keep in water basin; watch for borers.

53. Fuji-zakura (Mame-zakura); *see also* Sakura. 富士櫻, 豆櫻. Fuji flowering cherry. *Prunus incisa* Thunb. **Type:** T Dec BL FL. **Use:** *2–6 17 18 20 21 22 23 30 32.* **Way:** Div(2), Lay(2), Seed, Grf (3). **Pot:** early sprg or after blooming or early autm. **Trim:** D. **Wire:** late sprg to autm, paper wrap. **Note:** Full sun; half shade in sumr; water often; manure well; watch for caterpillars & borers.

54. Fukujisō (Ganjitsusō). 福壽草, 元日草. Adonis; pheasant's-eye. *A. amurensis* Regel et Radd. **Type:** G Pe FL. **Use:** *31.* **Way:** Div(5), Nat. **Pot:** twice yearly, after blooming & in late autm. **Note:** Full sun; water often in growing season.

55. Fukuro-mochi (Maruba-nezumimochi). Japanese ligustrum. *L. japonicum* Thunb. var. *rotundifolium* Blume. **Type:** T Egr BL FR. **Use:** *2 3 13 17 18.* **Way:** Cut, Lay(2). **Pot:** sprg. **Trim:** E. **Wire:** any time. **Note:** Full sun.

Fuyu-no-hanawarabi. *See* 130 Kan-warabi.

Fuyu-zuta. *See* 150 Ki-zuta.

— **G** —

56. Gaku-ajisai; *see also* 2 Ajisai. 額草. Hydrangea. *H. macrophylla* A. P. de Candolle var. *normalis* Wilson f.; *H. azisai* Sieb.; *H. macrophylla* Seringe. **Type:** S Dec BL FL. **Use:** *2–5 17 18 22–25.* **Way:** Cut, Div (1), Lay(2). **Pot:** early sprg. **Trim:** D. **Wire:** sprg to sumr, paper wrap. **Note:** Half shade in sumr; water often.

57. Gama-zumi (Yotsudome). 莢迷. Viburnum. *V. dilatatum* Thunb. **Type:** S Dec BL FL *FR.* **Use:** *2–5 13 17 18.* **Way:** Nat, Lay(2), Cut. **Pot:** early sprg. **Trim:** D. **Wire:** any time except wntr. **Note:** Full sun.

Ganjitsusō. 元日草. *See* 54 Fukujisō.

58. Gankōran. 岩高蘭. Empetrum; crowberry. *E. nigrum* L. **Type:** S Egr NE AP FL. **Use:** *14 28 30 32* Gr Min. **Way:** Nat, Div(3). **Trim:** every 2nd yr. **Note:** Half shade; water-spray foliage sprg to autm.

59. Gekkeiju. 月桂樹. Common laurel; sweet bay. *Laurus nobilis* L. **Type:** T Egr BL FR. **Use:** *2 3 4 17 18 22 23.* **Way:** Cut, Lay(2). **Pot:** late sprg. **Trim:** D. **Wire:** in growing season, paper wrap. **Note:** Full sun; water often.

Gigōkan. *See* 217 Nise-akashia.

60. Gin-baika. 銀梅花. True myrtle. *Myrtus communis* L. **Type:** S Egr BL FL. **Use:** *2 3 4 5 13 17 18.* **Way:** Cut, Lay(2), Div(2). **Pot:** sprg. **Trim:** D. **Wire:** in growing season; paper wrap. **Note:** Full sun; water often; keep warm in wntr.

61. Gin-mokusei (Mokusei); *see also* 144 Kin-mokusei. 木犀, 銀木犀. Sweet osmanthus. *O. fragrans* Lour. var. *latifolius* Makino; *O. asiaticus* Nakai. **Type:** T Egr BL FL DIO. **Use:** *2 3 4 5 17 18*. **Way:** Lay (1), Grf(3), Cut. **Pot:** early sprg. **Trim:** D. **Pot:** any time in growing season. **Note:** Half shade in sumr: water often.

Ginnan. 銀杏. *See* 112 Ichō.

Gōkamboku. *See* 213 Nemu.

62. Goyō-matsu (Kita-goyōmatsu); *see also* 92 Hime-komatsu. 五葉松, 北五葉松. Five-needle pine; Japanese white pine. *Pinus pentaphylla* Mayr.; *P. parviflora* Sieb. et Zucc. partim; *P. parviflora* Sieb. et Zucc. var. *pentaphylla* Henry. **Type:** T Egr NE. **Use:** all except 8; Min. **Way:** *Nat*, Lay(1), Seed, Grf(1, 2). **Pot:** sprg or autm. **Trim:** A & G for healthy plant. To make short needles and dense foliage, pull out all new needles after they open but before they get hard. **Wire:** autm to wntr. **Note:** Full sun & wind; keep somewhat dry; watch for mealy bugs.

Gumi. *See* 209(a) Natsu-gumi, 209(b) Nawashiro-gumi.

63. Gyoryū. 檉柳, 御柳, 三春柳. Juniper tamarix; tamarisk. *Tamarix chinensis* Lour.; *T. juniperina* Bunge. **Type:** T Dec NE(soft). **Use:** *2 3 4 5 13 14 17 18 22 23 30–32*. **Way:** Cut, Lay(2). **Pot:** sprg. **Trim:** keep long new shoots; cut way back in autm. **Wire:** sprg to sumr; paper wrap. **Note:** Keep wet all yr; keep warm in wntr.

— **H** —

Hachisu. *See* 200 Mukuge.

64. Hagi (Yama-hag); *see also* 89 Hime-hagi. 萩, 山萩. Japanese bush-clover. *Lespedeza bicolor* Turcz. var. *japonica* Nakai. **Type:** S Dec BL FL. **Use:** *2–5 13 14 17 18* MinDw. **Way:** Cut, Div(3), Seed. **Pot:** sprg. **Trim:** E; in late autm cut way back all branches at base. **Wire:** sprg to sumr. **Note:** Full sun; water often; watch for aphids on new shoots.

Hagoromo-matsu. 羽衣松. *See* 233 Rakuushō.

65. Hai-byakushin (Sonare); *see also* 108 Ibuki, 269 Shimpaku. 這柏槇, 磯馴. Japanese juniper. *Juniperus chinensis* L. var. *procumbens* Lindl.; *J. japonica* Hort.; *J. procumbens* Sieb. **Type:** S Egr NE DIO. **Use:** *4–7 9–15 17 18 20 21 28*. **Way:** Nat, Cut, Lay(2). **Pot:** any time except wntr. **Trim:** B. **Wire:** any time. **Note:** Full sun; water often; water-spray foliage sprg to autm; watch for red spiders.

66. Hai-matsu. 這松, 偃松. Pumila pine; creeping five-needle pine. *Pinus pumila* Regel.; *P. cembra* L. var. *pumila* Pall.; *P. parviflora* Sieb et Zucc. partim. **Type:** S Egr NE AP. **Use:** *4 5 7 9–15 17–21 28*. **Way:** Nat, Lay(1), Grf(1, 2). **Pot:** sprg or autm. **Trim:** same as no. 62 above. **Wire:** autm to wntr. **Note:** Full sun & wind; watch for mealy bugs.

Hai-nezu. *See* 306 Toshō.

67. Hakone-utsugi. 箱根空木. Weigele. *Weigela coraeensis* Thunb.; *W. grandiflora* Fortune; *Diervilla grandiflora* Sieb. et Zucc. **Type:** S Dec BL FL. **Use:** *2–5 17 18*. **Way:** Cut, Lay(2), Div(1). **Pot:** early sprg. **Trim:** D. **Wire:** sprg to sumr, paper wrap. **Note:** Half shade; water often.

68. Haku-chōge (Kōchōki). 白丁華, 香丁木. Japanese serissa. *S. japonica* Thunb. **Type:** S Egr BL FL. **Use:** *2–6 12–14 17 18 20 21 30 32* Min. **Way:** Cut, Div(1, 5); Lay(2). **Pot:** sprg. **Trim:** C. **Wire:** any time. **Note:** water often.

69. Haku-mokuren; *see also* 267 Shi-mokuren. 白木蘭, 玉蘭, 木蘭. Yulan. *Magnolia denudata* Desr.; *M. conspicua* Salisb. *M. yulan* Desf. **Type:** T Dec BL FL. **Use:** *2–5 17 18*. **Way:** Div(2), Lay(1). **Pot:** after blossoming. **Trim:** D. **Wire:** sprg to sumr, paper wrap. **Note:** Water often; shade in sumr.

70. Hakusan-shakunage; *see also* 96 Hime-shakunage, 260 Shakunage. 白山石南花. Rhododendron. *R. faauriae* Franch. **Type:** S Egr BL FL AP. **Use:** *2–5 13 14 17 18 20 21 22–27 28 30 32*. **Way:** Nat, Div(2), Lay (1). **Pot:** every 3rd sprg. **Trim:** not so necessary. **Wire:** sprg to sumr. **Note:** Half shade & keep damp.

71. Hama-mokkoku (Sharimbai). Rhaphiolepis. *R. umbellata* Makino var. *mertensii* Makino. **Type:** S Egr BL FR. **Use:** *2 3 17 18*. **Way:** Nat, Seed, Lay(1). **Pot:** every 3rd sprg. **Trim:** C. **Wire:** any time. **Note:** Full sun.

72. Hama-nashi (Hama-nasu). 玫瑰. Rugosa rose. *Rosa rugosa* Thunb. **Type:** S Dec BL FL FR. **Use:** *2–5 13 17 18*. **Way:** Cut, Nat. **Pot:** early each sprg. **Trim:** E; after berry finished, cut way back. **Wire:** in growing season. **Note:** Full sun.

73. Hana-kaidō (Suishi-kaidō, Nagasaki-ringo); *see also* 189 Miyama-kaidō. 花海棠, 垂絲海棠, 長崎苹果. Hall crab; Hall's crab-apple. *Malus halliana* Koehne; *Pyrus halliana* Voss. **Type:** T Dec BL *FL* FR. **Use:** *2–5 13 17 18*. **Way:** Lay(1), Div(5), Grf(3), Seed. **Pot:** once a yr in early sprg or after blossoming or in early autm. **Trim:** D. **Wire:** sprg to autm. **Note:** Full sun; water often; watch for aphids all during growing season.

74. Hana-tsukubaneutsugi. Glossy abelia. *A. grandiflora* Rehder. **Type:** S Dec BL FL. **Use:** *18*. **Way:** Cut, Div(2). **Pot:** sprg. **Trim:** E. **Wire:** in growing season. **Note:** Full sun.

75. Hana-zuhō. 紫荊. Chinese redbud. *Cercis chinensis* Bunge. **Type:** T Dec BL FL. **Use:** *2–4 17 18*. **Way:** Lay(1), Cut. **Pot:** early sprg. **Trim:** D. **Wire:** sprg to autm. **Note:** Full sun.

Hari-enju. *See* 217 Nise-akashia.

76. Hari-momi (Bara-momi). 針樅. Harimomi fir. *Picea polita* Carr. **Type:** T Egr NE. **Use:** *1 2–7 8 9 17 18 20–28*. **Way:** Nat, Cut, Seed, Lay(1). **Pot:** sprg or autm. **Trim:** B, but only once or twice a sprg. **Wire:** autm to wntr. **Note:** Half shade; water-spray sprg to sumr.

77. Haru-nire (Nire). 楡. Japanese elm. *Ulmus davidiana* Planch. var. *japonica* Nakai; *U. campestris* Sm. var. *japonica* Rehd.; *U. japonica* Sarg. **Type:** T Dec BL. **Use:** *2 3 8 17 18* 22–27. **Way:** Nat, Seed, Cut, Lay(2). **Pot:** early sprg. **Trim:** C; LT once in late sprg. **Wire:** sprg to sumr, paper wrap. **Note:** Full sun; half shade in sumr, watch for aphids on backs of leaves.

78. Haru-rindō; *see also* 51 Fude-rindō. 春龍膽, 石龍膽. Dwarf gentian. *Gentiana thunbergii* Griseb.; *G. japonica* Maxim. **Type:** G Bi FL. **Use:** 14 *30 32*. **Way:** Nat. **Note:** Half shade.

79. Hashibami. 榛. Japanese hazel. *Corylus heterophylla* Fish. var. *thunbergii* Blume. **Type:** S Dec BL FL FR. **Use:** *2 5* 13 14 17 18 20–30 *32*. **Way:** Nat, Cut, Lay(2). **Pot:** early sprg. **Trim:** D. **Wire:** sprg to sumr. **Note:** Full sun; half shade in sumr.

80. Hasu. 蓮. Lotus. *Nelumbo nucifera* Gaerth.; *N. seciosum* Willd. **Type:** G Dec Pe BL *FL* FR. **Use:** *32*. **Way:** Div(3). **Pot:** early each sprg. **Note:** Use clay or peat for soil; keep in water; watch for aphids.

81. Hatoya-bara; *see also* Bara. 鳩谷薔薇. Cherokee rose. *Rosa laevigata* Michaux f. **Type:** V Dec BL FL. **Use:** 2 3 4 5 13 14 *17–19* 21–23. **Way:** Cut, Lay(2, 3), Div(3). **Pot:** early each sprg. **Trim:** E. **Wire:** sprg to sumr. **Note:** Full sun; manure well; water often; watch for aphids all yr except wntr & for scale.

Hatsuyuki-kazura. 初雪桂. *See* 293 Teika-kazura.

82. Haze-no-ki (Tō-haze, Ryūkyū-haze). 黄櫨. Wax. *Rhus succedanea* L. **Type:** T Dec BL FR DIO. **Use:** *2 3* 13 *17 18* 22–27 (thin trunks) 30 *32*. **Way:** Seed, Cut, Lay(2). **Pot:** late sprg. **Trim:** C; late sprg to sumr cut all new shoots. **Wire:** sprg to sumr, paper wrap. **Note:** Half shade in sumr; water often; keep warm in wntr; female plant preferable.

Hempaku. 扁柏. *See* 101 Hinoki.

83. Hentō (Amentō). 西王母, 扁桃, 壽星桃. Peach. *Prunus amygdalus* Stockes. **Type:** T Dec BL FL *FR*. **Use:** *2 3 4 5 17* 18. **Way:** Lay(2), Grf(3, 2), Seed. **Pot:** early sprg or after blooming or early autm. **Trim:** D. **Wire:** sprg to sumr. **Note:** Full sun; water often; watch for borers.

Hiba. *See* 101 Hinoki, 16 Asunaro.

Hi-boke. 緋木瓜. *See* 25(b) Boke.

84. Higan-zakura; *see also* Sakura. 彼岸櫻. Flowering cherry. *Prunus subhirtella* Miq. **Type:** T Dec BL FL. **Use:** 2–5 *17–21* 22 23. **Way:** Div(2), Grf (3), Lay(1), Seed. **Pot:** early sprg or after blooming or early autm. **Trim:** D. **Wire:** sprg to autm, paper wrap. **Note:** Full sun; half shade in sumr; water often; manure well; watch for borers & caterpillars.

85. Hiiragi. 狗骨. Osmanthus; Japanese holly. *O. ilicifolius* Mouiffef; *O. aquifolium* Sieb. **Type:** S Egr BL(with needles) DIO. **Use:** 1 2 3 4 13 *17 18*. **Way:** Cut, Lay(2), Div(2). **Pot:** sprg. **Trim:** C. **Wire:** sprg to autm, paper wrap. **Note:** Full sun; female tree preferable.

86. Hiiragi-nanten. 十大功勞. Japanese holly-grape. *Mahonia japonica* DC.; *Berberis japonica* R.Br.; *Ilex japonica* Thunb. **Type:** S Egr BL FL FR. **Use:** 1 2 3 4 13 *17 18*. **Way:** Cut, Lay(2), Div(2). **Pot:** sprg. **Trim:** C. **Wire:** sprg to autm, paper wrap. **Note:** Full sun.

87. Hikage-no-kazura. 石松. Club moss. *Lycopodium clavatum* L. **Type:** G Egr Pe NE. **Use:** *14 30* 31 *32* Gr. **Way:** Div(3), Cut. **Pot:** sprg. **Note:** Half shade; water-spray often, keep always damp.

88. Himaraya-sugi. 印度杉. Deodar; true cedar; East Indian cedar. *Cedrus deodara* Loud.; *C. libanii* Barr. var. *deodara* Hook f.; *Pinus deodara* Roxb. **Type:** T Egr NE. **Use:** *1 9* 13 *17 18* 22–26. **Way:** Cut, Lay(1), Seed. **Pot:** sprg. **Trim:** B. **Wire:** any time. **Note:** Full sun.

Hime-bashō. *See* 19(b) Bashō.

Hime-fuji. *See* 153 Ko-fuji.

89. Hime-hagi (Koba-no-hagi); *see also* 64 Hagi. 姫萩. Dwarf bush-clover. *Desmodium microphylla* DC. **Type:** S Dec BL FL. **Use:** *2–5* 13 14 17 18 20 21 30–32 Min. **Way:** Cut, Div(3), Seed. **Pot:** early each sprg. **Trim:** E; in late autm cut off all stems at base. **Wire:** sprg to sumr. **Note:** Full sun; water often; watch for aphids on new shoots.

90. Hime-himuro (Himuro, Himuro-sugi). Himuro cypress. *Chamaecyparis pisifera* Endl. var. *squarrosa* Beissn. **Type:** T Egr NE. **Use:** 2 3 8 13 *14 17 18* 22–27 30. **Way:** Cut, Lay(2, 3), Div(1, 2). **Pot:** any time. **Trim:** B. **Wire:** any time. **Note:** full sun; always remove dead leaves.

91. Hime-kobushi (Beni-kobushi, Shide-kobushi); *see also* 151 Kobushi. 紅辛夷, 姫辛夷, 重華辛夷. Dwarf kobus magnolia. *M. stellata* Maxim. var. *keiskei* Makino. *Buergeria stellata* Sieb. et Zucc.; *M. stellata* Maxim. **Type:** S Dec BL FR. **Use:** *2–5 17 18*. **Way:** Div(2), Lay(1). **Pot:** once a yr in early sprg or just after blooming season or in early autm. **Wire:** sprg to sumr. **Note:** Full sun; water often.

92. Hime-komatsu; *see also* 62 Goyō-matsu. 姫小松. Himeko pine; five-needle pine. *Pinus pentaphylla* Mayr. var. *himekomatsu* Makino; *P. parviflora* Sieb. et Zucc.; *P. himekomatsu* Miyabe et Kudo; *P. mayri* Tatewaki. **Type:** T Egr NE. **Use:** all styles except 8; Min. **Way:** Nat, Lay(1), Seed, Grf(1, 2). **Pot:** sprg or autm. **Trim:** same as 62 Goyō-matsu. **Wire:** autm to wntr. **Note:** Full sun & wind; keep somewhat dry; watch for mealy bugs.

93. Hime-nokishinobu. 鎧蘭. Polypody. *Polypodium thunbergianum* Makino var. *onoei* Makino; *Lepisorus onoei* Ching; *P. lineare* Thunb. var. *onoei* Makino. **Type:** G Egr Pe. **Use:** 14 *30 32* Gr. **Way:** Div(3). **Pot:** sprg to autm. **Note:** Half shade; will grow in very little soil or in peat.

94. Hime-ringo (Ezo-ringo, Nagasaki-ringo, Ukezaki-kaidō). 姫苹果, 長崎苹果, 受唉海棠, 蝦夷苹果. Nagasaki crab-apple. *Malus cerasifera* Spach.; *M. micromalus* Makino. **Type:** T Dec BL FL *FR.* **Use:** *2–5 13 17 18* 30 32 Min. **Way:** Div(2, 5), Lay(1), Grf(3), Seed. **Pot:** early each sprg or in autm. **Trim:** D. **Wire:** sprg to autm; remove after 3–6 mos. to keep wire from scarring wood. **Note:** Full sun; water often; manure well; watch for aphids on new buds.

95. Hime-sekiryū (Chōsen-hime, Chōsen-sekiryū); *see also* 256 Sekiryū. 朝鮮姫, 姫石榴, 朝鮮石榴. Dwarf pomegranate. *Punica granatum* L. var. *nana* Pers. **Type:** S Dec BL FL FR. **Use:** *2–4 5 6 17 18 20 21* 22 23 30 32 Min. **Way:** Cut, Lay(2), Div(2), Seed. **Pot:** late sprg after new leaves open. **Trim:** E; immediately cut off new shoots at base of trunk. **Wire:** late sprg to sumr, paper wrap. **Note:** Keep very warm from late autm to early sprg; watch for aphids except in wntr.

96. Hime-shakunage. 姫石南花. Andromeda. *A. polifolia* L. **Type:** S Egr BL FL. **Use:** *14 18* 30 32 Min. **Way:** Cut, Div(3). **Pot:** each sprg. **Note:** Half shade; always keep damp.

97. Hime-shara (Ko-natsutsubaki); *see also* 211 Natsu-tsubaki. 姫娑羅. Dwarf stewartia. *S. monadelpha* Sieb. et Zucc. **Type:** T Dec BL FL. **Use:** *2 3 13 17 18* 22 23. **Way:** Cut, Lay(2), Div(2). **Pot:** sprg. **Trim:** D. **Wire:** sprg to sumr, paper wrap. **Note:** Full sun; half shade in sumr.

98. Hime-tokusa; *see also* 303 Tokusa. 姫木賊. Dwarf scouring rush. *Equisetum ramosissium* Desf. **Type:** G Egr Pe NE. **Use:** *30 32* Min. **Way:** Div(5). **Pot:** any time except wntr. **Trim:** pull out top if plant too tall. **Note:** Full shade; keep very wet.

99. Hime-tsuge (Kusa-tsuge); *see also* 311 Tsuge. 姫黄楊木, 草黄楊木. Box. *Buxus microphylla* Sieb. et Zucc. **Type:** S Egr BL FR. **Use:** *2–4 9 13 14 17 18* 30 Min. **Way:** Cut, Nat, Lay(2). **Pot:** sprg. **Trim:** C. **Wire:** any time. **Note:** Full sun; keep warm in wntr.

Hime-usuyukisō. *See* 193 Miyama-usuyukisō.

100. Himo-kazura. 紐蔓. Shakotan selaginella. *S. rupestris* Spring. var. *shakotanensis* Franch.; *S. shakotanensis* Miyabe et Kudo. **Type:** G Egr Pe. **Use:** 14 30 32 Gr Min. **Way:** Div(3), Cut. **Pot:** sprg to autm. **Note:** Always half shade; water-spray sprg to sumr.

Himuro. *See* 90 Hime-himuro.

Himuro-sugi. *See* 90 Hime-himuro.

Hina-gikyō. *See* 119 Ito-shajin.

101. Hinoki (Hempaku, Hiba). 檜, 扁柏. Hinoki cypress. *Chamaecyparis obtusa* Endl. **Type:** T Egr NE. **Use:** *1 13 17 18 20–29* Min. **Way:** Cut, Lay(1), Seed. **Pot:** any time. **Trim:** B. **Wire:** any time. **Note:** Half shade in sumr only; water-spray foliage sprg to late sumr; watch for red spiders.

Hon-buna. *See* 28(a) Buna.

Hon-maki. *See* 165 Kōya-maki.

Hon-tsuge. *See* 311 Tsuge.

102. Hotaru-bukuro. 山小菜, 螢蒙. Campanula. *C. punctata* Lam. **Type:** G Dec Pe BL FL. **Use:** *14 32.* **Way:** Div(3). **Pot:** every 2nd yr. **Note:** Full sun; half shade in sumr.

103. Hyakujikkō (Saru-suberi). 百日紅, 紫薇. **(a)** Common crape-myrtle. *Lagerstroemia indica* L. **(b)** White crape-myrtle. *L. indica* L. var. *alba* Nichl. **(c)** Purple crape-myrtle. *L. indica* L. var. *amabilis* Makino. **Type:** T Dec BL FL. **Use:** *2–4 6 17 18 19–21.* **Way:** Cut, Lay(2), Div(2). **Pot:** twice yearly in early sprg & early sumr. **Trim:** E. **Wire:** sprg to sumr, paper wrap. **Note:** Full sun; manure well; water often; keep warm in wntr; watch for aphids.

104. **(a)** Hyakunichisō. 百日草. Zinnia. *Z. elegans* L. **(b)** Hime-hyakunichisō. 姫百日草. Dwarf zinnia. *Z. pauciflora* L. **Type:** G An BL FL. **Use:** *31.* **Way:** Seed. **Note:** Full sun.

105. Hyōtamboku (Kingimboku); *see also* 319 Uguisu-kagura. 瓢簞木, 金銀木. Morrow honeysuckle. *Lonicera morrowii* A.Gray. **Type:** S Dec BL FL *FR.* **Use:** *2–5 13* 17 18. **Way:** Cut, Lay(1), Nat, Seed. **Pot:** early sprg. **Trim:** D. **Wire:** sprg to sumr. **Note:** Full sun.

106. Hyūga-mizuki (Iyo-mizuki). 日向水木, 伊豫水木. Buttercup winter hazel. *Corylopsis pauciflora* Sieb. et Zucc. **Type:** S Dec BL FL. **Use:** *2 3 13 17 18 20–25.* **Way:** Div(2), Lay(1), Nat. **Pot:** early sprg. **Trim:** D. **Wire:** sprg to sumr. **Note:** Full sun.

— I —

107. Ibota (Ibota-no-ki). 水蠟樹. Ibota ligustrum. *L. ibota* Sieb. var. *angustifolium* Blume. **Type:** S Semi-Dec BL FL FR. **Use:** *2 3 13 14* 17 18. **Way:** Cut, Lay(2), Seed. **Pot:** early each sprg. **Trim:** E. **Wire:** any time. **Note:** Full sun; watch for aphids.

108. Ibuki (Byakushin); *see also* 269 Shimpaku. 伊吹, 柏槙. Chinese juniper. *Juniperus chinensis* L. **Type:** T Egr NE DIO. **Use:** *2–7 9 10 12–15 17 18* 20 21 30. **Way:** Nat, Cut, Lay(1), Grf(2). **Pot:** any time. **Trim:** B, all yr. **Wire:** any time. **Note:** Full sun; good drainage; water-spray sprg to autm; watch for red spiders.

109. Ibuki-jakōsō (Jakōsō). Wild thyme; mother-of-thyme. *Thymus serphyllum* L. var. *przewalskii* Komar. **Type:** G Egr Pe BL. **Use:** *14* 30–32 Gr MinDw. **Way:** Div(3), Cut. **Pot:** any time. **Note:** Full sun.

110. Ichii (Onkō, Araragi). 紫杉, 一位. Japanese yew. *Taxus cuspidata* Sieb. et Zucc.; *T. baccata* L. var. *cuspidata* Carr.; *T. baccata* L. subsp. *cuspidata.* **Type:** T Egr NE FR DIO. **Use:** *1 2 9 17 18.* **Way:** Nat, Cut, Lay(1), Seed. **Pot:** sprg to autm. **Trim:** B, but if fruit wanted, wait until after blossoming to trim new shoots. **Wire:** any time except while in new bud. **Note:** Half shade; female plant preferable.

111. Ichijiku. 無花果. Fig. *Ficus carrica* L. **Type:** T Dec BL FR. **Use:** *2–4 5 13 17 18.* **Way:** Cut, Lay(2), **Pot:** early sprg. **Trim:** E. **Wire:** sprg to sumr, paper wrap. **Note:** Half shade; keep warm in wntr; watch for borers.

112. Ichō (Ginnan). 公孫樹, 銀杏. Maidenhair. *Ginkgo biloba* L. **Type:** T Dec BL FR DIO. **Use:** *2 8 17 18 20 21.* **Way:** Cut, Lay(2), Div(3), Grf (3). **Pot:** early sprg. **Trim:** E. **Wire:** in growing season. **Note:** Full sun; water often; female tree preferable.

Ii-giri. *See 206 Nanten-giri.*

Inu-akashia. *See 217 Nise-akashia.*

Inu-buna. *See 28(b) Buna.*

Inu-enju. *See 44 Enju.*

113. Inu-gaya. 粗榧, 油榧. Japanese plum-yew. *Cephalotaxus drupacea* Sieb. et Zucc. **Type:** T Egr NE FR DIO. **Use:** *1 2 9 17 18.* **Way:** Nat, Cut, Lay(1), Seed. **Pot:** sprg. **Trim:** same as 110 above. **Wire:** in growing season. **Note:** Full sun; female plant preferable.

114. Inu-maki (Maki, Hon-maki, Kusa-maki). 槙. Podocarpus yew; umbrella pine. *Podocarpus macrophylla* D.Don. **Type:** T Egr NE. **Use:** *1–3 17 18.* **Way:** Nat, Cut, Lay(1). **Pot:** sprg. **Trim:** B. **Wire:** in growing season. **Note:** Full sun.

115. Inu-shide (Soro); *see also* 5 Aka-shide, 169 Kuma-shide. Hornbeam; white-hair hornbeam. *Carpinus tschonoskii* Maxim.; *C. yedoensis* Maxim. **Type:** T Dec BL FR. **Use:** *2 3 4–6 13 17 18 22–27.* **Way:** Nat, Cut, Seed, Lay(2). **Pot:** early sprg. **Trim:** C. **Wire:** sprg to sumr. **Note:** Full sun; half shade in sumr.

116. Inu-tsuge. 犬黄楊. Box. *Ilex crenata* Thunb. **Type:** S Egr BL FR. **Use:** *2 3 4 5 9 13 14 17 18 30.* **Way:** Cut, Lay(2). **Pot:** early sprg. **Trim:** C. **Wire:** any time. **Note:** Full sun.

117. Inu-umemodoki. 犬落霜紅. Ilex. *I. serrata* Thunb. **Type:** S Dec BL FR DIO. **Use:** *2 3 4 5 13 17–19.* **Way:** Cut, Lay(2). **Pot:** early sprg. **Trim:** E. **Wire:** sprg to sumr. **Note:** Full sun; water often; watch for aphids & scale; female tree preferable.

Ishi-geyaki. *See 7 Aki-nire.*

118. Itadori. 虎杖. Polygonum. *P. reynoutria* Makino; *P. cuspidatum* Sieb. et Zucc.; *R. japonica* Houtt. **Type:** G Dec Pe BL FL. **Use:** 14 32 MinDw. **Way:** Div(3), Cut. **Pot:** each sprg. **Note:** Full sun; water often; watch for caterpillars.

119. Ito-shajin (Hina-gikyō). 糸沙参, 細葉沙参. Dwarf campanula. *C. wahlenbergia* A.DC.; *W. gracilis* A.DC. **Type:** G Dec Pe FL. **Use:** *14 30 32* Min. **Way:** Div(5), Seed, Nat. **Pot:** each sprg. **Note:** Full sun; half shade in sumr.

Ito-zakura. *See 263 Shidare-higanzakura.*

120. Iwa-chidori. 岩千鳥. Amitostigma. *A. keiskei.* Schlecht.; *Gymnadenia keiskei* Maxim. **Type:** G Dec Pe FL. **Use:** *14 32.* **Way:** Div(3), Seed, Nat. **Pot:** every 3rd yr. **Note:** Grows easily on rock.

121. Iwa-denda. 岩羊歯. Veitch fern. *Woodsia polystichoides* Eat. var. *veitchii* Hook et Baker; *W. veitchii* Hance. **Type:** G SemiDec Pe. **Use:** *14 30 32.* **Way:** Div(3), Nat. **Pot:** every 3rd yr. **Note:** Always half shade.

122. Iwa-hiba. 卷柏, 岩松. Selaginella. *S. involvens* Spring. **Type:** G Dec Pe NE(soft). **Use:** *14 30 32.* **Way:** Div(3), Cut, Seed, Nat. **Pot:** every 3rd yr. **Note:** Full shade; water-spray sprg to autm.

123. Iwa-uchiwa. Shortia. *S. uniflora* Maxim. **Type:** G Egr Pe BL FL. **Use:** *14 32.* **Way:** Nat, Div(3). **Pot:** every 3rd yr. **Note:** Half shade.

Iyo-mizuki. *See 106 Hyūga-mizuki.*

— J —

Jakōsō. *See 109 Ibuki-jakōsō.*

Jakuro. *See 256 Sekiryū.*

Jinchōge. *See 35 Chōji.*

— K —

Kaede (Momiji). 楓, 槭. *See 33 Chirimen-kaede,* 223 Nomura-kaede, 301 Tō-kaede, 332 Yama-momiji.

Kaidō. 海棠. Crab apple. *See 73 Hana-kaidō,* 94 Hime-ringo, 189 Miyama-kaidō.

124. Kaki; *see also* 181 Mame-gaki. 柿. Persimmon. *Diospyros kaki* L. fil. **Type:** T Dec BL FR. **Use:** *2–6 17 18 20 21.* **Way:** Grf(3), Lay(1). **Pot:** late each sprg. **Trim:** D. **Wire:** sprg to autm; branches break easily. **Note:** Full sun; water often.

125. Kakkō-azami. 藿香薊. Ageratum. *A. conyzoides* L. **Type:** G An FL. **Use:** *31.* **Way:** Seed. **Note:** Full sun.

Kamakura-hiba. *See 31 Chabo-hiba.*

126. Kamatsuka (Kenashi-ushikoroshi, Ushikoroshi). 鎌柄. Pourthiaea. *P. villosa* Decne. var. *laevis* Dipp.; *Crataegus laevis* Thunb. **Type:** T Dec BL FL *FR.* **Use:** *2 5 13 14 17 18 20–25 30 32.* **Way:** Seed, Lay(1). **Pot:** early each sprg. **Trim:** D. **Wire:** sprg to autm. **Note:** Full sun; watch for aphids on new buds and base of blossoms and fruit.

Kana-shide. *See 5 Aka-shide.*

127. Kanchiku. 寒竹. Winter bamboo. *Chimonobambusa marmorea* Makino; *Bambusa marmorea* Mitf. **Type:** G Egr Pe. **Use:** *13 14 18 22–27 32.* **Way:** Div(5). **Pot:** late each sprg. **Trim:** C; pull out central bud; LT in sumr. **Note:** Half shade; water often; keep warm in wntr; watch for scale and aphids.

128. Kan-giku. 寒菊. Winter chrysanthemum: **(a)**

Single flowered. *C. indicum* L. **(b)** Double flowered. *C. indicum* L. var. *hortense* Makino. **Type**: G Dec Pe BL FL. **Use**: *31*. **Way**: Div(3), Cut(autm). **Pot**: each yr. **Trim**: sprg to sumr. **Note**: Full sun; half shade in sumr; watch for aphids.

129. Kan-shinobu (Tachi-shinobu). 寒忍, 羊歯. Winter fern. *Onychium japonicum* Kunze; *Trichomanes japonicum* Thunb. **Type**: G Egr Pe. **Use**: *14 30–32*. **Way**: Div(3), Nat. **Trim**: when leaves grow too long cut all off at base. **Note**: Half shade. Easy to grow on rock.

130. Kan-warabi (Fuyu-no-hanawarabi). 寒厥. Botrychium *B. ternatum* Sw.; *Osmunda ternata* Thunb. **Type**: G Dec Pe FL. **Use**: *31 32*. **Way**: Nat, Div (5). **Pot**: each autm. **Note**: Half shade.

131. Kan-zakura; *see also* Sakura. 寒櫻. Winter flowering cherry. *Prunus campanulata* Maxim. **Type**: T Dec BL FR. **Use**: *2–4 5 17–21*. **Way**: Div(2), Grf(3), Lay(1). **Pot**: early sprg or after blossoming or early autm. **Trim**: D. **Wire**: late sprg to autm, paper wrap. **Note**: Full sun; water often; half shade in sumr; manure well; watch for caterpillars & borers.

Kara-boke. 唐木瓜. *See 25 Boke.*

Kara-kuwa. *See 330 Yamaboshi.*

132. Kara-matsu (Rakuyōshō). 落葉松. Japanese tamarack; larch. *Larix leptolepis* Murray; *Abies leptolepis* Sieb. et Zucc.; *L. japonica* Carr.; *L. kaempferi* Sarg. non Carr.; *Pinus kaempferi* Lamb. **Type**: T Dec NE(soft). **Use**: *1–3 9 10 13 14 17 18 22–27 32*. **Way**: Nat, Cut, Lay(1), Seed. **Pot**: early sprg. **Trim**: B. **Wire**: late sumr to autm. **Note**: Full sun; half shade in sumr.

133. Karatachi. 拘橘. Trifoliata citron. *Citrus trifoliata* L. *Poncirus trifoliata* Rafin. **Type**: S Egr BL FR. **Use**: *2–5 13 17 18*. **Way**: Cut, Lay(2), Grf(3). **Pot**: late sprg. **Trim**: E. **Wire**: late sprg to sumr, paper wrap. **Note**: Water often; keep very warm in wntr; watch for scale.

Kara-ume. *See 237 Rōbai.*

134. Karin. 榠樝, 花欄. Chinese quince. *Chaenomeles sinensis* Koehne; *Pseudocydonia sinensis* Schneid. **Type**: T Dec BL FR. **Use**: *2–5 13 17 18*. **Way**: Lay(2), Seed, Cut. **Pot**: very early sprg or in autm. **Trim**: D. **Wire**: sprg to autm, paper wrap. **Note**: Full sun; water often.

Kashi. *See 273 Shira-gashi.*

135. Kashiwa. 槲. Daimyo oak. *Quercus dentata* Thunb. **Type**: T Dec(dead leaves remain until sprg) BL FR. **Use**: *2–4 17 18*. **Way**: *Nat*, Lay(1), Div(2), Seed. **Pot**: early sprg. **Trim**: D. **Wire**: sprg to autm. **Note**: Full sun; half shade in wntr.

136. Kata-hiba (Kogane-shida). 兗州卷柏, 黃金羊歯. Golden fern; selaginella. *S. caulescens* Spring. **Type**: G Dec Pe. **Use**: *14 30–32* Min. **Way**: Div(3), Cut, Seed. **Trim**: when leaves grow too long, cut at base

of leaves before autm. **Note**: Half shade; grows easily on rock.

137. Kawara-nadeshiko (Nadeshiko). 河原撫子, 撫子. Wild pink; dianthus. *D. superbus* L. **Type**: G Dec Pe FL. **Use**: *31 32*. **Way**: Seed, Div(3), Cut. **Pot**: each sprg. **Note**: Full sun.

138. Kaya. 榧. Torreya. *T. nucifera* Sieb. et Zucc.; *Taxus nucifera* L. **Type**: T Egr NE FR DIO. **Use**: *1 2 9 17 18*. **Way**: Nat, Cut, Lay(1), Seed. **Pot**: sprg. **Trim**: A, but if fruits wanted E.

Kenashi-ushikoroshi. *See 126 Kamatsuka.*

139. Keyaki (Keaki). 欅. Japanese grey-bark elm; saw-leaved zelkova. *Z. serrata* Makino. **Type**: T Dec BL. **Use**: *8 13 17 18 24–27 30*. **Way**: Seed, Lay (2), Cut. **Pot**: early sprg. **Trim**: C; LT. **Wire**: any time except while budding. **Note**: Full sun; watch for aphids.

140. Kikyō. 桔梗. Chinese bellflower. *Platicodon grandiflorum* A.DC.; *Campanula grandiflora* Jacq.; *C. gruca* Thunb. **Type**: G Dec Pe FL. **Use**: *31*. **Way**: Div(5), Seed, Cut. **Pot**: each sprg. **Note**: Full sun; watch for aphids.

Ki-mokkōbara. 黄木香薔薇. *See 195 Mokkōbara.*

141. Kin-enokorosō. 金狗草. Foxtail. *Setaria lutescens* Hubbard; *Panicum lutescens* Weigel. **Type**: G An FL. **Use**: *32*. **Way**: Nat, Seed. **Note**: Full sun.

Kingimboku. *See 105 Hyōtamboku.*

142. Kan-jakka (Mure-suzume). 金雀花, 錦雞兒. Mongolian redshrub. *Caragana chamlagu* Lam. **Type**: S Dec BL FL. **Use**: *2–5 7 13 17 18*. **Way**: Cut, Div(3), Lay(3). **Pot**: early sprg. **Trim**: E. **Wire**: any time. **Note**: Full sun.

143. **(a)** Kinkan, Kinzu. 金豆柑, 金橘. Dwarf kumquat. *Fortunella japonica* Swingl.; *Citrus margarita* Lour. **(b)** Kinkan. 金柑, 金橘. Kumquat. *F. japonica* Swingl. var. *margarita* Makino; *F. margarita* Swingl. **Type**: S Egr BL FR. **Use**: *2–5 13 17 18* Min. **Way**: Cut, Lay(1), Grf(3), Seed. **Pot**: late sprg. **Trim**: E. **Wire**: late sprg to sumr, paper wrap. **Note**: Keep very warm in wntr; water often; watch for scale.

144. Kin-mokusei; *see also* 61 Gin-mokusei. 金木犀, 丹桂. Osmanthus. *O. aurantiacus* Nakai; *O. fragrans* Lour. var. *aurantiacus* Makino. **Type**: T Egr BL FL DIO. **Use**: *2 3 4 5 17 18*. **Way**: Lay(1), Grf(3), Cut. **Pot**: sprg. **Trim**: E. **Wire**: any time. **Note**: Full sun; half shade in sumr & water often.

145. Kin-rōbai (Kin-robai). 金露梅. Shrubby cinquefoil. *Dasyphora fruticosa* Rydberg; *Potentilla fruticosa* L. **Type**: S Dec BL FL. **Use**: *2 3–5 17 18*. **Way**: Cut, Div(2). **Pot**: sprg. **Trim**: E. **Wire**: any time except wntr. **Note**: Full sun.

146. Kinshi-nanten. 琴絲南天. Thin-leaf nandina. *N. domestica* Thunb. var. *capillaris* Makino. **Type**: S Egr BL FR. **Use**: *18 28* Min. **Way**: Cut, Div(2),

Grf(3). **Pot**: sprg. **Trim**: C. **Note**: Half shade.

Kinzu. *See* 143(a) Kinkan.

147. Kiri. 桐, 白桐. Royal paulownia. *P. tomentosa* Kanitz. **Type**: T Dec BL *FL* FR. **Use**: 2 3 17 18. **Way**: Lay(1), Seed. **Pot**: sprg. **Trim**: D. **Wire**: late sprg to sumr. **Note**: Full sun; half shade in sumr; water often.

148. Kirishima-tsutsuji. 霧島躑躅. Kirishima azalea. *Rhododendron obtusum* Planch.; *A. obtusa* Lindl. **Type**: S Egr BL FL. **Use**: *2–5 13 14 17 18 19 20 21 28 30 32* Min. **Way**: Cut, Lay(2), Div(2), Seed. **Pot**: late each sprg, after flowering. **Trim**: D. **Wire**: any time, no water half day before. **Note**: Half shade; water often; watch for scale on trunk; keep warm in wntr.

149. Ki-sokei; *see also* 224 Ōbai, 280 Sokei. 黄素馨. Jonquil-scented jasmine. *Jasminum odoratissimum* L. **Type**: S Egr BL FL. **Use**: *2–5 13* 17 18. **Way**: Cut, Lay(2), Div(2). **Pot**: late sprg. **Trim**: E; quickly cut off new shoots at base of trunk. **Wire**: late sprg to sumr, paper wrap. **Note**: Full sun; keep warm in wntr.

Kita-goyōmatsu. 北五葉松. *See* 62 Goyō-matsu.

150. Ki-zuta (Fuyu-zuta). 〔常春藤〕. Hedera ivy. *H. rhombea* Sieb. et Zucc.; *H. japonica* Tobler; *H. toblerii* Nakai. **Type**: V Egr BL. **Use**: 3 4 5 13 14 Min. **Way**: Cut, Lay(3). **Pot**: sprg. **Trim**: C. **Wire**: any time. **Note**: Full sun; water often.

Koba-no-hagi. *See* 89 Hime-hagi.

151. Kobushi; *see also* 91 Hime-kobushi. 辛夷. Kobus magnolia. *M. kobus* DC. **Type**: S Dec BL FL. **Use**: *2–5 13 17* 18. **Way**: Lay(1), Div(2). **Pot**: once a yr, early sprg or just after flowering season or early autm. **Trim**: D. **Wire**: sprg to sumr. **Note**: Full sun; water often.

Kō-chōki. *See* 68 Haku-chōge.

152. Ko-demari. 小手毬, 麻葉繍球. Reeves spiraea. *S. cantoniensis* Lour.; *S. reevesiana* Lindl. **Type**: S Dec BL FL. **Use**: *2–5 13 14 17 18 30 32*. **Way**: Div (1, 2), Cut. **Pot**: sprg. **Trim**: E. **Note**: Full sun.

153. Ko-fuji (Hime-fuji, Mekura-fuji). 小藤, 盲藤, 姫藤. Dwarf wisteria. *Millettia japonica* A.Gray var. *microphylla* Makino. **Type**: V Dec BL. **Use**: *2–5 13 14 17 18 21 22 30* Min. **Way**: Div(4), Cut, Lay(3). **Pot**: sprg. **Trim**: C. **Wire**: late sprg to autm. **Note**: Full sun; water often.

Kogane-shida. 黄金羊歯. *See* 136 Kata-hiba.

154. Koke-momo. 苔桃. Dwarf mossberry. *Vaccinium vitis-idaea* L. **Type**: G Egr BL Pe AP FR. **Use**: *14 30 32* Gr. **Way**: Nat, Div(2), Cut. **Pot**: every 3rd yr. **Note**: Full sun.

155. Koke-rindō. 苔龍膽. Moss gentian. *Gentiana squarrosa* Ledeb. **Type**: G Bi FL. **Use**: *14 30 32*. **Way**: Nat. **Note**: Half shade.

Kokuchiku. 黒竹. *See* 173 Kuro-chiku.

156. Ko-kuchinashi; *see also* 166 Kuchinashi. 小梔子. Dwarf gardenia. *G. radicans* Thunb. **Type**: S Egr BL FL FR. **Use**: *2–5 8 13 17 18 22–27*. **Way**: Cut, Lay(2), Div(1). **Pot**: late sprg. **Trim**: E. **Wire**: sprg to sumr, paper wrap. **Note**: Full sun; water often; keep warm in wntr; watch for caterpillars & aphids.

157. Kome-tsuga. 米栂. Hemlock. *Tsuga diversifolia* Mast.; *T. sieboldii* Carr. var. *nana* Carr. **Type**: T Egr NE. **Use**: *1 2 3 17 18* 20–28 30. **Way**: Nat, Cut. **Pot**: sprg. **Trim**: A. **Wire**: any time except while new shoots emerge. **Note**: Half shade.

158. Kome-tsutsuji. 米躑躅. Dwarf azalea. *Rhododendron tschonoskii* Maxim. **Type**: S Egr BL FL. **Use**: *3–6 11 13 14 18–21 28 30 32* Min. **Way**: Nat, Cut, Lay(2). **Pot**: late sprg, after flowering. **Trim**: D. **Wire**: any time, no water half day before. **Noet**: Half shade; water often.

159. Ko-nara (Nara). 枹, 橳. Oak. *Quercus serrata* Thunb.; *Q. glandulifera* Blume. **Type**: T Dec BL FR. **Use**: *2–4 17 18*. **Way**: Lay(1), Div(2), Seed. **Pot**: sprg. **Trim**: D. **Wire**: any time except wntr. **Note**: Full sun; half shade in sumr.

Ko-natsutsubaki. *See* 97 Hime-shara.

160. Konote-gashiwa. 側柏, 柏, 栢. Oriental arborvita. *Thuja orientalis* L. **Type**: T Egr NE. **Use**: *1 2 13 22–26*. **Way**: Cut, Lay(1). **Pot**: sprg or autm. **Trim**: B. **Wire**: any time. **Note**: Full sun; water-spray foliage sprg to sumr; watch for red spiders.

161. Kōrai-shiba. 高麗芝, 結縷草. Lawn grass. *Zoysia matrella* Merr. var. *tenuifolia* Dur. et Schinz.; *Z. tenuifolia* Wild. **Type**: G Egr NE(soft). **Use**: *14 30 32* Gr. **Way**: Div(3). **Pot**: Full sun; half shade in sumr; keep warm in wntr.

162. Korin-kuchinashi; *see also* 166 Kuchinashi. Dwarf gardenia. *G. jasminoides* Ellis. **Type**: S Egr BL FL FR. **Use**: *2–5 8 13 17 18 22–27*. **Way**: Cut, Lay(2), Div(1). **Pot**: late sprg. **Trim**: E. **Wire**: sprg to sumr, paper wrap. **Note**: Full sun; water often; keep warm in wntr; watch for caterpillars & aphids.

Kō-sanzashi. 紅山査子. *See* 246 Sanzashi.

163. Kōshin-bara; *see also* Bara. 庚申薔薇, 月季花, 長春花. Indian rose; Chinese rose. *Rosa chinensis* Jaquin. **Type**: V Egr BL FL. **Use**: *2–5 17 18 30 32* Min. **Way**: Cut, Div(3). **Pot**: early sprg or autm. **Trim**: E; immediately cut off new shoots at base of trunk. **Wire**: any time. **Note**: Full sun; keep warm in wntr; watch for aphids & scale.

164. Koshōbai. Dwarf Ilex. *I. serrata* Thunb. var. *subtilis* Loes. **Type**: S Dec BL FR DIO. **Use**: *2–5 13 14 17 18 30* Min. **Way**: Cut, Lay(1), Seed. **Pot**: early sprg. **Trim**: E. **Wire**: sprg to sumr. **Note**: Full sun; water often; female plant preferable; not very suitable for other than miniature use.

Kotoneastā. *See* 21 Beni-shitan.

Kotori-tomarazu. *See* 275 Shōbyaku.

Ko-tsukubaneutsugi. *See* 313 Tsukubaneutsugi.

165. Kōya-maki (Hon maki). 高野槇. Umbrella pine. *Sciadopitys verticillata* Sieb. et Zucc. **Type**: T Egr NE DIO. **Use**: *1-3 9 10 17* 18. **Way**: Cut, Lay(1). **Pot**: late sprg. **Trim**: B. **Wire**: any time. **Note**: Full sun.

Kōyō-zuta. *See* 212 Natsu-zuta.

166. Kuchinashi; *see also* 156 Ko-kuchinashi, 162 Korin-kuchinashi, 329 Yae-kuchinashi. 梔子花, 梔子, 巵子. Cape gardenia. *G. jasminoides* Ellis var. *grandiflora* Nakai; *G. florida* L. **Type**: S Egr BL FL FR. **Use**: *2-5* 8 13 17 *18* 22-27. **Way**: Cut, Lay(2), Div(1). **Pot**: late sprg. **Trim**: E. **Wire**: sprg to sumr, paper wrap. **Note**: Full sun; water often; keep warm in wntr; watch for caterpillars & aphids.

167. Kujaku-hiba. Kujaku cypress. *Chamaecyparis obtusa* Sieb. et Zucc. var. *filisoides* Mast. **Type**: T Egr NE. **Use**: *18 30*. **Way**: Cut, Lay(1). **Pot**: any time. **Trim**: B. **Wire**: any time. **Note**: Full sun.

168. Kuko. 拘杞. Boxthorn. *Lycium chinense* Mill. **Type**: S Dec BL FR. **Use**: *2 3-5 13 18*. **Way**: *Nat*, Cut, Div(3). **Pot**: late sprg. **Trim**: E. **Wire**: *late sprg to sumr*. **Note**: Full sun.

169. Kuma-shide (Shide); *see also* 5 Aka-shide, 115 Inu-shide. Hornbeam. *Carpinus carpinoides* Makino; *C. carpinus* Sarg.; *C. distegocarpus* Koidz.; *C. japonica* Bl.; *Distegocarpus carpinoides* Sieb. et Zucc. **Type**: T Dec BL FL FR. **Use**: *2 3 4-6 13* 17 18 22-27. **Way**: Nat, Cut, Lay(2), Seed. **Pot**: early sprg. **Trim**: D. **Wire**: sprg to sumr. **Note**: Full sun; half shade in sumr.

170. Kuma-zasa; *see also* Sasa. 熊笹. Bear bamboo; dwarf bamboo. *Sasa albo-marginata* Makino et Shibata. **Type**: G Egr BL Pe. **Use**: *14 30-32*. MinDw. **Way**: Div(5). **Pot**: late each sprg. **Trim**: pull out central bud; early sumr, cut all stems at base. **Note**: Half shade; water often; watch for scale.

171. Kurama-goke (Eizan-goke). 鞍馬苔. Kurama moss. *Selaginella japonica* Miq.; *S. remotifolia* Spr. var. *japonica* Koidz. **Type**: G Egr NE(soft) Pe. **Use**: *14 30-32* Gr MinDw. **Way**: Div(3), Cut. **Note**: Half shade.

172. Kuri. 栗. Japanese chestnut. *Castanea puvinervis* Schneid. **Type**: T Dec BL FR. **Use**: *2-4 17* 18 19. **Way**: Nat, Grf(3), Seed. **Pot**: sprg. **Trim**: E. **Wire**: sprg to autm. **Note**: Full sun.

Kurobe. *See* 215 Nezuko.

173. Kuro-chiku (Kokuchiku). 黒竹. Black bamboo. *Phyllostachys nigra* Munro; *Bambusa nigra* Munro; *Sinoarundinaria nigra* Ohwi. **Type**: G Egr Pe. **Use**: *14 18 32*. **Way**: Div(5). **Pot**: late sprg. **Trim**: pull out central bud; LT early sumr. **Note**: Half shade; keep warm in wntr; watch for scale.

174. Kuro-ezomatsu; *see also* 3 Aka-ezomatsu. 黒蝦夷松, 蝦夷松. Black Ezo spruce; Edo spruce; Yedo spruce; Yesso spruce. *Picea jezoensis* Carr.; *P. ajanensis* Fisch. **Type**: T Egr NE. **Use**: *1-7 9 10 13 14 17-30* 32. **Way**: Nat, Cut, Seed, Lay(1). **Pot**: sprg or early autm; keep in shade a wk after. **Trim**: B, once or twice a season, leaving few new needles at base. **Wire**: autm to wntr; do not twist too much. **Note**: Full sun; water-spray foliage sprg to autm.

175. Kuro-matsu (O-matsu). 黒松, 男松. Japanese black pine. *Pinus thunbergii* Parl. **Type**: T Egr NE. **Use**: *1-5 12-14 17-30* Min. **Way**: Nat, Seed, Grf (1, 2). **Pot**: sprg or autm. **Trim**: A; G. **Wire**: any time except while new buds soft. **Note**: Full sun & wind; keep somewhat dry; watch for aphids; well resists sea winds.

176. Kuro-umemodoki; *see also* 322 Umemodoki. 黒落霜紅, 鼠李. Rhamnus. *R. japonica* Maxim. **Type**: S Dec BL FR DIO. **Use**: *2 3 4 5 13 17 18*. **Way**: Cut, Lay(1), Nat. **Pot**: sprg. **Trim**: D. **Wire**: sprg. **Note**: Full sun; water often; female plant preferable.

177. Kurume-tsutsuji. 久留米躑躅. Kurume azalea. *Rhododendron kiusianum* Makino. **Type**: S Egr BL FL. **Use**: *2-5 13 14 17 18 19 20 21 28 30 32*. **Way**: Cut, Lay(2), Div(2). **Pot**: late sprg after flowers finished. **Trim**: D. **Wire**: sprg to autm; no water half day before. **Note**: Half shade; water often.

Kusa-boke. *See* 276 Shudome.

Kusa-maki. *See* 114 Inu-maki.

Kusa-tsuge. *See* 99 Hime-tsuge.

178. Kusu-no-ki. 樟. Camphor. *Cinnamomum camphora* Sieb. **Type**: T Egr BL. **Use**: *2 3 17* 18. **Way**: Nat, Seed, Lay(1). **Pot**: late sprg. **Trim**: C. **Wire**: any time except wntr. **Note**: Full sun; keep warm in wntr.

179. Kuwa. 桑. Mulberry. *Morus alba* L. **Type**: S Dec BL FR. **Use**: *2-5 13 17* 18. **Way**: Cut, Lay (2). **Pot**: sprg. **Trim**: E. **Wire**: sprg to sumr, paper wrap. **Note**: Full sun; water often.

180. Kyaraboku. 伽羅木. Umbrella yew; taxus. *T. cuspidata* Sieb. et Zucc. var. *umbraculifera* Makino; *T. adpressa* Gord.; *T. cuspidata* Sieb. et Zucc. var. *nana* Rehd. **Type**: S Egr NE DIO. **Use**: *1-3 17* 18. **Way**: Cut, Lay(2), Div(1). **Pot**: sprg. **Trim**: B. **Wire**: any time except when new buds soft. **Note**: Full sun.

— M —

Maki. 槇. *See* 114 Inu-maki.

181. Mame-gaki (Shinano-gaki). 君遷子. Date plum. *Diospyros lotus* L. **Type**: T Dec BL FR. **Use**: *2-5 13 17* 18 Min. **Way**: Grf(3), Lay(1). **Pot**: late each sprg. **Trim**: D. **Wire**: sprg to sumr, paper wrap. **Note**: Full sun; water often.

Mame-zakura. 豆櫻. *See* 53 Fuji-zakura.

182. Mame-zuta. 豆苔. Round moss; drymoglossum.

D. microphyllum C.Chr.; *Lemmaphyllum microphyllum* Presl. **Type**: G Egr Pe. **Use**: *14 30 32* Gr. **Way**: Div(5), Nat. **Note**: Half shade; grown on a rock.

183. Manryō. 萬兩. Coral ardisia. *A. crispa* A.DC. **Type**: S Egr BL FR. **Use**: *18 31*. **Way**: Cut, Div (2), Seed. **Pot**: sprg. **Trim**: C. **Note**: Half shade.

184. Mansaku. 金縷梅. Japanese witch-hazel. *Hama melis japonica* Sieb. et Zucc. **Type**: S Dec BL FL. **Use**: *2–5 13 18*. **Way**: Cut, Lay(2), Nat. **Pot**: early sprg. **Trim**: D. **Wire**: sprg. **Note**: Full sun.

Maruba-nezumimochi. *See* 55 Fukuro-mochi.

185. Marumero. 榲桲. Common quince. *Cydonia oblonga* Mill.; *C. vulgaris* Pers. **Type**: T Dec BL FL FR. **Use**: *2–5 17 18 20 21*. **Way**: Lay(1), Seed. **Pot**: sprg. **Trim**: D. **Wire**: sprg. **Note**: Full sun.

186. Mayumi; *see also* 315 Tsuribana-mayumi. 眞弓, 山錦木. Japanese spindle; Japanese strawberry-bush. *Euonymus sieboldiana* Blume. **Type**: S Dec BL FR. **Use**: *2–6 17 18 20 21 30 32*. **Way**: Cut, Lay(2), Seed, Nat. **Pot**: sprg. **Trim**: E. **Wire**: sprg to sumr. **Note**: Full sun.

Megi. 蘗木. *See* 275 Shōbyaku.

Mekura-fuji. 盲藤. *See* 153 Ko-fuji.

Me-matsu. 女松. *See* 4 Aka-matsu.

Me-mukunoki. *See* 46 Enoki.

187. Mikan. 蜜柑. Mandarin orange. *Citrus deliciosa* Tenore.; *C. unshiu* Marcov. **Type**: T Egr BL FR. **Use**: *2–5 17 18 20 21*. **Way**: Cut, Lay(1), Grf(3). **Pot**: late sprg. **Trim**: E. **Wire**: late sprg to sumr, paper wrap. **Note**: Water often; keep very warm in wntr; watch for scale.

188. Mine-zuhō. Loiseleuria. *L. procumbens* Desv.; *Azalea procumbens* L. **Type**: S Egr BL FL AP. **Use**: *14 32* Gr Min. **Way**: Nat, Div(3), Cut. **Pot**: every 3rd yr. **Note**: Half shade.

Misumisō. *See* 337 Yukiwarisō.

Miyama-azumagiku. *See* 18 Azuma-giku.

Miyama-byakushin. 深山柏槇. *See* 269 Shimpaku.

189. Miyama-kaidō (Zumi); *see also* 73 Hana-kaidō. 深山海棠, 三葉海棠, 棠梨. Wild crab-apple. *Malus toringo* Sieb.; *M. sieboldii* Rehd.; *Pyrus sieboldii* Regel.; *P. toringo* Sieb. **Type**: T Dec BL FL *FR*. **Use**: *2–5 13 17 18*. **Way**: Lay(1), Div(5), Grf(3), Seed. **Pot**: once a yr, early sprg or in autm. **Trim**: D. **Wire**: sprg to autm. **Note**: Full sun; water often; watch for aphids all through growing season.

190. Miyama-kirishima. 深山霧島. Dwarf azalea. *Rhododendron kiusianum* Makino. **Type**: S Egr BL FL. **Use**: *2–5 13 14 17 18 19 20 21 28 30 32* Min. **Way**: Cut, Lay(2), Div(2). **Pot**: late each sprg after flowering season. **Trim**: D. **Wire**: any time, no water half day before. **Note**: Half shade; water often; keep warm in wntr.

191. Miyama-odamaki. 深山苧環. Columbine. *Aquilegia akitensis* Huth. **Type**: G Dec BL FL Pe. **Use**: *32*. **Way**: Seed, Div(5), Nat. **Pot**: each sprg. **Note**: Full sun; half shade in sumr

192. Miyama-rindō. 深山龍膽. Alpine gentian. *Gentiana nipponica* Maxim. **Type**: G Dec BL FL Pe. **Use**: *31 32*. **Way**: Div(5), Nat. **Pot**: each sprg. **Note**: Half shade.

193. Miyama-usuyukisō (Hime-usuyukisō). Edelweiss. *Leontopodium alpinum* Cass. var. *fauriei* Beaun. **Type**: G Dec BL FL Pe AP. **Use**: *14 32* Min. **Way**: Div(5), Nat. **Pot**: every 3rd yr. **Note**: Half shade.

194. Mizuki. 水木, 橙台木. Controversa dogwood. *Cornus controversa* Hemsl. **Type**: T Dec BL FL. **Use**: *2 3 13 17 18*. **Way**: Div(2), Lay(1). **Pot**: sprg. **Trim**: D. **Wire**: sprg to autm, paper wrap. **Note**: Full sun; half shade in sumr.

195. Mokkō-bara (Sudare-bara, Ki-mokkōbara). 木香花, 木香薔薇, 黃木香薔薇. (a) Banksia rose. *Rosa banksiae* R.Brown var. *albo-plena* Rehder. (b) Yellow banksia rose. *R. banksiae* R.Brown. var. *lutea* Lindl. **Type**: V Dec BL FL. **Use**: *2–5 13 17 18*. **Way**: Cut, Lay(2), Div(5). **Pot**: early each sprg. **Trim**: E; after flowering finished, cut back all twigs. **Wire**: any time in growing season. **Note**: Full sun; manure well; water often; watch for aphids on new buds.

Mokuren. 木蘭. *See* 69 Haku-mokuren, 151 Kobushi, 267 Shi-mokuren.

Mokusei. 木犀. *See* 61 Gin-mokusei, 144 Kin-mokusei.

196. Momi; *see also* 76 Hari-momi. 樅. Momi fir. *Abies firma* Sieb. et Zucc. **Type**: T Egr NE. **Use**: *1–3 13 17 18 22–28*. **Way**: Nat, Cut, Lay(1). **Pot**: sprg. **Trim**: A. **Wire**: any time except when new buds soft. **Note**: Half shade; water-spray sprg to sumr.

Momiji. 楓. *See* 34 Chishio-momiji, 223 Nomura-kaede, 252 Seigen-momiji, 332 Yama-momiji.

197. Momo. 桃. Peach. *Prunus persica* Batsch.; *Amygdalus persica* L.; *Persica vulgaris* Mill. **Type**: T Dec BL FL FR. **Use**: *2–5 17 18 20 21*. **Way**: Lay(1), Grf(3), Seed. **Pot**: each sprg. **Trim**: D. **Wire**: sprg to sumr. **Note**: Full sun; manure well; watch for borers.

198. Mōsō-chiku. 猛宗竹. Heavy-stem bamboo. *Bambusa edulis* Carr.; *Phyllostachys edulis* A. et C. Riv.; *P. mitis* A. et C.Riv. **Type**: G Egr Pe. **Use**: *2 13 14 18 22–27 32*. **Way**: Div(5). **Pot**: late every 2nd sprg. **Trim**: pull out central new bud. **Note**: Half shade; water often; keep warm in wntr; watch for scale & aphids.

199. Mube (Tokiwa-akebi); *see also* 6 Akebi. 郁子, 木通, 常盤木通. Stauntonia. *S. hexaphylla* Dcne **Type**: V Egr BL FR. **Use**: *2 3 4 5 13*. **Way**: Lay(3, 2), Cut. **Pot**: each sprg. **Trim**: D. **Wire**: any time except wntr. **Note**: Full sun; water often.

200. Mukuge (Hachisu). 木槿. Shrub althea. *Hibiscus syriacus* L. **Type:** S Dec BL FL. **Use:** *2* 3 *17 18.* **Way:** Cut, Lay(2). **Pot:** each sprg. **Trim:** E. **Wire:** any time except wntr, paper wrap. **Note:** Full sun; water often.

201. Murasaki-hashidoi. Common lilac. *Syringa vulgaris* L. **Type:** S Dec BL FL. **Use:** *2–5* 13 *14 18 20 21 30.* **Way:** Cut, Div(1, 2), Lay(2). **Pot:** sprg. **Trim:** E; immediately cut off new shoots growing from base of trunk. **Wire:** sprg to sumr. **Note:** Full sun.

202. Murasakishikibu (Ko-murasakishikibu). 紫式部. Callicarpa. *C. dichotoma* Raeus.; *C. purpurea* Juss.; *C. gracilis* Sieb. et Zucc.; *Porphyra dichotoma* Lour. **Type:** S Dec BL FR. **Use:** *2–5 18 20 21 30.* **Way:** Div(1, 2), Lay(1). **Pot:** sprg. **Trim:** D. **Wire:** sprg to sumr, paper wrap. **Note:** Full sun.

Mure-suzume. *See* 142 Kin-jakka.

Muro. *See* 306 Toshō.

— N —

Nadeshiko. *See* 137 Kawara-nadeshiko.

Nagasaki-ringo. *See* 73 Hana-kaidō, 94 Hime-ringo.

203. Nagi. 梛, 竹柏. Japanese podocarpus. *P. nagi* Zoll. et Moritzi.; *Myrica nagi* Thunb.; *P. nageia* R. Br. **Type:** T Egr NE DIO. **Use:** *1 2 17 18.* **Way:** Cut, Lay(1). **Pot:** late sprg. **Trim:** B. **Wire:** sprg to sumr. **Note:** Half shade; keep warm in wntr.

204. Nana-kamado. 七竈. Japanese mountain ash. *Sorbus commixta* Hedlund.; *S. japonica* Koehne non Sieb. **Type:** S Dec BL FL. **Use:** *3–5* 17 *18 20 21.* **Way:** Cut, Lay(2). **Pot:** sprg. **Trim:** E. **Wire:** sprg to sumr. **Note:** Full sun; half shade in sumr.

Nankin-haze. *See* 320 Ukyū.

205. Nanten. 南天, 南天竹. Common nandina. *N. domestica* Thunb. **Type:** S Egr BL FR. **Use:** *18 30 31.* **Way:** Cut, Div(2), Grf(3), Seed. **Pot:** sprg. **Trim:** C. **Note:** Half shade.

206. Nanten-giri (Ii-giri). 南天桐, 椅. Idesia. *I. polycarpa* Maxim. **Type:** T Dec BL FR. **Use:** *2–5 17 18.* **Way:** Lay(1), Div(2), Seed. **Pot:** sprg. **Trim:** D. **Wire:** sprg to sumr. **Note:** Full sun; half shade in sumr; water often.

Nara. *See* 159 Ko-nara. 楢.

207. Nashi. 梨. Sand pear. *Pyrus simonii* Carr. **Type:** T Dec BL FL *FR.* **Use:** *2–5 17 18.* **Way:** Lay(1), Grf(3), Seed. **Pot:** early sprg. **Trim:** D. **Wire:** sprg to sumr. **Note:** Full sun; half shade in sumr; water often; watch for mildew & caterpillars.

208. Natsu-fuji (Doyō-fuji, Sakkō-fuji). 夏藤, 醋甲藤, 土用藤. Japanese millettia. *M. japonica* A. Gray. **Type:** V Egr BL *FL* FR. **Use:** *2–5 13 17* 18. **Way:** Cut, Lay(2), Div(4), Grf(3), Seed. **Pot:** early sprg.

Trim: D. **Wire:** sprg to sumr. **Note:** Water often even in wntr; in sumr keep in water basin; full sun; manure well; watch for borers.

209. **(a)** Natsu-gumi (Gumi, 〔Nawashiro-gumi〕). 木半夏. Elaeagnus. *E. multiflora* Thunb. **Type:** S Dec BL FR. **(b)** Nawashiro-gumi (Gumi, 〔Natsu-gumi〕). 胡頽子. Thorny elaeagnus. *E. pungens* Thunb. **Type:** S Egr BL FR. **Use:** *2–5 13 17* 18. **Way:** Cut, Lay(2), Seed. **Pot:** early sprg. **Trim:** D. **Wire:** sprg to sumr. **Note:** Full sun; water often; watch for borers.

210. Natsume. 棗. Jujube. *Zizyphus jujuba* Mill. var. *inermis* Rehd. **Type:** S Dec BL FR. **Use:** *2 3 4 5 13 17 18.* **Way:** Cut, Div(2), Lay(1), Seed. **Pot:** early sprg. **Trim:** D. **Wire:** sprg to sumr. **Note:** Full sun; water often.

211. Natsu-tsubaki (Shara-no-ki); *see also* 97 Hime-shara. 夏椿, 娑羅樹. Japanese stewartia. *S. pseudo-camellia* Maxim. **Type:** T Dec BL FL. **Use:** *2 3 13 17* 18. **Way:** Cut, Lay(1). **Pot:** early sprg. **Trim:** D. **Wire:** sprg to sumr, paper wrap. **Note:** Full sun; water often.

212. Natsu-zuta (Tsuta, Kōyō-zuta). 地錦, 蔦, 常春藤, 紅葉蔦. Boston ivy; Japanese ivy; Japanese creeper. *Parthenocissus thunbergii* Nakai; *Ampelopsis tricuspidata* Planch.; *P. tricuspidata* Planch. **Type:** V Dec BL. **Use:** 2 3 *4 5* 13 17 18 Min. **Way:** Cut, Lay(3, 2), Grf(3), Seed. **Pot:** early sprg. **Trim:** C; LT. **Wire:** sprg to sumr except while leaves soft. **Note:** Full sun; half shade in sumr; water-spray leaves in sumr; watch for caterpillars.

Nawashiro-gumi. *See* 209 Natsu-gumi.

213. Nemu (Gōkamboku). 合歡木. Silk; albizzia. *A. julibrissin* Dur. **Type:** S Dec BL FL. **Use:** *2 3 4 5 13 17 18.* **Way:** Cut, Div(2). **Pot:** late sprg. **Trim:** E. **Wire:** sprg to sumr. **Note:** Full sun; keep warm in wntr.

214. Ne-zasa; *see also* Sasa. 根笹. Dwarf bamboo; sharp-leafed dwarf bamboo. *Pleioblastus variegatus* Mak. var. *viridis* Mak. f. **Type:** G Egr Pe. **Use:** 14 *30–32* Gr Min. **Way:** Div(5). **Pot:** late sprg. **Trim:** pull out central new shoot; cut back all stems at base twice, sprg to sumr. **Note:** Half shade; water often; watch for scale.

Nezu. *See* 306 Toshō.

215. Nezuko (Kurobe). 檔. Thuja. *T. standishii* Carr.; *T. gigantea* Parl. var. *japonica* Franch. et Sav.; *T. japonica* Maxim. **Type:** T Egr NE. **Use:** *1* 2 3 17 18. **Way:** Cut, Lay(1), Nat. **Pot:** any time except wntr. **Trim:** B. **Wire:** any time. **Note:** Full sun.

216. Nindō (Suikazura). 多忍. Japanese honeysuckle. *Lonicera japonica* Thunb. **Type:** V Dec BL FL. **Use:** 2 3 *4 5* 17 18. **Way:** Cut, Lay(3, 2). **Pot:** early sprg. **Trim:** E. **Wire:** sprg to sumr. **Note:** Full sun.

Nire. 楡. *See* 7 Aki-nire, 77 Haru-nire.

Nire-geyaki. 楡欅. *See* 7 Aki-nire.

217. Nise-akashia (Gigōkan, [Akashia], Hari-enju, Inu-akashia). 擬合歓. Locust; common locust; false acacia. *Robinia pseudo-acacia* L. **Type:** S Dec FL. **Use:** *2 3 17 18.* **Way:** Cut, Lay(2), Div(2). **Pot:** sprg. **Trim:** E **Wire:** sprg to sumr. **Note:** Full sun.

218. Nishikigi. 衛矛, 鬼箭, 錦木. Winged euonymus; winged spindle. *E. alata.* Sieb. **Type:** S Dec BL FR. **Use:** 1 *2–6* 12 *13 14 17 18* 20 21 *30 32.* **Way:** Cut, Lay(2), Seed. **Pot:** sprg. **Trim:** E. **Wire:** sprg to sumr. **Note:** Full sun.

219. Nishiki-matsu. 錦松. Nishiki black pine; corticata pine. *Pinus thunbergii* Parl. var. *corticosa* Makino. **Type:** T Egr NE. **Use:** 1 *2–6 13 14 17* 18 20 21. **Way:** Grf(1, 2). **Pot:** sprg or early autm. **Trim:** A & G. **Wire:** autm to wntr. **Note:** Full sun; keep somewhat dry; resistant to sea winds; be careful not to damage rough bark on lower trunk.

220. Nishiki-zuta. 錦蔦. English ivy; common ivy. *Hedera helix* L. var. *tricolor* Hibberd. **Type:** V Dec BL. **Use:** *2 3 4 5* 13 17 18 Min. **Way:** Cut, Lay (3, 2), Grf(3), Seed. **Pot:** sprg. **Trim:** C. **Wire:** any time, paper wrap. **Note:** Half shade; water often; keep warm in wntr.

221. Niwa-ume. 郁李. Japanese single bush-cherry. *Prunus japonica* Thunb. **Type:** S Dec BL FL FR. **Use:** *2* 17 *18.* **Way:** Cut, Div(2), Lay(2). **Pot:** early sprg. **Trim:** D. **Wire:** sprg. **Note:** Full sun; water often.

222. Niwa-zakura. 多葉郁李. Japanese double bush-cherry. *Prunus japonica* Thunb. var. *multiplex* Makino. **Note:** Data same as for 221 above.

No-bara. 野薔薇. *See* 335 Yashōbi.

No-boke. 野木瓜. *See* 276 Shudome.

Noda-fuji. 野田藤. *See* 52 Fuji.

223. Nomura-kaede (Nomura-momiji). 野村楓, 野村槭. Japanese red maple. *Acer palmatum* Thunb. **Type:** T Dec BL. **Use:** *2 3–5* 13 17 18 20–29. **Way:** Seed, Grf(4, 3), Lay(1). **Pot:** early sprg. **Trim:** C; LT. **Wire:** late sprg, paper wrap; branches break easily. **Note:** Full sun; half shade in sumr; protect from strong winds; watch for aphids on new shoots in sprg.

— O —

224. Ōbai. 黄梅, 迎春花. Winter jasmine; naked-flower jasmine. *Jasminum nudiflorum* Lindl. **Type:** S(vinelike) Dec BL FL. **Use:** *2–5* 12–14 17 18 20 21. **Way:** Cut, Lay(2, 3), Div(2). **Pot:** early sprg. **Trim:** D; immediately cut off new shoots growing from base of trunk. **Wire:** sprg to sumr, paper wrap; branches break easily. **Note:** Half shade in sumr; water often; keep warm in wntr.

225. Ogatama-no-ki. [黄心樹]. Michelia. *M. com-*

pressa Maxim.; *Magnolia compressa* Maxim. **Type:** T Egr BL FL. **Use:** *2 3 4 5* 17 18. **Way:** Cut, Lay(2). **Pot:** late sprg. **Trim:** D. **Wire:** any time except wntr. **Note:** Full sun; water often; keep warm in wntr.

226. Ogi. 荻. Reed. *Miscanthus sacchariflorus* Benth. et Hook.; *Imperata sacchariflora* Maxim. **Type:** G Egr Pe. **Use:** 4 *5* 14 32. **Way:** Cut, Div(3). **Pot:** every 2nd yr. **Note:** Always keep damp & in full shade; keep warm in wntr.

227. Okame-zasa. 笹. Oval-leafed bamboo; dwarf bamboo. *Shibataea kumasasa* Makino; *Bambusa kumasasa* Zoll.; *Phyllostachys kumasasa* Munro. **Type:** G Egr Pe. **Use:** 14 30–32. **Way:** Div(5). **Pot:** late sprg. **Trim:** pull out central new shoot. **Note:** Half shade; always keep damp; keep warm in wntr; watch for scale.

O-matsu. 男松. *See* 175 Kuro-matsu.

228. Ominaeshi. 黄花龍芽, 女郎花, [敗醬]. Patrinia. *P. scabiosaefolia* Link. **Type:** G Dec Pe BL FL. **Use:** *31.* **Way:** Nat, Cut, Div(3). **Note:** Half shade.

229. Omoto. 萬年青. Rhodea. *R. japonica* Roth. **Type:** G Egr BL FR. **Use:** *32.* **Way:** Div(3), Seed. **Pot:** late each sprg. **Note:** Half shade; keep damp; keep warm in wntr; watch for scale on leaves.

230. Ōmura-tsutsuji (Ōmurasaki). Japanese azalea. *Rhododendron oomurasaki* Makino; *R. pulchrum* Sweet. **Type:** S Egr BL FL. **Use:** *2 3 4 5* 17 *18.* **Way:** Cut, Lay(2), Seed. **Pot:** late each sprg after flowering finished. **Trim:** D. **Wire:** sprg to autm; stop watering half day or day before. **Note:** Half shade; water often; keep warm in wntr; watch for scale on trunk & for caterpillars.

Onkō. *See* 110 Ichii.

231. Oroshima-chiku; *see also* Sasa. 笹. Dwarf bamboo; tiny-leafed bamboo. *Pleioblastus pygmaeus* Nakai var. *disitchus* Nakai. **Type:** G Egr Pe. **Use:** 14 30–32 Gr Min. **Way:** Div(5). **Pot:** late sprg. **Trim:** pull out central new shoot; sprg to sumr cut back all stems twice. **Note:** Half shade; water often; keep warm in wntr; watch for scale at base of leaves & for ants.

— P —

Piracansasu. *See* 289 Tachibanamodoki, 302 Tokiwa-sanzashi.

— R —

232. Rakan-maki. 羅漢槇, 羅漢松. Chinese podocarpus. *P. chinensis* Woll.; *P. macrophylla* D.Don var. *chinensis* Maxim.; *P. maki* Sieb. **Type:** T Egr NE DIO. **Use:** *1–3* 9 10 *17* 18. **Way:** Cut, Lay(1). **Pot:** late sprg. **Trim:** B. **Wire:** any time. **Note:** Full sun; keep warm in wntr.

233. Rakuushō (Amerika-suishō, Hagoromo-matsu). 落羽松, 羽衣松. Bald cypress; deciduous cypress.

Taxodium distichum Rich. **Type:** T Dec NE(soft). **Use:** *1–3* 9 10 *13* 14 *17* 18 22–27. **Way:** Nat, Cut, Lay(1), Seed. **Pot:** late sprg. **Trim:** B. **Wire:** late sprg to sumr. **Note:** Full sun; shade in sumr; always keep damp.

Rakuyōshō. 落葉松. *See* 132 Kara-matsu.

Ran. 蘭. *See* 278 Shun-ran.

234. Renge-tsutsuji. 〔羊躑躅〕. Japanese azalea; Chinese azalea. *Rhododendron molle* G.Don var. *japonicum* Makino; *R. japonicum* Seringe; *R. molle* G.Don. **Type:** S Dec BL FL. **Use:** *2* 3 4 5 *17* 18 19 20 21 28 *32*. **Way:** Nat, Cut, Lay(2), Seed. **Pot:** late sprg after flowering finished. **Trim:** D. **Wire:** late sprg to sumr. **Note:** Half shade.

235. Rengyō. 黃壽丹, 壽丹, 連翹. Golden bellflower; weeping forsythia. *F. suspensa* Vahl.; *Rangium suspensum* Ohwi. **Type:** S Dec BL FL. **Use:** 2 3 4 5 *13* 17 *18* 20 21 32. **Way:** Cut, Lay(3). **Pot:** after flowering finished. **Trim:** D. **Wire:** sprg to sumr. **Note:** Full sun.

236. Rindō. 龍膽. Common gentian. *Gentiana scabra* Bunge var. *buergeri* Maxim. **Type:** G Dec Pe BL FL. **Use:** *31 32*. **Way:** Div(3), Cut, Nat. **Pot:** sprg. **Note:** Half shade.

Ringo. 苹果. *See* 326 Wa-ringo.

237. Rōbai (Kara-ume). 蠟梅. Allspice; winter sweet. *Meratia praecox* Rehd. et Wils. **Type:** S Dec BL FL. **Use:** *2–5* 6 13 *17–21*. **Way:** Cut, Div(2), Lay(1), Nat. **Pot:** after flowers finished. **Trim:** D. **Wire:** sprg to autm. **Note:** Full sun; half shade in sumr.

Rokkakudō-yanagi. 六角堂柳. *See* 264 Shidare-yanagi.

Ryūkyū-haze. *See* 82 Haze-no-ki.

238. Ryūkyū-tsutsuji. 琉球躑躅. Ryukyu azalea. *Rhododendron mucronatum* G.Don. **Type:** S Egr BL FL. **Use:** *2–5 13* 14 17 *18* 19 *20 21* 28 30 *32* Min. **Way:** Cut, Lay(2), Div(2), Seed. **Pot:** yearly after flowers finished. **Trim:** D. **Wire:** sprg to autm; no water half day before. **Note:** Half shade; water often; keep warm in wntr; watch for scale on trunk & for caterpillars.

239. Ryū-no-hige (Bakumontō). 龍鬚, 麥門冬. Ophipogon. *O. japonicus* Ker-Grawl. **Type:** G Egr Pe FL FR. **Use:** *32*. **Way:** Div(3). **Pot:** every 2nd yr. **Note:** Half shade.

— S —

240. Saboten. 仙人掌, 霸王樹. Cactus. *Cactaceae*. **Type:** G Egr Pe FL. **Use:** *30*. **Way:** Cut, Div(3), Grf(1). Seed. **Pot:** every 3 to 5 yrs. **Note:** Keep very dry & very warm.

241. Sagisō. 鷺草. Pecteilis. *P. radiata* Rafin.; *Habenaria radiata* Spreng.; *Orchis radiata* Thunb. **Type:** G Dec Pe FL. **Use:** *31 32*. **Way:** Div(5), Nat. **Pot:** every 3-5 yrs. **Note:** Keep in water basin; half shade.

Saifuriboku. *See* 265 Shide-zakura.

242. Sakaki. 榊. Euryale. *Cleyera ochnacea* DC. **Type:** S Egr BL FR. **Use:** *2* 3 *13* 17 18. **Way:** Cut, Lay(1), Seed. **Pot:** sprg. **Trim:** E. **Wire:** any time. **Note:** Keep in half shade; keep warm in wntr.

Sakkō-fuji. 醋甲藤. *See* 208 Natsu-fuji.

Sakura. 櫻. Cherry. *See* 26 Botan-zakura, 41 Edo-higanzakura, 53 Fuji-zakura (Mame-zakura), 84 Higan-zakura, 131 Kan-zakura, 248 Sato-zakura, 253 Seiyō-mizakura, 263 Shidare-higanzakura (Ito-zakura), 290 Taiwan-hizakura, 334 Yama-zakura.

243. Sakurasō. 櫻草. Primrose. *Primula sieboldii* Morren f. *spontanea* Takeda. **Type:** G Dec Pe BL FL. **Use:** *32*. **Way:** Div(4), Seed. **Pot:** yearly after flowering finished. **Note:** Half shade.

Sane-kazura. *See* 22 Binan-kazura.

Sankaku-kaede. 三角楓. *See* 301 Tō-kaede.

244. Sanshō. 蜀椒. Chinese pepper. *Xanthoxylum piperitum* DC. **Type:** S Dec BL FR DIO. **Use:** *2* 3 4 5 12 *13 17 18* 20 21 Min. **Way:** Seed, Cut, Lay(2). **Pot:** sprg. **Trim:** D. **Wire:** sprg to sumr. **Note:** Full sun; female plant preferable.

245. Sanshuyu. 山茱萸. Japanese cornelian cherry. *Cornus officinalis* Sieb. et Zucc.; *Macrocarpium officinale* Nakai. **Type:** S Dec BL FL FR. **Use:** *2–5 13* 17 *18* 20 21. **Way:** Div(2), Lay(1), Seed. **Pot:** early sprg or early autm. **Trim:** D. **Wire:** sprg to sumr. **Note:** Full sun; half shade in sumr.

246. Sanzashi (Kō-sanzashi); *see also* 254 Seiyō-sanzashi. 山査子, 紅山査子, 山樝. Nippon hawthorn. *Crataegus cuneata* Sieb. et Zucc. **Type:** S Dec BL FL *FR*. **Use:** *2–5 13* 17 18 20 21 30. **Way:** Div(2), Lay(1), Seed. **Pot:** early sprg or early autm. **Trim:** D. **Wire:** sprg to sumr. **Note:** Full sun; half shade in sumr; water often; watch for aphids.

247. Sarasa-renge (Sarasa-mokuren). 紗更蓮華. Magnolia. *M. conspicua* Salisb. var. *purpurascens* Maxim.; *M. purpurascens* Makino. **Type:** T Dec BL FL. **Use:** *2–5 17* 18. **Way:** Div(2), Lay(1). **Pot:** after flowering season. **Trim:** D. **Wire:** sprg to sumr, paper wrap. **Note:** Full sun; half shade in sumr; water often.

Saru-suberi. *See* 103 Hyakujikkō.

Sasa. 笹. Dwarf bamboo. *See* 32 Chigo-zasa, 170 Kuma-zasa, 214 Ne-zasa, 227 Okame-zasa, 231 Oroshima-chiku.

248. Sato-zakura. 里櫻. Flowering cherry. *Prunus lannesiana* Wilson; *P. donarium* Sieb. **Type:** T Dec BL FL. **Use:** *2–6 17–21*. **Way:** Div(2), Grf(3), Lay(1). **Pot:** yearly, early sprg or after flowering or early autm. **Trim:** D. **Wire:** sprg to sumr, paper wrap. **Note:** Full sun; half shade in sumr; water often; manure well; watch for borers & caterpillars.

249. Satsuki-tsutsuji (Satsuki). 皐月, 杜鵑花. Satsuki azalea. *Rhododendron lateritium* Planch. **Type:** S Egr BL FL. **Use:** *1 2–6 9 13 14 17–21 28 30.* **Way:** Cut, Lay(2), Div(2), Seed. **Pot:** late each sprg after flowering finished. **Trim:** D. **Wire:** sprg to sumr; branches break easily so no water half day or day before. **Note:** Half shade; keep warm in wntr; water **often**; watch for scale on trunk.

Satsuma-kongiku. *See* 48 Ezo-giku.

250. Sawara. 椹, 花柏. Sawara cypress; sawara retinospora. *Chamaecyparis pisifera* Endl.; *Cupressus pisifera* K.Koch; *R. pisifera* Sieb. et Zucc. **Type:** T Egr NE. **Use:** *1 13 17 18 22–29* Min. **Way:** Cut, Lay(1), Seed. **Pot:** any time except wntr. **Trim:** B. **Wire:** any time. **Note:** Half shade; water often; watch for red spiders.

251. Sazanka. 山茶花. Sasanqua tea. *Camellia sasanqua* Thunb. **Type:** T Egr BL FL. **Use:** *2–6 13 17 18 19–21.* **Way:** Cut, Lay(2), Seed. **Pot:** late sprg. **Trim:** D. **Wire:** any time; paper wrap. **Note:** Half shade; keep warm in wntr; watch for aphids on new buds.

252. Seigen-momiji; *see also* Momiji. 清玄槭. Japanese red maple. *Acer palmatum* Thunb. **Type:** T Dec BL. **Use:** *2–5 13 17 18 20–29.* **Way:** Seed, Grf(4, 3), Lay(1). **Pot:** sprg. **Trim:** C. **LT** late sprg to early sumr. **Wire:** late sprg to sumr, paper wrap; branches break easily. **Note:** Shade in sumr; in growing season, particularly when in new bud, protect from strong winds; watch for aphids on new buds and backs of leaves.

Seiko-no-ashi. *See* 14 Ashi.

253. Seiyō-mizakura; *see also* Sakura. 櫻桃. Cherry. *Prunus pseudo-cerasus* Lindl. **Type:** T Dec BL FL FR. **Use:** *2–4 6 17 18 19–21.* **Way:** Div(2), Grf(3), Lay(1), Seed. **Pot:** early sprg or after flowering. **Trim:** D. **Wire:** sprg to sumr, paper wrap. **Note:** Full sun; half shade in sumr; water often; manure well; watch for borers & caterpillars.

254. Seiyō-sanzashi; *see also* 246 Sanzashi. 西洋山査子. English hawthorn; common hawthorn; may; maybush. *Crataegus oxyacantha* L. **Type:** S Dec BL FL. **Use:** *2–5 13 17 18 20 21.* **Way:** Div(2), Lay(1), Grf(3). **Pot:** early sprg or early autm. **Trim:** D. **Wire:** sprg to autm. **Note:** Full sun; half shade in sumr; water often; watch for aphids.

255. Seiyō-suguri; *see also* 284 Suguri. 西洋須具利. English gooseberry. *Ribes grossularia* L. **Type:** S Dec BL FR. **Use:** *2–5 13 17 18.* **Way:** Cut, Div(2), Lay(2). **Pot:** each sprg. **Trim:** D. **Wire:** any time. **Note:** Full sun; half shade in sumr; keep warm in wntr.

256. Sekiryū (Jakuro, Zakuro). 石榴, 柘榴, 安石榴. Common pomegranate. *Punica granatum* L. **Type:** T Dec BL FL FR. **Use:** *2–6 13 15 17 18 20 21 22 23.* **Way:** Lay(2), Cut, Div(2), Seed. **Pot:** late sprg. **Trim:** E. **Wire:** late sprg to sumr, paper wrap.

Note: Full sun; half shade in sumr; keep warm in wntr; watch for aphids on new shoots & for caterpillars.

257. Sekishō. 石菖蒲. Dwarf sweet-rush; dwarf sweet-flag. *Acorus gramineus* Soland. **Type:** G Egr Pe. **Use:** *14 30 32.* **Way:** Div(3). **Pot:** late sprg. **Trim:** twice yearly; late sprg to sumr, cut off all leaves at base. **Note:** Full shade; keep always moist; keep warm in wntr.

258. Sekkoku. 石斛. Dendrobium. *D. monile* Kranzl. **Type:** G Egr Pe FL. **Use:** *14 32.* **Way:** Div(3), Nat. **Pot:** late sprg. **Note:** Full shade; not too wet; keep warm; watch for scale.

259. Sennichisō. 千日草, 千日紅. Gomphrena. *G. globosa* L. **Type:** G An BL FL. **Use:** *31.* **Way:** Seed. **Note:** Full sun.

260. Shakunage (Shakunagi); *see also* 70 Hakusan-shakunage, 96 Hime-shakunage, 314 Tsukushi-shakunage. 石南花. Dwarf rhododendron. *R. degronianum* Carr. **Type:** S Egr BL FL. **Use:** *2 3 4 5 17 18 28 32.* **Way:** Nat, Lay(1), Div(2). **Pot:** late every 3rd sprg. **Trim:** D, but not so necessary. **Wire:** sprg to sumr. **Note:** Half shade; keep damp.

261. Shamo-hiba. Shamo cypress. *Chamaecyparis obtusa* Sieb. et Zucc. var. *lycopodioides* Carr. **Type:** T Egr NE. **Use:** *1 2 3 13 14 17 18 30.* **Way:** Cut, Lay(1). **Pot:** any time. **Trim:** B. **Wire:** any time. **Note:** Full sun; half shade in sumr.

Shara-no-ki. 娑羅樹. *See* 211 Natsu-tsubaki.

Sharimbai. *See* 71 Hama-mokkoku.

262. Sharintō (Shitanju). 紫檀樹. Cotoneaster. *C. rotundifolia* Wall. var. *lanata* Schneid. **Type:** S Egr BL FL FR. **Use:** *2–6 12 13 14 17 18 21 22 30 32.* **Way:** Cut, Lay(2), Div(2). **Pot:** any time in growing season. **Trim:** C. **Wire:** any time in growing season. **Note:** Full sun; water often; watch for aphids & scale.

Shida. 羊歯. Fern. *See* 121 Iwa-denda, 129 Kan-shinobu, 136 Kata-hiba (Kogane-shida), 324 Urajiro-shida.

263. Shidare-higanzakura (Ito-zakura); *see also* Sakura. 枝垂彼岸櫻, 糸櫻. Weeping flowering-cherry. *Prunus itosakura* Sieb. **Type:** T Dec BL FL. **Use:** *2–5 17–21 22 23.* **Way:** Div(2), Grf(3), Lay(1), Seed. **Pot:** every 2nd yr, in early sprg or after flowering or in early autm. **Trim:** D. **Wire:** late sprg to autm, paper wrap. **Note:** Full sun; half shade in sumr; water often; manure well; watch for borers & caterpillars.

264. Shidare-yanagi (Yanagi, Rokkakudō-yanagi). 枝垂柳, 六角堂柳. Babylon weeping-willow; weeping willow. *Salix babylonica* L. **Type:** T Dec BL DIO. **Use:** *2–5 13 14 17 32.* **Way:** Cut, Lay(2). **Pot:** early sprg & early sumr. **Trim:** cut back long new shoots only when repotting & in late autm. **Wire:** sprg to sumr, paper wrap; hand-shaping also effective.

Note: Half shade; always keep damp; keep in water basin in sumr; watch for aphids & caterpillars.

Shide. *See* 169 Kuma-shide.

Shide-kobushi. 重華辛夷. *See* 91 Hime-kobushi.

265. Shide-zakura (Zaifuriboku, Saifuriboku). 茱振木, 弊櫻. Japanese Juneberry. *Amelanchier asiatica* Endl. **Type:** T Dec BL FL. **Use:** *2–5* 13 *17* 18 20 21. **Way:** Grf(3), Lay(1). **Pot:** early each sprg. **Trim:** D. **Wire:** late sprg to autm, paper wrap. **Note:** Full sun; water often.

266. Shii. 椎. Japanese chinquapin. *Shiia sieboldii* Makino. **Type:** T Egr BL FR. **Use:** *2 3 17* 18. **Way:** Nat, Lay(1), Seed. **Pot:** sprg. **Trim:** D. **Wire:** any time. **Note:** Half shade; watch for borers.

267. Shi-mokuren; *see also* 69 Haku-mokuren. 紫木蘭, 辛夷. Lily magnolia; Japanese magnolia. *M. liliflora* Desr. **Type:** T Dec BL FL. **Use:** *2–5 17* 18. **Way:** Div(2), Lay(1). **Pot:** after flowering season. **Trim:** D. **Wire:** sprg to autm, paper wrap. **Note:** Full sun; half shade in sumr; water often.

268. Shimotsuke. 下野. Japanese spiraea. *S. japonica* L. **Type:** S Dec BL FL. **Use:** *2–5 18 30 32*. **Way:** Div(2, 3), Cut. **Pot:** sprg. **Trim:** E. **Note:** Full sun; water often; watch for aphids & caterpillars.

269. Shimpaku (Miyama-byakushin); *see also* 108 Ibuki. 眞柏, 檜柏, 深山柏槙. Sargent juniper [Chinese juniper]. *Juniperus chinensis* L. var. *sargentii* Henry; *J. chinensis* L. var. *procumbens* Takeda; *J. sargentii* Takeda. **Type:** T Egr NE DIO. **Use:** *2–7 10 12–15 17 18 20 21 30* Min. **Way:** Nat, Cut, Lay(1). **Pot:** any time except wntr. **Trim:** B. **Wire:** any time, particularly autm to wntr. **Note:** Full sun; water-spray foliage sprg to sumr; watch for red spiders.

Shina-enju. *See* 44 Enju.

Shinano-gaki. *See* 181 Mame-gaki.

270. Shina-tsukubaneutsugi (Tsukubane-utsugi). Chinese abelia. *A. chinensis* R.Brown. **Type:** S Dec BL FL. **Use:** 3–5 17 *18*. **Way:** Div(1), Cut. **Pot:** sprg. **Trim:** E. **Wire:** sprg to autm. **Note:** Full sun.

271. Shinobu-hiba. Shinobu cypress. *Chamaecyparis pisifera* Endl. var. *plumosa* Beissn. **Type:** T Egr NE. **Use:** *1 2 3* 13 14 *17 18 30*. **Way:** Cut, Lay(1). **Pot:** any time except wntr. **Trim:** B. **Wire:** any time. **Note:** Half shade.

272. Shirakaba. 白樺. White birch. *Betula tauschii* Koidz.; *B. alba* L. var. *japonica* Miq.; *B. alba* L. var. *tauschii* DC.; *B. japonica* Sieb. **Type:** T Dec BL. **Use:** 2 3 *17 18* 20 21 *22–29*. **Way:** Nat, Div(2). **Pot:** sprg. **Trim:** C; immediately cut off new shoots from base of trunk. **Wire:** sprg to sumr, paper wrap. **Note:** Full sun; water often.

273. Shira-kashi. 白樫, 鐵橵, 鉤栗. Oak; quercus. *Q. myrsinaefolia* Blume. **Type:** T Egr BL FR. **Use:**

2 3 17 18. **Way:** Nat, Seed. **Pot:** sprg. **Trim:** E. **Wire:** any time. **Note:** Half shade.

Shiro-buna. *See* 28(a) Buna.

Shiro-chiku. 棕櫚竹. *See* 279 Shuro-chiku.

274. Shiro-umemodoki; *see also* 322 Umemodoki. 白落霜紅. White English holly. *Ilex serrata* Thunb. var. *sieboldii* Loes f. *leucocarpa* Makino. **Type:** S Dec BL FR DIO. **Use:** *2–6 13 14 17–21* Min. **Way:** Cut, Lay(1), Seed. **Pot:** early sprg. **Trim:** E. **Wire:** sprg to early sumr, paper wrap; branches break easily. **Note:** Full sun; half shade in sumr; water often; watch for aphids & scale; female plant preferable.

Shitanju. 紫檀樹. *See* 262 Sharintō.

275. Shōbyaku (Megi, Kotori-tomarazu). 小蘗, 鸞木. Thunberg berberry; coral barberry. *Berberis thunbergii* DC. **Type:** S Dec BL FR. **Use:** *2–5 7 13 14 17 18* 20 21 *30 32* MinDw. **Way:** Cut, Lay(2), Div(2). **Pot:** early sprg. **Trim:** C. **Wire:** any time. **Note:** Full sun; watch for scale.

276. Shudome (No-boke, Kusa-boke, Chojubai). 朱止, 野木瓜, 草木瓜, 長壽梅. Flowering quince. *Chaenomeles maulei* Lavall.; *C. japonica* Lindl. **Type:** S Dec BL FL FR. **Use:** *2–5 12–14 17* 18 20 21 *30 32* MinDw. **Way:** Cut, Div(2, 5). **Pot:** early sprg. **Trim:** C. **Wire:** any time. **Note:** Full sun; half shade in sumr; water often; watch for aphids & scale.

277. Shūkaidō. 秋海棠. Begonia. *B. evansiana* Andr. **Type:** G Dec Pe BL FL. **Use:** *14 32*. **Way:** Div(5), Cut. **Pot:** late sprg. **Note:** Full shade; water often.

278. Shun-ran. 春蘭. Japanese ground-orchid. *Cymbidium virescens* Lindl. **Type:** G Egr Pe *FL* FR. **Use:** *31 32*. **Way:** Nat, Div(5). **Pot:** late sprg. **Note:** Full shade; watch for scale on leaves.

279. Shuro-chiku (Shiro-chiku). 棕櫚竹. Hemp palm; reed rhapis. *R. humilis* Blume. **Type:** G Egr Pe BL. **Use:** *13 14 18 22–27 32*. **Way:** Div(2). **Pot:** every 3rd sprg. **Note:** Full shade; keep warm in wntr.

280. Sokei; *see also* 149 Ki-sokei, 224 Ōbai. 素馨, 秀英. Common white jasmine. *Jasminum officinale* L. **Type:** S Egr BL FL. **Use:** *2–5 13* 17 18. **Way:** Cut, Lay(2), Div(2). **Pot:** late each sprg. **Trim:** E. **Wire:** late sprg to sumr, paper wrap. **Note:** Full sun; keep warm in wntr.

Sonare. 磯馴. *See* 65 Hai-byakushin.

Soro. *See* 5 Aka-shide, 115 Inu-shide.

281. Sotetsu. 蘇鐵. Cycad. *Cycas revoluta* Thunb. **Type:** S Egr NE DIO. **Use:** 13 14 18 *22–27 32*. **Way:** Div(5), Nat. **Pot:** late sprg. **Note:** Full shade; keep warm in wntr.

282. Sugi. 杉. Common cryptomeria. *C. japonica* D.Don. **Type:** T Egr NE **Use:** *1 13 17 18 20–27 30 32*. **Way:** Cut, Lay(2). **Pot:** late sprg. **Trim:**

B; not too late in autm. **Wire:** late sprg to sumr. **Note:** Half shade; water often; keep warm in wntr; watch for red spiders & scale.

283. Sugi-goke. 杉苔. Cryptomeria moss. *Polytrichum commune* L. **Type:** G Egr NE(soft). **Use:** *14 30 32* Gr Min. **Way:** Div(3). **Pot:** any time. **Note:** Full shade.

284. Suguri; *see also* 255 Seiyō-suguri. 須具利. Gooseberry. *Ribes grossularioides* Maxim. **Type:** S Dec BL FR. **Use:** *2–5 13 17 18.* **Way:** Cut, Div(2), Lay(2). **Pot:** sprg. **Trim:** D. **Wire:** any time except wntr. **Note:** Full sun.

Suikazura. *See* 216 Nindō.

Suishi-kaidō. 垂枝海棠. *See* 73 Hana-kaidō.

285. Sumire. 菫. Violet. *Viola mandshurica* W. Beck. **Type:** G Dec Pe FL. **Use:** *14 30–32.* **Way:** Seed, Div(5). **Pot:** early each sprg. **Note:** Half shade.

286. Sumomo. 李. Plum. *Prunus salicina* Lindl.; *P. triflora* Roxb. **Type:** T Dec BL FL FR. **Use:** *2–5 17 18.* **Way:** Lay(2), Cut, Grf(3), Seed. **Pot:** early each sprg. **Trim:** D. **Wire:** sprg to sumr. **Note:** Full sun; half shade in sumr; watch for borers & aphids.

287. Susuki. 芒. Miscanthus. *M. sinensis* Anderss. **Type:** G Dec Pe FL. **Use:** *14 31 32* MinDw. **Way:** Div(3). **Pot:** early each sprg. **Trim:** cut back in late sprg & late autm. **Note:** Full sun.

288. Suzuran. 鈴蘭, 君影草. Lily of the valley. *Convallaria majalis* L. var. *keiskei* Makino; *C. keiskei* Miq. **Type:** G Dec Pe BL FL. **Use:** *32.* **Way:** Div (3), Nat. **Pot:** yearly after flowering finished. **Note:** Half shade.

— T —

289. Tachibanamodoki (Piracansasu). 橘擬. Narrow-leafed fire thorn. *Pyracantha angustifolia* Schneid. **Type:** S Egr BL FL *FR.* **Use:** *2–5 13 14 17 18 30 32.* **Way:** Cut, Lay(2), Div(1, 2). **Pot:** sprg. **Trim:** E. **Wire:** any time. **Note:** Full sun; water often; watch for scale.

Tachi-shinobu. *See* 129 Kan-shinobu.

290. Taiwan-hizakura; *see also* Sakura. 台灣緋櫻. Flowering cherry. *Prunus campanulata* Maxim. **Type:** T Dec BL FL. **Use:** *2–4 5 17–21.* **Way:** Div(2), Grf(3), Lay(1). **Pot:** early sprg or after flowering or early autm. **Trim:** D. **Wire:** sprg to sumr; paper wrap. **Note:** Full sun; half shade in sumr; water often; manure well; watch for borers & caterpillars.

Take. 竹. Bamboo. *See* 127 Kan-chiku, 173 Kuro-chiku; 198 Mōsō-chiku, 328 Ya-dake.

291. Tanchōboku (Danchōge). 丹頂木. Serissa. *S. crassiramea* Makino. **Type:** S Egr BL FL. **Use:** *2–6 12–14 17 18 20 21 30 32* Min. **Way:** Cut, Div(1,

5), Lay(2). **Pot:** sprg. **Trim:** C. **Wire:** any time. **Note:** Full sun.

292. Taniwatari-no-ki. 谷渡木. Nauclea. *N. Orientalis* L; *Adina globiflora* Salisb. **Type:** T Egr BL FL. **Use:** *2–5 13 14 17 18* Min. **Way:** Cut, Div(2). **Pot:** late sprg. **Trim:** E. **Wire:** any time except wntr. **Note:** Full sun; keep warm in wntr.

293. Teika-kazura (Hatsuyuki-kazura, Chōji-kazura, Chirimen-kazura). 初雪桂, 絡石, 縮緬葛, 白花藤, 丁字桂. Star jasmine. *Trachelospermum asiaticum* Nakai var. *intermedium* Nakai; *T. jasminoides* Franch. et Sav. non Lem; *Malouetia asiatica* Sieb. et Zucc. **Type:** V Egr BL FL. **Use:** *2–6 13 14 17 18 30 32* MinDw. **Way:** Cut, Lay(3), Div(3). **Pot:** late sprg to autm. **Trim:** E. **Wire:** any time except wntr. **Note:** Water often; keep warm in wntr.

294. Tennō-ume. 小石積, 磯山椒. Osteomeles. *O. subrotunda* C.Koch. **Type:** S Egr BL FL. **Use:** *2–6 13 14 17 18 30 32* Min. **Way:** Cut, Lay(3), Div(3). **Pot:** late sprg to autm. **Trim:** D; when new bud grows at base of trunk, cut off immediately. **Wire:** any time except wntr. **Note:** Water often; keep warm in wntr.

295. Teriha-noibara. 照葉野薔薇. Dog rose. *Rosa wichuraiana* Crep. **Type:** V Dec BL FL FR. **Use:** *2–6 13 14 17 18 30 32* Min. **Way:** Cut, Lay(3), Div (3), Seed. **Pot:** early sprg or early autm. **Trim:** E; when new bud grows at base of trunk, cut off immediately. **Wire:** any time except wntr. **Note:** Full sun; watch for aphids on new buds.

296. Tobera. 海桐花. Tobira. *Pittosporum tobira* Aiton. **Type:** S Egr BL FL DIO. **Use:** *2–4 13 17 18 20 21.* **Way:** Cut, Div(2), Seed. **Pot:** sprg. **Trim:** E. **Wire:** any time except wntr. **Note:** Full sun; female plant preferable.

297. Tochi-no-ki. 七葉樹, 橡, 栃. Japanese horse chestnut. *Aesculus turbinata* Blume. **Type:** T Dec BL *FL* FR. **Use:** *2 3 17 18.* **Way:** Seed, Lay(1). **Pot:** sprg. **Trim:** D. **Wire:** sprg to sumr, paper wrap. **Note:** Half shade.

298. Todo-matsu. 椴松, 青根. Sakhalin fir. *Abies sachalinensis* Mast. **Type:** T Egr NE. **Use:** *1–7 9 10 13 14 17–30 32.* **Way:** Nat, Cut, Seed, Lay(1). **Pot:** sprg or autm. **Trim:** B. **Wire:** any time except while new buds soft. **Note:** Half shade; water-spray sprg to sumr.

Toga. *See* 309 Tsuga.

299. Toga-sawara. Pseudotsuga. *P. japonica* Shiras.; *Tsuga japonica* Shiras. **Note:** Data same as for 298 above. Watch for red spiders.

Tō-gaya. *See* 36 Chōsen-gaya.

Tō-haze. *See* 82 Haze-no-ki.

300. Tōhi. 唐檜. Hondo spruce. *Picea jezoensis* Carr. var. *hondoensis* Rehd. **Type:** T Egr NE. **Use:** *1 2–7 9 10 13 17 18 20–29.* **Way:** Nat, Cut, Seed, Lay

(1). **Pot:** sprg or autm. **Trim:** B. **Wire:** any time except while new buds soft. **Note:** Half shade; water-spray foliage sprg to sumr; watch for red spiders.

301. Tō-kaede (Kaede, Sankaku-kaede). 唐楓, 楓, 三角楓. Trident maple. *Acer buergerianum* Miq. **Type:** T Dec BL. **Use:** *1–6 7 12–14 17–30 32* Min. **Way:** Cut, Lay(2), Seed. **Pot:** early sprg. **Trim:** C; LT late sprg to sumr. **Wire:** late sprg to autm, preferably during LT; paper wrap. **Note:** Full sun; half shade in sumr; water often.

Tokiwa-akebi. *See* 199 Mube.

302. Tokiwa-sanzashi (Piracansasu). Scarlet fire-thorn. *Pyracantha coccinea* Roemer. **Type:** S Egr BL FL *FR*. **Use:** *2–5 13 14 17 18 30 32*. **Way:** Cut, Lay(2), Div(1, 2). **Pot:** any time. **Trim:** E. **Wire:** any time. **Note:** Full sun; water often; keep a little warm in wntr; watch for scale.

303. Tokusa. 木賊. Scouring rush; Japanese scouring rush. *Equisetum hiemale* L. var. *japonicum* Milde. **Type:** G Egr Pe NE(soft). **Use:** *14 30 32* Min. **Way:** Div (5, 3). **Pot:** yearly, any time. **Trim:** Pull out top when it grows too tall. **Note:** Full shade; keep very wet.

304. Toneriko. 枔. Ground ash. *Fraxinus sieboldiana* Blume. **Type:** T Dec BL FL FR DIO. **Use:** *2 3 17 18*. **Way:** Lay(1), Seed. **Pot:** sprg. **Trim:** D. **Wire:** sprg to sumr, paper wrap. **Note:** Full sun; water often; female plant preferable.

305. Tosa-mizuki. 土佐水木. Spike winter-hazel. *Corylopsis spicata* Sieb. et Zucc. **Type:** S Dec BL FL. **Use:** *2–4 13 17 18 20–23*. **Way:** Div(2), Lay(1), Cut. **Pot:** after flowering finished. **Trim:** D. **Wire:** sprg to sumr, paper wrap. **Note:** Full sun; half shade in sumr; water often.

306. Toshō (Nezu, Muro, Hai-nezu). 杜松, 這杜松. Needle juniper. *Juniperus rigida* Sieb. et Zucc. **Type:** T Egr NE DIO. **Use:** *1–6 7 9 10 13–15 17–30* MinDw. **Way:** Nat, Cut, Lay(1), Seed. **Pot:** late sprg. **Trim:** B. **Wire:** any time except early sprg. **Note:** Full sun; water often; watch for red spiders.

307. Tō-tsubaki. 唐椿. Reticulata camellia. *C. reticulata* Lindl. **Type:** T Egr BL FL. **Use:** *2–6 13 17 18 19–21*. **Way:** Cut, Lay(2), Seed. **Pot:** late sprg. **Trim:** D. **Wire:** any time except early sprg; paper wrap; branches break easily. **Note:** Half shade; keep little warm in wntr; watch for aphids on new buds.

308. Tsubaki. 山茶, 椿. Common camellia; garden camellia. *C. japonica* L. var. *hortensis* Makino. **Type, use, way, trim, & note:** same as 307 above. **Pot:** yearly, late sprg.

309. Tsuga (Toga). 樛木. Siebold hemlock. *Tsuga sieboldii* Carr.; *Abies tsuga* Sieb. et Zucc. **Type:** T Egr NE. **Use:** *1–3 13 17 18 22–29*. **Way:** Nat, Cut, Lay(1). **Pot:** late each sprg. **Trim:** B. **Wire:** any time except while new shoots soft. **Note:** Half shade; water-spray sprg to sumr.

310. Tsuga-zakura. Phyllodoce. *P. nipponica* Makino. **Type:** S Egr NE FL AP. **Use:** *14 30 32* Gr. **Way:** Nat, Div(5). **Pot:** sprg. **Note:** Half shade; water-spray sprg to autm.

311. Tsuge (Asama-tsuge, Hon-tsuge); *see also* 99 Hime-tsuge. 柘植, 黃楊木. Japanese box. *Buxus microphylla* Sieb. et Zucc. var. *suffruticosa* Makino. **Type:** S Egr BL. **Use:** *2–5 6 9 13 14 17 18 30* Min. **Way:** Nat, Cut, Lay(2). **Pot:** late sprg. **Trim:** C. **Wire:** late sprg to sumr. **Note:** Half shade; keep little warm in wntr.

312. Tsukinuki-nindō; *see also* 105 Hyōtamboku, 319 Uguisu-kagura. Trumpet honeysuckle. *Lonicera sempervirens* Aiton. **Type:** V Dec BL FL. **Use:** *2 3 4 5 17 18*. **Way:** Cut, Lay(3, 2). **Pot:** late sprg. **Trim:** E. **Wire:** late sprg to sumr. **Note:** Full sun; half shade in sumr.

313. Tsukubane-utsugi (Ko-tsukubaneutsugi); *see also* 269 Shina-tsukubaneutsugi. Abelia. *A. spathulata* Sieb. et Zucc. **Type:** S Dec BL FL. **Use:** *3–5 17 18*. **Way:** Div(1), Cut. **Pot:** sprg. **Trim:** E. **Wire:** late sprg to sumr. **Note:** Full sun; half shade in sumr.

314. Tsukushi-shakunage; *see also* 260 Shakunage. Leatherleaf rhododendron. *R. metternichii* Sieb. et Zucc. **Type:** S Egr BL FL AP. **Use:** *2 3 4 5 6 17 18 28 32*. **Way:** Nat, Lay(1), Div(2). **Pot:** sprg. **Trim:** D, but not so necessary. **Note:** Half shade; keep damp.

315. Tsuribana-mayumi; *see also* 186 Mayumi. 吊花 眞弓. Euonymus. *E. oxyphylla* Miq. **Type:** S Dec BL FR. **Use:** *2–6 12 13 17 18*. **Way:** Cut, Lay(2), Div(2). **Pot:** sprg. **Trim:** E. **Wire:** sprg to sumr, paper wrap. **Note:** Full sun; half shade in sumr; water often.

316. Tsuru-kokemomo. 蔓苔桃. Mossberry. *Vaccinium oxycoccus* L.; *O. palustris* Pers. **Type:** G Egr NE (heavy, not sharp) FR. **Use:** *5 14 32* Gr. **Way:** Cut, Div(2). **Pot:** every 3rd yr. **Note:** Half shade; water-spray sprg to autm.

317. Tsuru-masaki. 扶芳藤. Euonymus. *E. radicans* Sieb.; *E. japonica* Thunb. var. *radicans* Miq. **Type:** V Egr BL FR. **Use:** *2 3 4 5 13*. **Way:** Cut, Lay (3). **Pot:** sprg. **Trim:** E. **Wire:** sprg to autm. **Note:** Half shade; water often.

318. Tsuru-umemodoki (Tsuru-modoki). 蔓梅擬. False bittersweet; Oriental bittersweet. *Celastrus orbiculatus* Thunb. **Type:** V Dec BL FR DIO. **Use:** *2–6 13 14 17 18 20 21 30 32*. **Way:** Cut, Lay(3, 2). **Pot:** sprg. **Trim:** E. **Wire:** sprg to autm. **Note:** Full sun; half shade in sumr; water often; watch for aphids; female plant preferable.

Tsuta. 蔦. *See* 150 Ki-zuta, 212 Natsu-zuta.

Tsutsuji. *See* 234 Renge-tsutsuji.

— U —

319. Uguisu-kagura (Uguisuboku); *see also* 105

Hyōtamboku. 鶯木. Honeysuckle. *Lonicera gracilipes* Miq. var. *glabra* Miq. **Type**: S Dec BL FL *FR*. **Use**: *2–6* 13 *17* 18. **Way**: Cut, Lay(2, 3). **Pot**: sprg. **Trim**: E. **Wire**: sprg to autm. **Note**: Full sun; half shade in sumr; water often.

Ukezaki-kaidō. *See* 94 Hime-ringo.

320. Ukyū (Nankin-haze). 鳥臼. Chinese tallow. *Sapium sebiferum* Roxb. **Type**: T Dec BL. **Use**: *2–4 17* 18. **Way**: Nat, Cut, Lay(2). **Pot**: late sprg. **Trim**: C. **Wire**: late sprg to sumr. **Note**: Full sun; keep warm in wntr.

321. Ume. 梅. Japanese flowering apricot [plum; apricot]. *Prunus mume* Sieb. et Zucc. **Type**: T Dec BL *FL* FR. **Use**: *2–7 9* 10 *13 14 17* 18 *20–25* 26 27 *30 31*. **Way**: Cut, Lay(1), Grf(3). **Pot**: early each sprg just after flowering finished. **Trim**: F. **Wire**: late sprg to sumr. **Note**: Full sun; manure well; watch for aphids, scale, caterpillars, & borers.

322. Umemodoki; *see also* 176 Kuro-umemodoki, 274 Shiro-umemodoki. 落霜紅, 梅擬.. English holly; fine-tooth holly; Seibold ilex. *I. serrata* Thunb. var. *sieboldii* Loes. **Type**: S Dec BL FR DIO. **Use**: *2–6* 13 14 *17–21 28 30 31* Min. **Way**: Cut, Lay(1), Div (2), Nat. **Pot**: early each sprg. **Trim**: E; immediately cut off new shoots growing from base of trunk. **Wire**: late sprg to sumr, paper wrap; branches break very easily. **Note**: Full sun; water often; watch for aphids & scale; female plant preferable.

323. Unzen-tsutsuji. 雲仙躑躅. Unzen azalea; wild-thyme azalea. *Rhododendron serpyllifolium* Miq. **Type**: S Egr BL FL. **Use**: *2–6* 13 14 *17–21 28 30 32* Min. **Way**: Cut, Lay(2), Div(2), Nat. **Pot**: yearly after flowering finished. **Trim**: D; immediately cut off new shoots growing from base of trunk. **Wire**: sprg to sumr; branches break easily. **Note**: Half shade; water often; keep warm in wntr.

Urahagusa. *See* 50 Fūchisō.

324. Urajiro-shida. 裏白羊歯. Urajiro fern. *Cheilanthes argentea* Kunze.; *Pteris argentea* Gmel. **Type**: G Egr Pe. **Use**: *14 32*. **Way**: Div(3), Nat. **Pot**: every 3rd yr. **Note**: Full shade; keep warm in wntr.

Ushikoroshi. *See* 126 Kamatsuka.

325. Utsugi. 空木花. Deutzia. *D. crenata* Sieb. et Zucc. f. *angustifolia* Regel. **Type**: S Dec BL FL. **Use**: *2–5 17* 18. **Way**: Cut, Lay(2), Div(1). **Pot**: each sprg. **Trim**: D. **Wire**: sprg to sumr. **Note**: Full sun; shade in sumr; water often.

— W —

326. Wa-ringo (Ringo). 和苹果, 苹果. Apple. *Malus pumila* Mill var. *dulcissima* Koidz. **Type**: T Dec BL FL *FR*. **Use**: *2–5* 13 *17* 18. **Way**: Div(2), Lay(1), Grf(3), Seed. **Pot**: early sprg or early autm. **Trim**: D. **Wire**: sprg to sumr, paper wrap. **Note**: Full sun; water often; manure well; watch for aphids & borers.

— Y —

327. Yabukōji. 紫金牛. Ardisia; bladhia. *A. japonica* Blume. **Type**: S Egr BL FR. **Use**: *31 32*. **Way**: Div(5), Cut. **Pot**: any time. **Note**: Half shade.

328. Ya-dake; *see also* Take. 矢竹. Sharp-leafed bamboo. *Pseudosasa japonica* Makino. **Type**: G Egr Pe. **Use**: *14* 18 *32*. **Way**: Div(5). **Pot**: late sprg. **Note**: Half shade; keep damp; keep warm in wntr; watch for scale on base of leaves.

329. Yae-kuchinashi; *see also* 166 Kuchinashi. 八重梔子花, 水梔子, 黄枝. Double-flower gardenia; gardenia. *G. jasminoides* Ellis. var. *radicans* Makino. **Type**: S Egr BL FL. **Use**: *2–5* 8 13 17 *18* 22–27. **Way**: Cut, Lay(1), Div(1). **Pot**: late sprg. **Wire**: late sprg to sumr, paper wrap. **Note**: Full sun; half shade in sumr; keep warm; watch for aphids on new shoots & for caterpillars.

330. Yamabōshi (Kara-kuwa). 四照花. Kousa dogwood. *Cornus kousa* Buerg. **Type**: S Dec BL FL FR. **Use**: *2–5 17* 18. **Way**: Cut, Lay(2), Div(1). **Pot**: sprg. **Trim**: D. **Wire**: sprg to autm. **Note**: Full sun; half shade in sumr.

331. Yama-fuji; *see also* 52 Fuji. 山藤. Japanese mountain wisteria. *Wistaria brachybotrys* Sieb. et Zucc. **Type**: V Dec BL *FL* FR. **Use**: 3 4 5 7 13. **Way**: Cut, Div(4), Lay(2, 3), Grf(3), Seed. **Pot**: sprg. **Trim**: D. **Wire**: sprg to autm. **Note**: Full sun; half shade in sumr; water often even in wntr.

Yama-giri. 山桐. *See* 1 Abura-giri.

Yama-hagi. 山萩. *See* 64 Hagi.

332. Yama-momiji (Momiji); *see also* Momiji. 山槭, 槭樹, 槭. Japanese maple; Japanese mountain maple. *Acer palmatum* Thunb. **Type**: T Dec BL. **Use**: *2–6* 13 *14 17–30 32*. **Way**: Seed, Nat, Lay(2), Cut. **Pot**: sprg or after LT. **Trim**: C; LT. **Wire**: sprg to sumr during LT, paper wrap; branches break easily. **Note**: Full sun; half shade in sumr; water often; watch for aphids on new buds & backs of leaves, scale on trunk, & caterpillars.

333. Yama-tsutsuji. 山躑躅. Azalea. *Rhododendron obtusum* Planch. var. *kaempferi* Wils.; *A. kaempferi* K.Andre.; *R. indicum* L. var. *kaempferi* Maxim.; *R. kaempferi* Planch. **Type**: S SemiDec BL FL. **Use**: 2 3 *4–6* 13 *17* 18 *19–21 28* 32. **Way**: Nat, Cut, Lay (2), Div(2). **Pot**: late each sprg when flowering finished. **Trim**: D. **Wire**: sprg to sumr. **Note**: Half shade; water often.

334. Yama-zakura; *see also* Sakura. 山櫻. Mountain flowering-cherry. *Prunus donarium* Sieb. var. *spontanea* Makino. **Type**: T Dec BL FL. **Use**: *2–6 17–21*. **Way**: Div(2), Grf(3), Lay(1). **Pot**: yearly after flowering finished or early autm. **Trim**: D. **Wire**: sprg to sumr, paper wrap. **Note**: Full sun; half shade in sumr; manure well; watch for borers & caterpillars.

Yanagi. 柳. *See* 264 Shidare-yanagi.

335. Yashōbi (No-bara); *see also* Bara, 295 Teriha-noibara. 野薔薇. Dog rose. *Rosa multiflora* Thunb.; *R. polyantha* Sieb. et Zucc. **Type：** V Dec BL FL FR. **Use：** *2–6 13 14 17 18 30 32* MinDw. **Way：** Nat, Cut, Lay(3), Div(3), Seed. **Pot：** very early each sprg. **Trim：** E; do not keep strong new.shoots which grow from base of trunk. **Wire：** any time. **Note：** Full sun; watch for aphids on new shoots.

　　　Yotsudome. *See* 57 Gama-zumi.

336. Yukinoshita. 虎耳草. Saxifraga. *S. stolonifera* Meerb.; *S. sarmentosa* L. f. **Type：** G Egr Pe BL FL. **Use：** *32*. **Way：** Div(5). **Pot：** every 3rd yr. **Note：** Full shade.

337. Yukiwarisō (Misumisō). 雪割草. Bird's-eye. *Hepatica acuta* Britton.; *H. triloba* Charix var. *acuta* Pursh.; *H. acutiloba* DC. **Type：** G Dec Pe BL FL. **Use：** *31*. **Way：** Div(5), Nat. **Pot：** in sprg after flowering finished or in late autm. **Note：** Half shade.

338. Yuki-yanagi. 雪柳. Thunberg spiraea; snow wisteria. *S. thunbergii* Sieb. **Type：** S Dec BL FL.

Use： *13 14 18 30 32* Min. **Way：** Div(2), Cut, Seed. **Pot：** sprg. **Trim：** E. **Note：** Full sun; watch for aphids

339. Yusura-ume. 山櫻桃, 〔櫻桃〕, 英桃. Korean bush-cherry. *Prunus tomentosa* Thunb. **Type：** S Dec BL FL *FR*. **Use：** *2–5* 6 13 *17* 18 *20 21*. **Way：** Cut, Lay(2), Seed. **Pot：** sprg. **Trim：** D. **Wire：** sprg to sumr.**Note：** Full sun; half shade in sumr

340. Yuzu. 抽子, 抽. True citron. *Citrus junos* Tanaka; *C. medica* b. *junos* Sieb. **Type：** T Egr BL FR. **Use：** 2 3 4 5 17 18. **Way：** Cut, Lay(1), Grf (3). **Pot：** late sprg. **Trim：** E. **Wire：** sumr, paper wrap. **Note：** Half shade; keep warm in wntr; watch for scale.

— Z —

Zaifuriboku. *See* 265 Shide-zakura.

Zakuro. *See* 256 Sekiryū.

Zumi. *See* 189 Miyama-kaidō.

PLANT INDEX BY ENGLISH & SCIENTIFIC NAMES

In the following index of bonsai plants by their English and scientific names, the numerical references are to the basic data on plants in Appendix 3.

APPENDIX 5

PLANT INDEX BY CHINESE-JAPANESE CHARACTERS

The following index of bonsai plants by Chinese-Japanese characters is arranged according to the total number of strokes in the first character. The numerical references are to the basic data on plants in Appendix 3.   Plants whose names are correctly written in the *kana* syllabary are not included here, as they may be found directly in Appendix 3.

GENERAL INDEX

The following is an index of only the main text and the introductions to the appendices. References to plates and figures will be found at appropriate places in the text itself; references to the 340 plants on which basic data are given will be found alphabetically arranged in Appendices 3 and 4.

Trunk, styles of *(continued)*
   twin, 65–66
   twisted, 65
Tsukami-yose; see Clustered-
   group style
Twin-trunk style, 65–66
Twisted-trunk style, 65
Two-tree style, 66

Ume; see Apricot, flowering
Upright style, 63–65
Urine, and damaged leaves, 154

Variegated leaves, propagation, 23
Vegetable manures, 124, 127

Water
   cool, 151
   chlorinated, 147
   types used, 57, 147
Watering; *see also* Spraying
   can, 147
   cuttings, 28
   and damaged leaf buds, 153
   and damaged leaves, 153
   and damaged roots, 153
   group plantings, 145
   leaving space for, 53
   after potting, 57

Watering *(continued)*
   regular care, 147–51
   rock plantings, 134
   of seed, 26
   of specific plants, 185 ff.
   syringe, 151
   too much or too little, 61
   before wiring, 112
Wax, used in treating pests, 160
Weeding, 151
Weeping styles, exhibiting, 171, 172
Willow, 19
   layering, 35
   pruning, 116
   repotting, 47
   soils for, 50
   wiring, 113
Wind
   and damaged leaves, 153
   protection from, 57, 134, 147
Wind-swept style, 65
   choice of pot for, 129
   from lopsided tree, 118
Winter care, 151, 152
Wire, copper
   annealing of, 112–13
   pinning down surface roots, 53
   proper sizes, 113

Wire, copper *(continued)*
   as tourniquet in layering, 35
Wiring
   to correct branch defects, 118–21
   to fix tree in pot, 53, 54–57, 132
   group plantings, 145
   of natural dwarfs, 25–26
   to preserve shape, 62
   rock plantings, 145
   scars, 167
   of specific plants, 185 ff.
   in training, 111–15
Wisteria, 21–22
Wood ash, as manure and soil conditioner, 124–27, 128
Wood shaving, 26, 57
Worms, 61

Yabukôji; see Ardisia
Yamayori; see Natural-group style
Yose-ue; see Group plantings, bonsai styles of; Multiple-tree style
Yukiwari-sô; see Hepatica

Zelkova, 50, 121, 137